Bill Overmyer has authored four books.

THE DEAD CAT BOUNCE MAKE MONEY FAST

A no nonsense, cut to the chase, heads up description of the environment of a steep stock market decline. This work will enable a first time investor to develop the skills to assess the correct time to buy and sell stock and realize an amazing profit within two years. So called market sophisticates might turn down their noses and say this book is crass. Nothing could be further from the truth.

OVER THE ROAD TRUCK DRIVING POEMS

A collection of poems related to the trials and tribulations of the over the road truck drivers.

BRONZE MINER

This romance novel takes place in a remote mountain town. The shared interests between the two lovers are a bronze foundry work place, a recreational ski area, the great outdoors and a student parachute center.

THE CRASH OF 2017

An in depth description of the environment at the of the top of the market when most people, according to the Consumer Confidence Index, think that the economy is in good shape. SURVEY SAYS!

The
CRASH OF
2017

The Set Up!

BILL OVERMYER

 iUniverse®

THE CRASH OF 2017
THE SET UP!

iUniverse books may be ordered through booksellers or by contacting:

iUniverse
1663 Liberty Drive
Bloomington, IN 47403
www.iuniverse.com
1-800-Authors (1-800-288-4677)

ISBN: 978-1-5320-2338-5 (sc)
ISBN: 978-1-5320-2339-2 (e)

Library of Congress Control Number: 2017906892

Print information available on the last page.

iUniverse rev. date: 06/29/2017

DEDICATION

THIS BOOK IS DEDICTED TO ALL MEN AND
WOMEN WHO PROUDLY WEAR

THE UNIFORMS OF THE ARMED FORCES OF
THE UNITED STATES OF AMERICA

ACKNOWLEDGEMENTS

Securities Research Company (SRC) grants permission for their charts to be used in this publication. The views expressed in this publication are solely the view of the author and do not reflect the views of SRC. SRC hereby disclaims any responsibility for any content within this publication. Photo copy or reproduction of any material (SRC charts) within this publication by any means and without prior approval and written consent by SRC is prohibited and punishable by law.

Please visit www.srcstockcharts.com.

CONTENTS

SUNDAY BRUNCH 1

HALLOWEEN WEEK 68

LUNCH.. 93

LIVERMORE.. 106

SHORT THE MARKET... 125

WALL STREET DIGEST.. 142

LIGHTS OUT TRICK 175

THE LIBRARY 197

EPILOGUE.. 215

APPENDIX 217

GLOSSARY 219

SUNDAY BRUNCH

It was another great Sunday brunch with church members from The Lost Souls of the Evangelical Church. New neighbors for just two months now, the Thompson and Whiting foursome were at the end of three long tables that had been joined together. The Whiting's were in their middle fifties. Richard and Veronica kept their salt and pepper hair a medium length and they were very conservative in their personal and public opinions. The Whiting's worked for themselves. They were not hurting as far as financial matters were concerned. They were financially independent. The Whiting's had just moved to Iowa from Arizona. They purchased the house that was up for sale next to the Thompson's and now they were getting acquainted as good neighbors. This was the second Sunday brunch they attended together.

Jeff and Angelique just turned thirty. Jeff drove a concrete truck for a living. He carried ten extra pounds of body weight that he could stand to lose. His black hair was short and curly and he occasionally wore white sun glasses. His wife, Angelique worked part time in administration for the school district. A pleasant looking brunette, Angelique was somewhat at odds with her lackluster surroundings. Since childhood, she had always felt that she would live in suburban splendor.

"I love this Sunday brunch get together," Veronica stated with satisfaction. "I love the salads and the endless choices."

Angelique gave her a crooked smile. "Oh, Ronnie, wouldn't you rather be at home watching all of the pregame analysis?" They both agreed that football was a waste of time and they shared a laugh while their husbands tried to repress scowls. "JT is actually helping around the house a little more than usual. Imagine that!" The church group was beginning to disperse, but the Whiting's and the Thompson's continued to huddle at the end of the third table.

The Whiting's began to bet in the stock market twenty seven years ago. Richard's uncle had been a stockbroker for ten years before he returned to a regular job. Jeff hoped to glean as much advice from the Whiting's as they were willing to share. Yesterday, Jeff had phoned Richard with a couple of stock market questions.

"What do you say Jeff? Want to kick the stock market around a little bit?"

"Sure Richard. Let me grab a cup of coffee." Richard sometimes liked to show off his knowledge of the markets. Jeff never held it against him. He hoped to learn some wise things from Richard. More than that, Jeff hoped to glean as much as he could from their success. He wanted to ask Richard what that steep, 500 point sell off last Thursday was all about. It was the largest single point drop in a day since the drops in 2007 and 2008. Jeff decided to hold that question for now. He was hoping that this brunch would be the golden opportunity to get his wife involved in the stock market. **Hopefully**, Angelique would develop an active interest if she and Veronica became friends. Jeff sauntered back to the group, sipped his hot coffee and opened up the discussion. "Does this market seem strange to you, Richard?"

"That is kind of a large statement, Jeff. Could you be more specific?"

"A couple of years ago it seemed that stock prices were headed upward with a little bit of steam and zest, but now prices are kind of, well, not stagnant, but more like dragging along and not really moving up."

Veronica finished her salad. "The market moves up rapidly after a good drubbing. It always has a quick rise in stock prices after a crash."

Richard agreed. "Ronnie is right. All stocks moved up pretty fast from the last market crash, and now, four years later, the advance has slowed. There is not as much of that broad, all inclusive, across the board action. By that I mean *not all companies are participating in any upward move that the **DJIA Index** happens to make.* **Half** of the NYSE stocks are languishing. Not all of the different industry groups are moving up in share price. The only action going on right at this particular moment are the very high priced company stock swaps to buy out competitors or merge with them."

"Sometimes they do that to eliminate competition," Ronnie smiled.

Richard continued. "Companies like to make acquisitions while the stock prices are high. They believe that it helps to justify the current lofty share prices, *and*, if a company stock price is up two or three times higher in price, then the company only has to offer half as much stock for the acquisition. Maybe."

"What do think about diversification? Is it a smart thing to do?"

"I don't believe any investor is diversified at all, if they keep plowing any stock market gains back into the market. It is just the wrong thing to do." Richard munched some potato salad. "Stocks are intangibles in a sense. Right now, there is nothing but inflated paper prices at this stage in the game. There is **more downside** risk right now than any **upside** potential." Richard paused for a sip of coffee. "Stock market diversification is just an ancient ploy. It is a slick trick thought up by the financial guru's at the big brokerage houses. When a novice investor makes money in the market they are often encouraged to put it right back into other stocks. Salesmen tell them to buy stocks in every sector of the market. If one sector drops, supposedly the stocks held in the other sectors of the market will stay up or even increase in value. **Supposedly**, the investor portfolio will manage to maintain the same value dollar wise as one or two stocks drop and two or three rise in price." Richard cleared his throat and sipped his coffee. "This idea is wishful thinking, but *it is presented and sold to gullible investors as a reliable, foolproof strategy* that will protect their portfolio balance. The sales force likes to say there will always be one sector that performs *beyond expectations*. One sector will always *outperform* all of the others. It is a believable suggestion for gullible investors. What the heck! The broker just wants another commission."

"What if the market takes a nose dive?"

"That is just the point, Jeff. All sectors will take the dive. Basically, you shoot yourself in the foot if you invest only in the stock market. The paper profits will dry up and shrink dramatically. Ownership in gold and silver would be a true hedge against a stock market sell off or catastrophic crash. Some people buy hedge funds, but hedge funds typically pan out after two years and so will your hard earned money."

Veronica wanted to elaborate on phraseology. "The term '*outperform*' that Richard used is financially correct for conversational dialogue. Notice the positive spin on the phrase '*outperform the market*' or '*perform beyond expectations*'. This kind of wording is used to enhance the perception that the market research letters you receive, and the sales rep lingo, is astute and sophisticated. The words are introduced to make the investor think they are learning something, when actually they are not. There are other phrases that have neutral meanings. Take the phrases '*below expectations*' or '*performed moderately well*'. They are designed to keep investors from panicking and to keep them holding on to their stocks for the long run."

Angelique stared into Veronica's eyes. "I guess that does sound a whole lot better than saying, '*Your stocks suck!*'" Laughter erupted at the table. Jeff was floored by his wife's comment.

Richard was not finished. "Stock prices are intangibles to some degree, and paper profits will vanish in a market crash. To diversify, you need to buy something for yourself. A franchise. Start a business. Buy land and fence it. Use it for boat or RV storage. Or start with six units and add on when you can afford to. Raise livestock. Open a salvage yard if you can get approval from the county. Buy real property."

Veronica added, "How can there be true diversification of your investments, if everything is still in the stock market? Be like Jay Leno. Buy some classic cars and artwork. Look at the market as an opportunity to make money and then get out with your cash. You have to cash out and get to real property. Real tangibles." Ronnie sipped her iced tea. "Also, Jeff. If you are cornered with a bad selection, if you made a bad trade, then yes, you will get the impression that the market is doing nothing Anytime you are weighed down with a loser, it will seem like nothing is going on. It will frustrate you and make you grumpy. You get to watch all of the other stocks *outperform* your loser." Jeff choked into his hot coffee just as he took a sip.

Richard confirmed Ronnie's statement. "That is right, Jeff. A loser blows everything out of proportion. It ruins your perspective and your thinking. The negative emotion and anger that build up will override any honest, neutral assessment needed to invest wisely." Richard looked into Jeff's eyes. "Sell the dogs, Jeff. Don't think twice. Then you will be able to sleep at night."

Ronnie returned to Jeff's question. "Jeff. Let me venture back to your question. I bet you are wondering about all of the under currents in our world now from politics, to the Fed, to the economy, to the average American citizen? Are you wondering if these things are going to pull the market down?"

Jeff gave her a perplexed look. Things were not always as they seemed. "Well. That is partly what I was asking. I am thinking the market is running out of steam. The market is not as exciting as it used to be."

Angie dutifully informed the Whiting's. "My husband bought stock at the very bottom of the market. He just got lucky and he has been cranky and hard to live with ever since then."

Richard gave Angelique a look. Veronica was intrigued. "So, Jeff. You got lucky on your first stock investment. How did that happen? Did you have any help?"

Jeff reached into his shirt pocket and pulled out his white sunglasses. He casually slipped them on to enhance his image. He spoke only with the slightest trace of condescension and disdain. "Well, Veronica." Jeff paused for effect. "Even a blind man gets lucky once in a while." Richard laughed out loud. Ronnie's eyes widened. She was slightly taken aback, but she replied, "Angie, you are fortunate to have married a man with a sense of humor."

Angie cautioned. "Don't pay any attention to him Ronnie! He thinks he's so cool when he plays the dirty Italian greaser."

Jeff smiled and wallowed in smugness. "I will have to show you my studio some day. I am self educated. I read and learned about the market crashes from a book called *The Dead Cat Bounce Make Money Fast*." Jeff gave Angie the evil eye, and Angie returned it.

Richard picked up from the point of digression. "Let me guess, Jeff. The Dow Jones Average is jumping around in a narrow range and your stocks are not advancing. The *30* stocks in the *DJIA Index* are holding and advancing slowly, but there is no broad market advance like there was after the crash in 2008. Is that your question?"

Ronnie threw in a few political issues. "Plus, if you consider all of the uncertainty of jihad, ebola, and the Russians crossing into the Ukraine, things are looking a little bit grim. It may not be worthwhile to have any stocks at this time."

Angie stared Ronnie. "Does all of that terrorist stuff matter to the market?"

Ronnie smiled knowingly. "Yes, Angie. It can have an influence."

Richard butted in. "Jeff, let me say something philosophical to test your degree of knowledge. Your goal is to determine the overall market movement. Now, here is the question. Are you riding a building surge of water? Is it forming a large wave? Are the waves uniform in big long rows, one right after the other? Are they marching in unison straight towards the beach with a porpoise?" Giggles surfaced at the table. Richard was playing with them now.

Jeff decided to take the high road. "Well, Richard. In the spirit of your ocean wave analysis, I think we are on the crest of a gigantic wave. No! I should say we are on the crest of a giant swell. It is just a giant swell and it has dissipated some. It shrinks in size somewhat and then swells to return to the original height. There are no more long rows of waves behind it. And now, the giant swell dissipates into just choppy water. The sea is calm."

Richard stared Jeff directly in the eyes, in a menacing fashion. "Have you ever surfed the big ones in the ocean, Jeff? What size board do you use?" The girls were chuckling now. Richard loved to entertain and the girls were enjoying it.

Jeff's eyes were crossed. "Richard. You are messing with me. I won't have you treating me like a clown. But, yes, how wonderfully insightful you are. Every once in a while, there is a swell. But it wanes and disappears rapidly. And to make matters worse, it moves in no particular direction that I can follow." Jeff paused and took a sip of coffee. "Have you ever watched the surfers hop up on the boards, and notice that the wave is petering out? The surfers change their minds on the spot. They sit down, spin around and paddle back out to sea to look for a *real wave* to catch." Jeff's brow furrowed. "Let me say it this way, Richard. I think we are getting pretty near the top of the Dow Jones and the S+P 500. This is it. This is the top of the market. This big wave is just beginning to flatten out. There are no other waves behind it. There are only swells. And, one more thing, Richard." Jeff gave Richard a hard stare. "I want desperately to learn how to sell the market short and play the downside."

Richard offered. "Ah ha! *You have surfed the big ones*! You **have** become knowledgeable. Well. I've got news for you, boy. The market is a totally different creature now. Here is the answer to your question. Your analogy is correct. The surf is no longer up! The thundering herd has vanished! Only the illusions remain. Remember that! The market and the gyrations we have now are a mixed bag. Stock prices are three times what they were just four years ago. My uncle can remember when everyone was satisfied with two times their money."

Richard paused and sipped his coffee. "The brokerage houses have to pay more to keep stock in their inventories. During their daily routine of house trading and trying to make a buck by buying and selling, all they are looking at is scraps. Small potatoes. **But,** it buoys the belief that the market is still alive." Richard sipped more coffee. "Another thing, Jeff. The marching band is louder now than ever before. This band does not know if the market is going to tank or not. It does not care. But, they have to keep after it on a positive note. It is their job. Besides Jeff, let's face things realistically. Aren't you glad? It gives a schlob like you a chance to make a buck." Bursts of laughter flowed from the girls.

Jeff gave Richard a serious look. "I'm getting tired of your petty put downs, Richard. Don't push me too far, or I will break you in half."

Ronnie tried to smooth any startled emotions. "He wasn't that way when I first married him, Jeff." She smiled. "The stock market has slightly twisted his demeanor."

Richard bounced back. "Point taken, Jeff. I apologize. Let me ask you this question. Do you have a lust in your heart for vast riches?"

Angelique verified, "That is not the half of it!"

Jeff suppressed a tremor. "He just can't leave it alone, can he, Veronica?" Jeff raised his eyebrows. "Ronnie, do you think the crest will turn down to a large fast crash? Or will it just fizzle out over distance and time and disappear like the high tide?"

Veronica couldn't resist. "Richard is having too much fun with you, Jeff. Please forgive him. You know, I actually think that the market will really begin to churn for at least a year. To use Richard's analysis, I think the waters are choppy and that we are headed downstream into the rapids." Veronica looked at everyone. "And then, we will dramatically slip over the waterfall."

Angelique was startled by Ronnie's choice of words. "My! Ronnie, you certainly paint a dreadful picture!"

Richard sat back in his chair and smiled broadly at his wife. "I see. Any idea how far downstream this waterfall is, Professor?"

Jeff replied, "That is exactly the question I am asking you two."

Richard spoke thoughtfully. "It is going to be awhile before we hit the waterfall, Jeff. The game changes at the top and so, you have to change your strategy. You play the dips. Stock prices drop and then they rebound back. This happens several times over the course of a year, especially around the earnings announcements. The earnings announcements are all the rage. The only upside in this next DJIA leg upward will be a narrow trading range of, say, a twenty percent increase in a few stock prices."

Ronnie explained to Angelique. "When Americans stop spending, the companies have to cut back production to survive. The hiring freeze is imposed. Resigning workers are not replaced. Disappointing earnings reports and lower than expected profits begin to appear when the economy slows down. Consumers buy only necessities. People stop spending. They barely have enough money to make ends meet and pay utility bills. So, what you do now is, you wait for the rallies to fizzle out and for the share prices to drop. Then you buy a small amount and wait for the next move up. A rebound. If it happens, then you sell for a small short term profit. It will be ten percent if you are lucky. You should stay with the big stocks that trade actively and are still producing operating profits. You have to understand that *the market is a short term creature now*. Only a few stocks are bobbing on the surface. That is the main thing. **The long term machine is dead.**"

Richard looked deep in perplexed thought. He reiterated a second time. "The game changes. Your strategy has to change. You become *a short term investor*. You buy the drops in prices after any bad news sends prices down. *This is not the time to put a large wad of cash in for the long haul*. The market is no big deal at this point. You should sell your stocks. *You should be in cash*. Stocks are overpriced. Fewer people are buying. The market no longer has the ability to make a strong, broad advance of all stock share prices. No one is putting any money in the market anymore."

Ronnie picked up the thought. "Now, say only 25% of the stocks will advance from now to the end of the year instead of 100%. People will sell and take their winnings to the bank. *This is what is actually happening.* Next year, it will be only 15% advancing, just figuratively speaking. After that, *only the DJIA Index* will advance and it will be smaller than before, say only 5 %. Maybe 10 %. Trading volumes will be smaller. Gradually, the stock *price **losses** will increase in size* as you near the waterfall. They will become more severe. The drops will no longer be 5 or 10%. They will be 15 to 20%. And the next rallies will not see a full price recovery to what the prices were before. So don't play the dips on the downside."

Richard looked at Angie and Jeff. "While the stocks are churning during this slow time at the top, the big boys are quietly selling. They keep their fingers crossed and pray that the market does not sell off very fast so they will able to liquidate more of their holdings. In other words, they sell out. You have to understand that this is not done in a day, a week or a month. It takes six months to a year. They turn those intangible stock quotes and paper profits into hard cash. During this period, any stock that takes off like a rocket gets media coverage like it is the first born baby of the new year."

Veronica raised her hands in the air. Her wrist bracelets were shiny and tinkling. "And then the hype starts up. You hear classic, timeless quotes from the gods of finance. *'The market isn't dead yet. You should still be in stocks! The bear isn't here yet. We still have a long way to go'.*"

Richard tried to explain in more detail. "You also have two different things going on at this time. There are two different perspectives. They are very confusing. Analysts of economics, and genuine economics professors, will state in their publications that the economy is still bullish. Now, this is the GDP *economy* they are talking about. This is **not** *the stock market industry or the stock market economy.* Investors are confused by this because what you have is a **bullish goods economy** that is going to continue to expand for more years. How many does not matter. It is merely an expansion of our nation's growth, mostly due to population growth and replacement of worn out goods. At times the *national goods economy* may slow and actually stagnate. A year or two of no growth. A mild recession. Yet the *goods economy* is still poised to grow and the economists are still professing expansion over the coming years. There is no depression coming up in the foreseeable future. But, the stagnation might slow the trading in the stock market economy. You should realize that **expansion** is a misused word."

Ronnie added two cents. "The stock market gurus and finance wizards will say **the stock market** is still bullish. That is not true. The stock market will turn down whenever the goods economy slows or recedes and the quarterly earnings drop. Our national economic growth is maybe one percent right now and that includes government projects in the statistic. So, actually the GDP may be less than one percent or even zero right now."

"Please, let me finish, please!" Richard paused and cleared his throat. "Now, this second perspective is the stock business. This is where the stock market guru's fail to explain to investors that *the stock market economy* is far different from *the goods economy*. The gurus don't bother to explain that share prices have topped out and that no one wants to buy expensive stocks anymore. *And this is primarily because stocks are trading at three or four times higher than they did four years ago.* The guru's will tell investors that a *correction* in share prices is imminent, but it will only be a small correction. *They do not tell investors to **sell**.* Gurus advise investors to hold onto their stocks and, after the drop, they tell investors to accumulate more shares. They claim that the share prices are more fairly valued. Once they get their jaws warmed up, they even predict that stocks will rally back and the economy will expand. To them, it is still a bull market in stocks. This is a ruse, but it is one that is presented every time."

Ronnie smiled and confirmed her husband's analysis. "There you have it. The great big deception of smoke and mirrors." She drew a deep breath for an announcement. Angie stared in silence. She was amazed by Veronica's ability to communicate. "Boys, I have something I want to give to Angelique." She reached into her large carry all bag with the big round plastic handles. She pulled out a 400 page book and passed it across the table. "Angelique. I have brought a present to give you. Richard gave me this book several years ago. It was a gift from his uncle, the stock broker. You will find it interesting even at the very beginning. The first sixty pages will hold your attention. After that, you might want to skim it and hop around a little bit." Veronica passed the book across the table to Angie. Richard chuckled when he saw the book and passed a quick wink to Jeff.

Richard explained, "She was dogging me hard about throwing away her hard earned money. She said gambling on stocks was not Christian. She would yell at me too. It made me want to cry."

"Pay no attention to him, Angie." Veronica insisted. "It is time you took an interest and learned a little about the market. You need to understand and appreciate what Jeff is trying to do. You might even find yourself getting involved in this endeavor. And you should be." Jeff suppressed a smile. He had an urge to leap across the table and kiss Veronica twenty or thirty times.

Angelique read the title out loud. "*The Ultimate Safe Money Guide* by Martin Weiss, PHD. Why this, Ronnie?"

"Now, don't get mad at what I am going to say, Angie. We are not children here. I know you are suspicious and full of distrust about the market. That is basically because you have no knowledge or understanding of what the market is all about." Angie's eyes widened and she gasped. Veronica continued. "I was the same way, dear. No one trusts anything they do not understand. The book will give you a different perspective of the securities industry, and one that you will like. It will vastly increase your knowledge, very quickly and quite easily. It will add balance to your reasoning while you search for answers to questions on stocks and the market. It will give you the knowledge to appreciate Jeff's efforts. We don't want the securities industry to pull you two apart. You two are too good of a couple for that." Chuckles arose back and forth across the table. Richard slapped his knee and sniffed, "Oh, Lord! Where is my hanky?"

"Oh! Well!" Angelique huffed. She was slightly irritated with a gift that she did not really believe she would use. "I guess there were times in that first year, while I was washing dishes in my dull, drab kitchen, when I often thought about taking the big kitchen knife and stabbing

Jeff in the heart fifty or sixty times. How did you know?" There were chuckles from the men.

Veronica ignored the confession and continued as if she had not been interrupted. "Weiss is a PHD and a connoisseur of finance and economics. 'The Safe Money Guide' is an encyclopedia of first rate conservative investments. The returns are not spectacular, but the risks are far less than Jeff's approach. This will help you keep each other in check in a knowledgeable, educated fashion, and it will keep you working as a team. Then you won't have to indulge yourselves in those horribly pointless and emotionally overwhelming *blood feuds to the sudden death.*" More laughter rose from the table. They all shared smiles at Ronnie's rebuttal. "The Weiss Research Department is large and unbiased. He rates and ranks securities and issues his own reports. It really is an excellent book. It is a huge accomplishment and no words are minced."

Angie reached across the table to get the book, "Oh, How wonderful! Thank you." Angie took the book and muttered under her breath. Her voice trailed off with disgust. "I will get even with you for doing this to me, Ronnie." There was more laughter from the guys.

Ronnie rebounded sourly, "You needn't be so grateful, Angelique. It is the least I can do." The guys were howling and hooting now.

Angelique quickly responded. "Well. I have news for you two Whiting's. Jeff has made me the *vice* president, and he has given me the power of the savings department. It is a token gesture of goodwill to keep me interested and let him continue his dream to become a bag thrower." Richard howled and Angie ignored him. "He lets me control the savings account. I just stare at the balance and put it in the file. Maybe we will put some savings in our IRAs or maybe we will find a good mutual fund manager. But I warned Jeff. If he steals as much as one penny out of the savings, without my consent, then I will pull the Loraina Bobbit trick on him while he is sleeping. I will snip off his berries and of course, after that, the divorce papers will be served."

Richard had a mystified look on his face. "Wait a minute! I thought we were all Christians here? Are not we not loving, caring people?"

Ronnie chimed in. "A bag thrower, huh? Ha ha ha hah! Tell me about that one would you, Jeff?"

Jeff retorted, "I just included her so she will quit nagging me about wasting all my time doing research in my strategy room. She thinks I am hiding from her. And, yes, Ronnie. I do plan to have limousines and chauffeurs. The entire financial community will hold their breath to hear my every word and all of my confidential whispers. The brokerage houses will beg and plead with me not to sell the market short." Richard laughed and snorted loudly.

Angie leered at her husband and raised her voice in mock anger to cut him off. "The only way you will ever ride in a limo is if you are the chauffer."

Richard replied, "I have just the book for you two to read."

Angie came to her senses and apologized for her outburst. "I have to admit that I was quite mad at Jeff when he first put money in the stock market instead of remodeling the house and getting a new car for me. I thought he had gone mental. I made it pretty obvious that I did not agree with his what he was doing. I was going to close the gates to my playground." Angie paused as if deep in thought and weighing the gravity of the situation. "I was totally against Jeff's interest in the market. I did not agree with his endeavor at all. I thought he had no more interest in me. What is this book about, Ronnie?"

"You will find that this book addresses the fears and suspicions about the stock market. Once you read it, you will understand how you can make extra cash to pay down your bills and build a nest egg. And this would be without risk. It will keep you ahead of inflation. It will introduce you to tax free interest on municipal bonds."

"You mean Jeff and I won't have to live in squalor for the rest of our lives?"

Jeff stepped in. "I tried to change Angie's point of view, but I failed miserably. And that is because I was not able to dream up an approach like this conversation we are having now. I couldn't come up with a tactful conversation that would keep us on a neutral path of discussion without anger or resentment surfacing between us. I am just a poor communicator! I could not, *for the life of me*, figure out what to say or how to explain the market in a favorable way to Angelique. I am very grateful to both of you. Finally, my wife and I can live in an investment environment without bitterness between us." Angie looked at him cross eyed. "You and I are going to have a talk when we get home, *Mr. Jeffy.*"

"You will appreciate the approach, Jeff." Richard nodded his head. "I know you will. Marty Weiss is one of the more brilliant income portfolio managers in the world. He addresses the shenanigans that abound in the nation's financial community. He does not tolerate the manipulations or deceptions that are made by the dishonest elements in the business world. I guess I may as well say *theft and lying.*" Richard advised Jeff. "When you have extra cash burning a hole in your pocket, you might tuck it away in one of Martin's recommendations. That is what Ronnie has always done for me. She reviews the recommendations and leaves me notes on the situations that she feels are promising."

Veronica had not finished her rant. "You know the market research reports from the brokerage houses and other advisors in the financial community are fluff. They are overly positive. There is never even the slightest hint of a negative situation. If an unfavorable situation occurs, it is addressed immediately. It is glossed over as if there is nothing to be worried about. This is, of course, is not quite the lie, but not quite the truth either. The reports are not actually blatant lies, but they do border on deception. The bad news is edited out.

"There have been plenty of out and out lies." Richard added. "Blatant lies. Enron. Cendant (See appendix). Madoff, the Savings and Loan disaster. Dan Quayle's spelling of potato. All of this is similar to what goes on in the political arena. One of the sad things about the industry is that the brokers are too lazy to verify the statements in the research reports. They just pass the research reports out to the unwitting and unsuspecting clients and look the other way. The managers make the reports sound like a big deal. They tell their sales reps, 'I got the research reports for you sales people. They are classified. These are in house reports only. Do not show them to your clients.'" Richard sat back. "Of course everyone knows that the sales reps mail photo copies to their clients right away."

Veronica added, "Managers worry that what is printed could be used against the sales staff in a court of law. *That fact alone* should scare you silly. The house traders can buy up any company stock at a low price and fill their house inventory to the max. It costs them a pretty dime.

Then they preach that the company is in a turnaround situation or that there is a new product or an improvement in operational efficiency. The sales people fire up their client's ears and get them primed to invest. The broker house raises the bid and ask along the way. The house makes a tidy profit and then later the stock falls flat. As unlikely as it may seem, they get away with it time and time again."

Richard added, "Brokers just regurgitate the rumors passed around the house. Brokers never do their own research. Here is a line that has been used for over forty years now. It goes like this, '*Coleman and Brunswick are going to merge*.'"

Jeff spoke up. "I want to get to the library to go over the articles in the financial newspapers. They stock Barron's weekly, the Economist magazine, Popular Science and others. I can save some pennies that way. The business reference book section is right there to look up company financials in Moody's and Standard and Poor's. You can delve into the hard financial statistics that you don't find on the internet. Corporate plans for instance."

Jeff paused and asked, "What is up with this PE ratio business? If a PE ratio is ten, then it takes ten years of earnings per share for the earnings to add up to the price of one share of stock? I guess that is not all bad, but what about a PE of 26 or 30? If a stock's earning per share is a dollar and the stock price is thirty dollars, it would take thirty years for the earnings to pay for one share of stock. Yet the account executives swear that it is an important measure to go by. What is so hot about this PE stuff?"

Veronica spoke up. "You are right, Jeff. It is just a simple mathematical relation. But, brokers like to say if the stock is not trading above a PE of 22 or so, then no one is interested in trading the stock. Stock prices get bid up when trading actively, especially if there is more buying than selling. It is nothing more than a simple statement that an actively traded stock is going to have a Price to Earnings ratio of 28 or so. There is no mystery to it. The more a stock is traded and sought after by investors, the more its share price is bid upward. Likewise, *the PE ratio also increases*. That is all. Plain and simple. Actively traded stocks will have a higher PE ratio because the share prices have moved up higher."

Richard added, "It is a sales pitch used to influence clients to buy a stock. It is just more financial speak and sales pitch. There is nothing "scientific" about it. Here is a funny truth though. Wall Street claims that today's current stock prices reflect the '*future value*' of the share price. Conservative investors call this '*speculation*'. Yet, at the bottom of the market when share prices have crashed you will find that 90% of the companies have a PE ratio of 6. Would a PE of 6 be a better representation of '*future value*'?" Chuckles rose around the table.

"What ever happened to book value?"

Veronica handled the question. "Well, Jeff, it depends on the situation. Many companies do not have tons of buildings and equipment anymore. They are what is known as *light industry*. Their fixed costs and overhead are low. Their operations can produce a ton of profit. Not many investors care about book value any more. Some high tech firms are asset lean. They have a low overhead and do gazillions in revenues producing parts for the fancy new cell phones and other telecommunication gizmos. Their asset value in plant, property and equipment is less than heavy manufacturing, like the auto and trucking industries for example. Some companies have billions of shares now and their book values are less than five dollars a share. What else, Jeff?"

"What is this *one tenth of one percent*? The market is up by one tenth of one percent? It seems like I hear or read that every day. I bet most people think it is ten percent."

Richard responded. "Great question. Now keep in mind we are talking here about *index* numbers of the Dow Jones Industrials. One point does not equal one dollar. So, if the Dow is 500, then 10 % would be 50 index points and one per cent would be 5 index points. One tenth of one percent (.001) would be less than one index point. How about them apples?"

Veronica took her turn. "Let me explain it another way. If the market rose one DJIA Index point every day, then after 200 days the market would be up 200 points for the year. That is the easiest way to think of it. Non investors who hear the rant that the market has been steadily moving upward all year long do not bother to compare the difference between the beginning and ending index numbers. The market is up by 200 points. This is no big deal, right? The **underlying deception** *is that* *only the **DJIA Index** is moving up **and not the rest of the 2500 NYSE stocks**.*"

Angie understood. "Someone who is unknowing or totally in the dark might think that all of the stocks on the New York Exchange were going up every day, huh? Making great strides towards the moon!"

"Yes, Angie. Think about it. They announce through the media that the market broke another record today. Up by a whole one tenth of a percent. And they beat the drum like it was just another day with the market climbing like a rocket. In reality, the DJIA Index is just barely holding ground while investors with profits are cashing out."

Jeff asked Veronica, "Is one year the minimum amount of time that the big-time investors, the mutual funds and corporations, need to sneak the billions of dollars out of the market and turn those paper holdings into cash?" Ronnie answered, "Richard and I think it is more than one year. This is all part of the illusion and deception. The market appears to go sideways, **the *index* that is**, until the evil deed is done. After the big boys have cashed out, the market drops. "See how conditioned I am to using the general words? The **real market**, the other 2500 stocks will drop before the DJIA Index drops. They are already down 15% or more. Then, finally, near the end the DJIA index begins its drop."

Veronica paused. "Let me say something about diversification. Richard and I buy mining stocks that produce gold and silver. Sometimes these two elements are just by products of the main metal that is being mined. But there are other ways to diversify. Buy collectible art. Collectible autos. Better yet, buy a franchise! Or buy a plot of dirt and put a fence around it and use your husband for the junkyard dog. Put up a small metal building. Start with just the frame. Later you can add a roof. You can finish it off as you can afford it. Repair autos, atvs, lawn mowers, weed whips. Use the land for storage units or store boats and RV's. Start with six small storage units and add more when you have extra cash. Buy a Barbie Doll and leave it in the original packaging. Dig a hole for a basement on your vacant plot of land one summer. Two summers later you can pour the basement floor and walls. Then call the carpenters in two years later for a small, one story structure. Three years later you can build a single story add on or perhaps a second story. You save for these projects a little bit at a time and you work on them when you can afford it. You can teach your family the construction trade and how to become a general contractor. In fifteen years you will have a house that is completely paid for. You can sell it or rent it out. Instead of $150,000, you pay no interest on a mortgage and it will only cost you $65,000."

Richard questioned Jeff. "Do you have seller's remorse?"

"There is always this nagging feeling that I should have sold sooner and attempted a couple more trades along the way."

"JT, don't think anything of it. You won. You did it. You have held out to the very end and captured the big returns. You didn't lose any money chasing the market rumors. You did terrific! Angie, You should be proud of JT."

JT replied, "That is the way I see it and that is what I hope to do in the future. Right now I just wonder sometimes what is going on in the market. It seems to be holding. There is good news out now and then. I guess I am wondering if I should take another chance and by stock. Every once in a while the news spits out that there may be an opportunity in 'so and so' stock."

"Don't keep me in suspense. Give me a name."

JT wrinkled up his forehead. "Well, this was a couple of months ago. April, I think. There was some ranting in Barron's about Samsung stock price making a comeback. They didn't quite meet earning expectations and the stock sold off to a pretty low price. Competition beat them up pretty bad and their earnings suffered. Analysts in Barron's were predicting a possible 50 % share price comeback if you bought shares back in April. Samsung is touting a new system or at least a more competitive design on their flat screen or the cell phone. Something like that. I can't remember. They are getting ready to kick off a big media blitz, blah, blah, blah, but, the product isn't in the store yet."

Richard listened to his new neighbor and nodded his head. "When you can't find any information from your usual sources, *you should just pick up the phone and* **call the headquarters**. Ask them to send out any information they can. Or you can always call the marketing department. *You won't believe it!* They will fill your ear. My uncle used to brag about calling Lee Iacoca's secretary when Chrysler was in bankruptcy." Richard sipped his coffee. "You did really well your first time out, Jeff. Not everyone is so lucky. Never forget that. The market has kind of stalled right now. It is looking for a breather. I talked with Walt last week and he seems to think that we will be all right through the end of the year."

"You know, that is what I am worried about. Is this market going to drop before the end of the year?"

"Let me tell you exactly what my uncle said. The midterm elections are coming up this November, 2014. The right wing radical Tea Party and Ralph Reed's Christian Coalition are fed up with the Dumbos. They will be out in big numbers to vote and get Republicans elected to take control of the Senate." Jeff started to speak, but Richard waved him off. "There won't be any significant effect on the market. The news will be nothing spectacular and it will have no effect." Jeff nodded and Richard continued. "Then we will coast through the holidays." Richard squirmed in the seat to adjust his posture. "Next year could be slim pickings though. Walt is pretty certain that the mutual fund trading will continue on a short term investing posture that will carry the market through to June, 2015. He isn't certain about the last half of the year, *but* with the presidential election coming up in 2016, and all the nomination hoopla, he thinks the DJIA and S+P 500 Indexes will 'stagger' towards the end of the year 2016 without a total collapse on the DOW or the Standard and Poors Indexes."

Jeff scratched his head and chin. "You know that sounds like a pretty good forecast."

Ronnie reminded Richard of the tax loss selling. "You are going to have selling in December for tax purposes. Investors will sell their short term losses and get a capital loss deduction on their tax returns. The capital gains deduction. I think all of that has to be done by the 15th of December by IRS rule. That should get the sale on your December securities statement. The same positions are often bought later in the new year, hopefully at a lower price. You know, I really am not sure about the date and come to think of it, the law may have changed. I can't remember."

"What about the banks?"

Richard gazed at the ceiling. "Banks? Banks are the great mirage. They actually own all the commercial and residential properties that are mortgaged. The homeowners make a huge monthly interest payment and only a small amount of the monthly payment goes to pay down the loan balance."

Ronnie interrupted. "Banks have a list of unrecoverable loans, but they are never listed in the financial pages or annual reports. It really makes no difference. They have the title to the property. The unrecoverable loans should cause an adjustment to the Current Interest Income and the Current Principle Income accounts and the Long Term Interest and Principle Income accounts. All they need to do is get the houses and commercial property auctioned off. The auctions are cash at sale time."

"But what happens when the foreclosures set in?"

"I am not an expert in this area. Let me try to say it a different way. The bank technically owns the structure but they do not mark their financial statements with the number of unoccupied houses or buildings. They just have less income for the balance sheet and the income statements. Jeff, I would really have to look at a bank annual report. That would be the way to find out. But, I don't think that they list their bad loans or their unrecoverable loans. The figures might be too confusing to shareholders or potential investors. Maybe some use the 'Uncollectible Accounts' position on their financials or some guestimate of unmortgaged asset value. Some merely write them off and they do not include any figures. But never fear! You can bet your house that a list is turned over to the bank collection department."

"What about credit cards?"

"Again. I don't know. There is no forgiveness of loan unless you go bankrupt here in the USA or offer a good sized payment to close out the account if the card company agrees. Same with a home loan. Sometimes in financial meltdowns a persistent homeowner can strike a deal on the remaining home balance. Deals can be struck for 75%, sometimes 70% of the remaining balance if teetering on foreclosure. The banks are trying to capture money if they can. You have to catch an authorized representative, a real company official with the power to make the deal. Don't waste your breath with a call center representative."

"Are international loans by bank syndicates to international countries similar to this situation?"

"International loan syndicates go back over 100 years. They can include some fashion of barter and trade. There are syndications between banks by contractual terms, and consortiums by two or three companies and maybe some private concerns by contractual agreement. Of course there is the World Bank. Again, I am just guessing here. Defaults or losses in international agreements could turn into sanctions, but, if I am correct, the financiers sometimes have to eat and digest a situation they don't like. They don't have much choice. They have to rebound. They have to get out and about and have some luncheons. They have to talk to old enemies and sniff out some new deals."

The restaurant workers began to scurry around to close the buffet and clean up. Ronnie announced, "Hey gang! It's about time to wind up this brunch. What say for some easy fun we schedule that croquet game we have been talking about?"

"Good idea. Hey!" Jeff threw in. "We can throw bull about the financial world. Or horse shoes."

Angie proposed an idea. "Let's use both back yards and set up a giant croquet field."

Richard approved. "That could be a blast. The Halloween vacation starts Wednesday. How about Thursday around noonish? We might have to play in the snow, but who cares?"

Angie laughed. "I will bring the snow shovel and the hot toddy mix. I sure had a good time today. You two know tons about the market."

Contented, happy and knowledgeable, they shared laughter and said their goodbyes in the parking lot. Angie had been taken aback at Veronica's gift and the Whiting's long time knowledge of the market. Jeff hoped that this Sunday brunch session would pull Angie closer to the investing world.

Back at the house, Jeff headed to the utility room. Just about five years ago, he set up his strategy desk in a little used corner of the living room. After three months Angelique moved his desk into the small utility room between the clothes dryer and the hot water heater. Jeff's desk had always been out of place in the living room.

The other rooms in the house were dedicated to more important activities.

As for now, he was determined to spend several hours in his private strategy room this afternoon to try and get a handle on the market. It was a dismal setting, but he had gotten used to it. He switched on the overhead light and a small one on the desk. It wasn't a totally worthless arrangement. At least he had one and he had found refuge and knowledge in his pursuit.

As always, Jeff stood in front of his desk and gazed at the two by three foot chart he had tacked to the wall above his desk. He bought the 50 year chart from Securities Research Company in July, 2014. At the same time he purchased the SRC Blue Book. Price had not been a factor. The chart showed six chart paths over the last 50 years from January, 1964 to July 2014. One chart for the Dow Jones Industrial Index. One for the Dow Transportation Index. One for the Dow Utilities Index. The NYSE Composite Index. The NASD Composite index. The S+P 500 Composite Index. It was impressive.

Jeff stared at his home made triangles underneath the chart. They reminded him of nuclear radiation symbols in the bomb shelter logo from his younger years. Like sirens that beckoned ships that sailed the Mediterranean 2000 years ago, the symbols beckoned to him. The triangles were as big as his hand. They were seven inches on each side. The bottom triangle was secured to the wall. At the top of the triangles, one small nail held the two together. This allowed Jeff to spin the top triangle upside down over the bottom triangle. Sometimes he would spin the top one just for fun and diversion. The triangles and the chart were valuable tools. Jeff could not make winning trades in the stock market without them.

When the top triangle was upside down over the peak of the bottom triangle, it was obvious that all hell was going to break loose. Just like the Dead Cat Bounce predicted. Jeff had finally figured out the total overall symbolism of these elementary shapes. There is no way to sell all of the shares in the upside down triangle for the high prices in the D Area of the bottom triangle. It would cause the market to crash. Prices would drop like a rock, especially if no one was buying stocks.

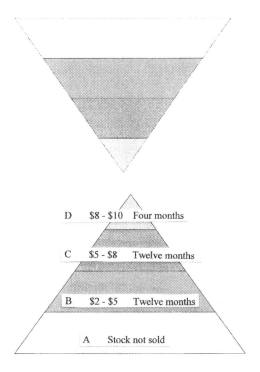

D	$8 - $10	Four months
C	$5 - $8	Twelve months
B	$2 - $5	Twelve months
A	Stock not sold	

DEAD CAT BOUNCE

He closed his eyes to clear his mind and focus on the task at hand. He was going to catch up with the current environment of the stock market. He was troubled by the 500 point drop Thursday (October 4, 2014) and he was determined to figure out what actions precipitated the drop. He opened his eyes and gazed at the desk. If the desk could speak it would voice a couple of sentences of discontent. *Where have you been?* It is about time you showed up. *You have neglected me.* **You are guilty**.

He knocked the dust off two books of financial fiction by Paul Erdman. The Crash of 1979 and The Crash of 1989. Erdman was a Canadian by birth. Eventually he became an American banker who opened *the very first American bank in Switzerland*. Paul was caught trading coffee futures in the bank's account. He used bank holdings as collateral. He served jail time and wrote about his exploits and parlayed his knowledge into tales of financial fiction. Erdman sold over 5.5 million books of financial fiction worldwide. He could spin a great yarn of the flow of money moving back and forth in the world of financial loans. He took you into the lives of the board of directors, the operating chiefs, the dictators, the owners and managers of the world's biggest corporations, including banks. What an eye opener! It provided Jeff with inspiration to escape the rut of his current situation and it gave him control of his dreams and his financial future. If he could become financially independent, then he and Angelique would have more time together.

Jeff was grateful for the reading habit he developed. It took him out of his present world and took him into the lives of politicians, the rich and famous and their greed. Their difficulties. Their vanities and their determination. Biographies of policemen, military leaders, soldier's lives, firemen, and detectives were testament to human intelligence, dedication, courage and survival. Books had given Jeff a new view of the world. He was actually able to understand what was really going on. Reading books had changed his life. To Jeff, *television was a **real downer**.*

His reading began with Steven Koontz and Steven King novels. Any national best seller had an exciting story to tell. Books allowed his mind to work. To Jeff, movies were no comparison to a good book, unless you liked all of your emotions stretched as thin as a wire in 80 minutes. Movie scenes these days were nothing but fast action, a lot of jive talk and full tilt blood baths. Movies are crass. Books bit Jeff right in the brain. Books are intelligent. Books can improve your life.

Reading allowed Jeff to become worldly and educated. He knew more now than the new investors who were putting some of their hard earned money into the market this very day. Little did they realize that they were *paying 3.5 to 4 times more* than the stocks cost after the last market crash four years ago. Jeff felt that the current prices had little or no chance of going higher. He felt good. He had a new global perspective. He understood what was going on. He was worldly and sophisticated and knowledgeable in areas that he previously knew nothing about. He was way ahead of his coworkers. And now, he held a healthy disdain for unions.

Jeff held a knowledge of the economies of the world and some of the corporate shenanigans within many countries. Books had given him a surge of self-confidence and a renewed awakening of his self-esteem. He dusted off *The Dead Cat Bounce*. He was grateful for *The Dead Cat*

Bounce. It outlined the flow of the market from the worst disaster day to the top of the crest of the stock cycle. No smoke and mirrors here. No ambiguities existed. The book was totally unbiased and full of market truth.

The Dead Cat Bounce was the impetus that moved Jeff off his duff and started him thinking that he could buy a stock, all by himself, and win, all by himself. He never thought he would understand the stock market or have enough confidence to invest on his own. Like a hunting dog, the Dead Cat Bounce had led Jeff to the incredibly low stock share prices at the bottom of the market crash in 2009. It had all been a miracle. Just five short years ago. He still pinched himself. This cycle might occur every seven or eight years for the rest of his life. And that would be the big payoff. He could easily have four more chances to catch the bottom of the market.

The information Jeff gleaned from The Dead Cat Bounce kept him more focused and goal oriented than a big mosquito on a camel's ass. His discipline had been unswerving. He had sold one stock fourteen months after the crash. It netted him a bundle of money. It wasn't a fortune, but it could keep the wolves away for a while. If he and Angie ever lost their jobs, it would prevent foreclosure on their house. And for the first time in his life, Jeff knew that he would always, without fail, have extra money set aside for the *disaster shopping day* in the stock market.

He gazed at the stack of newspapers on the floor. The stack consisted of pages torn out of the local newspaper business section. There were news clippings about earnings reports. There were predictions of the direction of share prices made by analysts from brokerage houses. There were opinions of independent analysts and wealthy players of the stock market. It made his head spin. There was always more than one opinion as to why there was an upward move in the market. Many different reasons were given as to why one event happened. It was all here. The positive and the negative and it all overlapped and occupied the same time and dimension. It was all intermingled in a swirl like the daiquiris and ice in the kitchen blender. Both substances literally melted his mind to mush.

The pile was about six months old. The articles were his ongoing diary of market action and new things to learn. He monitored the accuracy of these statements made by the TV news and the printed press news for financial truth. *Did real investors respond to world newspaper or TV*? Or *is the media just a scoreboard that smart investors avoid*? Jeff had proof that the media was just a scoreboard of *after the fact statements*. More importantly, the information was often **highly incorrect** analysis. It was all stacked on the floor beside his desk. He had seen it all!

Jeff had put two and two together and assessed that the media prints views from both sides of the event, positive and negative. In this strategy, the newspapers don't get sued and everyone has a feel good day because everyone is able to read their own view and opinion and then continue on with their assumption that all is right with the world. If a reader does not like what he reads, then he just has to turn the page and read about the same event with a different viewpoint. The articles report a reason that a particular stock or business sector moved up or down. It was just a scoreboard of runs, goals, kicks, hits, and errors until '*game over*' was declared.

Jeff decided he would catch up with current events and skim the stack before he attached any conclusions to the reason for the sudden 500 point drop in the DJIA Index last week. It was the largest drop in one day of trading since the dark clouds formed over the market in 2007. Jeff Picked up the stack and placed it in the center of his desk.

As he skimmed the articles, he decided to separate the pile into two stacks. He would put the newspaper clippings from the business page of the local paper on the left. This pile included stock prices, index statistics and the Associated Press articles that printed a reason for the previous days advance or decline. Those clippings went in a pile on the left side.

On the right side he would put the professional summations of market events from the financial community. There were finance magazines, market research reports from the marketing departments of brokerage houses and newsletters from gurus. Mutual fund managers near term market predictions for the year were included. This was the very serious hot poop from the professionals. The most educated opinions, guesses and what ifs. The skinny. The true statistics. The good stuff from the more knowledgeable advisors. All of these golden predictions and explanations would go in the pile on the right.

The enormity of it all was vast. The articles on the left were the usual weather reports. Partly sunny. Partly cloudy. Maybe rain tomorrow maybe sunshine. Maybe both. It was as if the stories and articles were alphabetized and kept in a long row of vertical file cabinets so they could be pulled out and used again and again by the newspaper staff writers, decade after decade. These articles were the same mundane, inaccurate, superficial explanations used in every stock market cycle rise and fall in the last 75 years. It was all angled to explain a little incident and to pacify any frightful event. It was all very misleading fluff to the new investor.

For individuals who have to run around in their daily work routines, and try to make a paycheck to survive for another month, the articles provided enough information to put the citizenry at ease. The news told them what was going on. Things were okay. No real problems existed. The forecast was great weather all this week. A few partly cloudy days. A few great summer days with sunshine. Good week to plan outings and spend money. Get out of the house for the weekend, but be sure to watch for that occasional picnic spoiler, the tornado or hurricane. Life goes on. That pretty much covered all the uncertainties and erased all the doubt for those whose knowledge and commitment was superficial. Read this and go about your lives without worry. You are protected.

Once finished, Jeff stared and pondered both stacks.

The significance of the local newspaper to Jeff was that it listed sixty popular companies that traded nationally and a few local companies in the state. The advantage of this page to him was the way the stocks were presented. The first column was the sixty corporate names and symbols. The second column was the 52 week HI and LO stock price. There was a small horizontal line connecting the two. On the line between the high price and the low price was a small dot that indicated *current price*. Jeff could check the location of the dot and know where the current price was in relation to the 52 week HI and LO. With just a quick glance, he could identify any drastic changes in market direction. For instance, Jeff could determine immediately that one third of the companies were at their high. One third were in the middle and on third were at their low. This was all within the last twelve months. Most of the DJIA Index companies were near their 52 week highs. Twenty companies at their 52 week low and 20 companies were in the middle. A mixed bag.

However, Jeff had discovered two very big mistakes with this presentation. Once two years of time had strolled by, the **direction** *of a stock price* **trend** *could be lost.* Jeff would no longer be able to tell if the stock was two or three times higher than it was two years ago. The same would be true if a stock had fallen from grace. The only other thing that bothered Jeff was that most of these stocks were S+P 500 and DJIA Index companies. The very big companies. Aside from that point, the stocks *trading in the middle* of their 52 week high and low were plodding along. Business as usual. No real problems sales wise or earnings wise at this time. They were '*marginally performing*' as the brokers would say. And the ones at the yearly high? Well, these stocks were very actively trading and they just continued to bob up and down at their 52 week highs. There was plenty of volume to pick the share price back up if it dropped 5 % because the broker house just might beef up their inventory, set a rumor loose on the street and sell into the rise in price when the new buying came in and the bid and ask were raised. Near term investors were always trying to get 3 to 5 % every hour of the day in 100 markets around the world. Mutual funds managers traded short term. USA company managers traded short term. Bank managers traded short term. All were trying to steal whatever they could.

Jeff felt that all the dots would soon be on the left side, the 52 week low side, with the exception of the DJIA companies. Everything possible was done to keep the DJIA Index afloat. His gut feeling was that the market was cresting. He scanned the names of the companies whose dots were on the right. The companies at their 52 week high share price were the large nationals and a few companies that made up the DJIA Index. That made sense to Jeff. Obviously, the market was near the top just four years out from the last market crash. Would it be downhill for two years from now on? That is what The *Dead Cat Bounce* said. *From the market crest, it would take two years to get to the disaster day shopping spree.*

He looked at the stack on the right. Over the last ten months, whenever he was in the big city, he had picked up a couple of copies of Barron's, some Forbes, the Economist magazine and Popular Science. The articles in these issues had a little more meat, a little more depth backed by credible facts and conclusions. These articles were vibrant.

They held sound explanations from the most educated and respected sources in the financial community.

It didn't look as if there was going to be a Black Monday or a Black Friday during this October of 2014. Trading stocks in the USA markets by investors from every nation in the world was not about to dry up right now. No depression today. The stock brokers of the world would not be jumping out of buildings this year. The elections by both political parties for the House of Representatives and the Senate that make up the two houses in the USA Congress were coming up in November, 2014. This was just one month away. In one more year the presidential candidates from both political parties would announce their run for President of the USA. Jeff felt it was possible that the market would drop at that time. If not, he thought March of 2017 would see the sharp drop after the new president was sworn into office. According to the wall chart, it was usually the year after the election.

Some companies had announced a slowdown in the economy. A few had suggested that earnings would not increase. The quarterly reports surfacing for the third quarter stated that their earnings '*did not meet expectations*' and were '*lower than projected*'. Where was the pizzazz? The earnings were bland and uneventful. There were piles of reasons given for this dilemma to sooth the worried investors. More than likely, investors were safe for now, but there was no doubt in Jeff's mind that share prices were going to begin to recede slowly, just like the tide.

The USA was still trying to recover from a horrific drop in 2009. It was actually a **mini depression**, but no one wants to hear the D word, especially the current administration. Everyone must use the socially correct words. By all means, the truth would be suppressed and remain hidden for at least two or three years before **this blow out** was declared the '**Great Recession**'. This predicament was one of the anxieties that subconsciously annoyed him. Don't rattle the pots and pans or make too much noise. Be quite as a mouse and keep the lid on. Status quo, as it should be. Jeff knew it should be called **The Mini Depression**. The subject was openly debated. Blame was still being heaped on the previous republican administration. Both Jeff and Angie were hurting for the promised stimulus money from the Obama administration.

Today, Jeff could feel a stock market correction looming. He was relieved and he realized that it was time for him to get out of the market.

He had money in his brokerage account. He refused to think about it. He was trying to go cold turkey and not to do any trading. He had left it alone for three years now. He had acquired discipline against the addictive lure to make a stock trade, just to experience *the cheap thrill of gambling or self importance*. There was a big difference between **imagining** that one could win and **calmly making the right choice at the right time**.

Jeff recalled that the Dead Bounce warned against this overwhelming urge to chase stocks as long as one was breathing. By chasing stocks, Jeff would be just another gambling hall drifter who wandered aimlessly around the market and the investment advisors, hopping from one *'hot stock tout'* to another ringing slot machine. He would lose his hard earned money a little bit at a time. It would trickle through his fingers. His cash balance would dwindle right before his very eyes.

The psychological effects of winning in the stock market are similar to the false confidence that tin horn gamblers experience at the limited stakes gambling casino. The over confident winner will swagger around the machines. He sneers at all the losers while *stalking his next hot one arm victim*. He revels in his winnings and may slam a drink and flirt with the cocktail waitress as he restores his energy for the next hit and run assault on the casino machines. He walks the isles, tossing his chips from one had to the other. The strong desire for a cheap, easy thrill always wins over a weakening resistance and resolve. The total addiction is here. He should stuff his winnings in his pocket and run screaming to his car in the parking lot. If there is no discipline, then all of the hard earned money is lost to the mental craving, to the itch.

Jeff did not want to be a loser. Initially, he made the commitment to stay away from short term trades and chasing stocks in his first venture into the market. He felt that it was important to concentrate on his main goal to learn and experience the market. **Preservation of capital was the number one goal**. He knew he could lose his shirt trying to play short term swings in the market. He did not have the necessary experience or understanding to trade without losing his money. But now, after four years of observation, he felt that he could make short term trades with a small amount of money. Still, he was worried it would fuel a desire to 'bet the pot' for the big win and lose everything. Jeff feared that mistake more than anything.

JT had actually held an investment and watched it move up and back down in the $3 to $5 range for a year and then, in a twenty dollar range between $30 to $50 during the next year, after the stock had a *10 for 1 reverse split*. It was unnerving but educational. He believed it helped to establish some discipline and resist the urge to chase stocks. It wasn't quite the twelve step program that the alcoholics attended, but it did have a sobering effect.

The near term investors fight for every dollar they grab. They are knowledgeable. They take risks. They are a tenacious, disciplined bunch who know how to steal money from the market. Now that jeff was learning more, he would play these near term swings with ten percent of his money the next time around.

He recalled that two years after the crash in 09 and 10 that the economy had faltered again in 2012. The DJIA Index had moved from the 6500-7000 area up close to 13000. A very sharp rebound. There was a big tout on the Street in 2011 that the DOW was headed to 13000. The question was posed, 'Could the DOW hit 13000?' Well, it did for a short time, maybe a week, and in October, 2012 the market **very unexpectedly** lost some ground. Jeff thought it was due to stimulus bailout money having to be repaid by the rescued banks.

There were six events that had led to the uncertainties in the market. The talking heads on the TV business news teams hinted that there might be a double dip recession and they expected it to occur within a year or six months from 2010. Some did not believe that the '*Stimulus Package*' would work. Oil was continuing to climb in price. This fuel expense was added into the inflated cost of transporting goods. As a result, the prices of food, most retail items and other commodities increased everywhere. There was a lot of conjecture among Middle East and other OPEC countries about using a middle east dinar to replace the USA dollar as *the world's **oil currency standard***. The USA dollars just were not good enough. The POTUS pulled the troops out of Iraq and that led to a resurgence of jihad terror attacks all over the world. The socialist Affordable Care Act in the USA had been introduced. Businesses were not in favor of it and they moved millions of workers to less than 40 hours a week. Workers were classified as part time employees and required to find their own health insurance policies.

My gosh? Did the democrats stop to think that taxes (government revenues) on payrolls to the I R S would shrink by quite a large amount? Heck no!! These government program designers did not have the ability to think a problem through and pick out any resulting problem area that might render the effort useless. They do not possess analytical skills. Their solution is 'Never mind! Let the creation live!' There is nothing special about the intelligence of politicians. They are geared to their retirement benefits and raising taxes. The hell with the people they serve! Throw tax money at it! I mean you just can't please Americans these days. That is why Bill Clinton had James Carvell as a press secretary. James phoo phooed the radical right wing conservative extremists who wanted to rule the country. James belittled them all.

One of the other events was the Russian invasion of Ukraine. And if that was not enough there was the Boston Marathon bombing. EBOLA was going to wipe out a significant portion of the population in Africa and eventually move over to America. Wasn't that like the year 2000 and Y2K computer date sequence failure? A bunch of uncertainty from out of nowhere. All kinds of news talk to present an interesting story to read. The articles contained no substance or hard factual data. Just supposings. Just the usual alarming routines to juice up the public's need for sensational news. Pick any reason you can accept or understand. Any reason will do for justification to drop share prices. Can't you see? The brokerage houses were laughing while they scooped up stocks to beef up their inventories. They would sell the shares back to the public and make a small house profit once the market got rolling again. *Investor fears would be sedated by the marching band* along with the new Wall Street explanation for the short pullback. The recovery was quick. Many analysts thought the drop in the market was not really warranted. Really? During this time, Jeff watched his Citigroup go up and down. He learned firsthand how much bad news could slow market trading and drop share prices.

At this point in October, 2014, Jeff felt like the market was over. He was not certain what to do. He wasn't lost. He was trying to figure out what was going to happen next. What must he do now? This was his big concern that was making it tough to sleep at night. It made him uneasy and it burned a hole in his head. The Dead Cat Bounce had not provided much of a description about the nature and characteristics of the top of the market. It did claim that the DJIA Index would begin to decline if **negative earnings** reports for the fiscal quarter began to turn up. When **negative earnings** for the quarters were back to back, then the crash would be close at hand. Jeff realized that was not the case right now as far as quarterly earnings reports and job layoffs were concerned. Yet he felt the slowdown was at hand and that a crash was possibly just one year away.

It was time to change his thoughts and his approach to the market. He felt an inexplicable stirring, a questioning in his head and heart. He felt that money could be made. He could feel it in his gut and his bones and his mind. He looked at The Dead Cat Bounce. The book had briefly mentioned that investors had the ability to play the downside of the market. This was what Jeff wanted to do. One could bet that the market was going to decline and indeed make investments accordingly. There were profits to be made.

Jeff wanted to have that bet. It was time for him to change goals, attitudes and direction. He would get the bet in place now. The market was going to drop lower within one year from now and then it would go over the cliff. And once again, an overwhelming itch to gamble began to plague him! This was the thought that was haunting him and it was scarier than anything that he had ever read in Dean Koontz or Stephen King.

He grabbed his trusty spiral notebook. He needed a new one. He would dedicate it to the downside of the market and learning how to short a stock. He would learn to short stocks by doing his homework. He would learn everything until he could regurgitate pure 100 % correct knowledge of how to make a short trade. On the next clean page, he printed in large block letters, 'A Change of Thought'. He added, 'A Change of direction', and 'A New Goal'. He had to lock it in his spiral diary, on paper. Now that it was on the 'TO DO' list, there was only one problem. Jeff did not know how to play a market slide. How in the world do you short stocks? He was going to find out. He would search the internet and if that did not work he would call the brokerage houses.

Jeff was going to learn to short and he was going to be the scourge of the street. A heavy hitter. No stock would be safe! He would defeat his feeling of uncertainty with knowledge. Knowledge brought him successfully to his present position. Knowledge was his guardian. His defense. His protector. Knowledge was the key difference between blindly jumping in and losing every hard earned nickel he had, or staying calm and remaining out of the fray. He would pick the right time and circumstance to accumulate a position. This was what separated him from new upstarts and made him a seasoned veteran. Making money by investing in a falling market was Jeff's new ambition in life. And he owed it all to *The Dead Cat Bounce Make Money Fast.*

He was aware that he could bet on the market drop and win. He picked up his spiral and wrote down the first thing he was going to do. Sell all stocks. He had to sell his stocks and collect his winnings to protect what he had earned the easy way. The second was to search the internet and read every article that explained how to short stock. The third was to call brokerage houses until he found a reliable broker or a reliable source of knowledge on how to make successful short trades.

The new spiral would highlight this new decision and new direction. The title would be 'How to Play the downside of the Market'. And like his old spiral, it would start at subject A and proceed painfully to subject Z for however long it would take him to learn everything.

He would do this and he would have to honor the promises that he made to his wife. They would pay down the principle on the home loan. They would do everything to get the house paid off ten years faster. Just stay calm and stick to the game plan. Stay positive. Stay disciplined and stay focused. Jeff felt a flood of relief the more he pondered this thought and this new direction. He knew he was right. He just did not know how to get it done.

He yawned and stretched. He needed to get some exercise. He was grateful that he had purchased some stock in a manufacturing concern. His 280 shares of Texas Instruments were traded at $17.00 back in 2009. He hated the thought of giving them up. The shares were currently trading in the $45 to $50 area. He was happy and content with them. They provided mental security. He felt that this company could just go on to the stars, but, having witnessed the bottom of the market, Jeff knew that most stocks were going to drop again during the next two years. Just like they did in 2008. He felt TXN would not fall as much as the others. He had held the stock almost four years and so far it had performed much better than Citigroup. Citigroup had given him gas as well as fits and starts and a nervous twitch. It wasn't easy digesting the ups and downs. It had stressed him out.

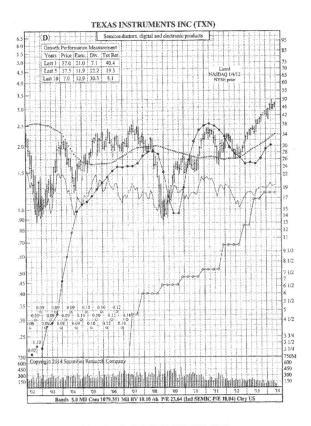

TEXAS INSTRUMENTS
Chart provided by Securities Research Company
(SRC). Please visit www.srcstockcharts.com

Jeff allowed himself to reminisce a bit. He had done well in his initial round of investing when he went disaster shopping four years ago, or was it five, in 2009. He bought Citigroup at $1.50. Right on the disaster day price. 3300 shares for $5000.00. Citi jumped back to $5 a share in just 5 months. A little over $16,000.00. A tidy profit of $11,000. His selection had doubled in just 5 months. Wasn't that what investors try to do in three or four years? **YES!** *Of course it is!*

But Citigroup had given Jeff a quick lesson. One thing Citi Corporation had done for Jeff's benefit was to drop from $5 back to $3 a share.

He thought about Citi for a moment. Citi was no better off now after the bailout. There were pending class action law suits from the foreclosed mortgage customers who had suffered hardships. They had been totally disregarded. These things happen. Lawsuits and mistakes occur now and then. It forced the company to make an announcement. *We are confident that the lawsuits will have **no impact** on current performance.* Blah, blah, blah. The company officials predicted that Citi stock was resilient. Jeff knew otherwise. Jeff knew Citi was going to drop.

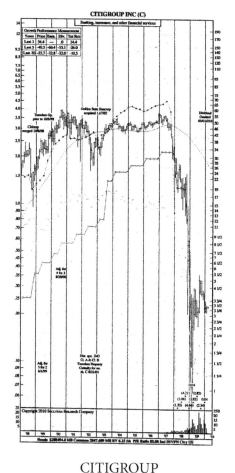

CITIGROUP
Chart provided by Securities Research Company
(SRC). Please visit www.srcstockcharts.com

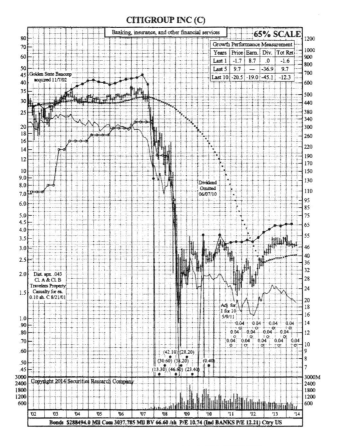

CITIGROUP REVERSE SPLIT
Chart provided by Securities Research Company
(SRC). Please visit www.srcstockcharts.com

Just four months after he bought CITI Jeff was busy strutting around, dressing fashionably, sporting his white sun glasses, smoking cigars and playing the wise investor to all his friends. He began to think he was bullet proof. He didn't have enough doubt about the exorbitant number of outstanding shares at the time. Only what? **26 billion** or so of Citigroup shares?

He didn't understand what to do with his paper profit. If he ever had a paper profit that moved two times higher in five months again, then he would capture part of those golden profits. But in 2009, Jeff figured there was another two years to the top of the share price. Two years up and two years down. Just like the four year business cycle analogy in The Dead Cat Bounce. But *that analogy was a dream scene*, wasn't it? Just a hopeful example. It was far from being exact on the timing. *In reality, it could be six or seven years depending on surrounding events and world economies at the time.* The ultimate peak of the market would always be elusive.

A year and a half later, in 2011 there was a reverse split of ten shares of Citi Group for every one share he held. This would drop the outstanding common shares from **26 billion** back to a reasonable **2.6 billion**. 2.6 billion could be dealt with. Easier for record keeping even in the age of super computers.

After the reverse split, the stock declined in 2011 and 2012. It had been a lesson for him. It dampened his gambling fever and greed craving. It helped him to learn how to keep control of his emotions. It helped him to understand and come to grips with the hard fact that after stocks run up in price, paper profits would be cashed out. After profits were taken, the share prices would slide back. And then, ***possibly***, the shares could be bought again for a rebound back to the high price ***provided*** the company was delivering good quarterly profits.

Instead of selling his winner of three times his money in 5 months, JT watched Citi fall back to the $3.25 area. It was still a winner. He still had the stock. Four years later he still had 330 shares and JT was going to sell them for $18,000.00.

The downward move in Citi value had shook him awake to the perilous situation that the bank stocks and mortgage companies were still in a dangerous position, even after the Federal bailout. Jeff lost his nerve with bank stocks at that instant. There were impending class action suits floating around. So, like a homeowner gets rid of mice and roaches, he quickly got rid of the Bank of America stock and he did so at $15.00 after it slipped down from $17. Jeff dumped his 2000 shares of Bank America that he bought for $3 a share (a total of $6,000) during the disaster day shopping sale. He cleared his position for a payout of $30,000. This was solid gain of $24,000.00 on a $6,000.00 investment in just over 12 months. Jeff smoked a couple of cigars after that one. He actually had his first long term gain in just a year and a half.

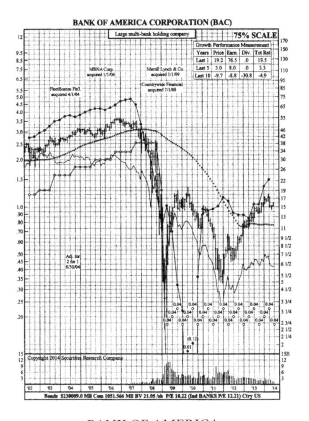

BANK OF AMERICA
Chart provided by Securities Research Company
(SRC). Please visit www.srcstockcharts.com

One year after the sale, as a victim of the problems in the industry at the time, Bank America had fallen back to $5. Jeff wasn't sure if he should buy the stock again. The whole industry had been saved by the bailout. Yet the problems had not gone away and this bothered him.

Angie walked by the utility room and peeked in. "Hey, love. While you are in there controlling the financial world, would you please find some time to sweep the floors and empty the waste baskets in the house?"

"Sure, dear." *What is it about women that keeps their husbands trudging along?*

For the past six months Jeff had ignored the market. *The Dead Cat Bounce* advised him to keep weekly notes but it was just too boring after a while. He had some things to do and wanted to enjoy the summer of weekend vacations that Angie had planned for them. There had been no reason to worry. Now here it was the middle of October. Now he knew why the brokers played a lot of golf every day in the summer. Their coworkers were the ever important support system, not the office. Escape is good for everyone. Not just convicts.

Right now, he had to escape to his cleaning routine. First things first. He forced himself to leave the strategy room and trudged down the hall to the kitchen. He started a fresh pot of coffee. Angie joined him in the kitchen with the 'The Ultimate Safe Money Guide' in hand.

She rolled her eyes to the dull drab ceiling and then back to her husband. "I know you are going back to your study, so I am going to the living room and read all about this Weiss guy."

"You mean Wise guy?"

"Whatever. I know Ronnie will be nagging me about my thoughts so I have to make some attempt." Angie poured herself a glass of wine. "I am going to the living room to watch TV and read." She turned and left for the living room.

Jeff kept his brain rummaging through the facts and conditions of investing while doing the chores. He quickly broomed the vinyl kitchen floor. He vacuumed the rugs in the hallway and then he emptied the wastebaskets in the house. He then moved the vacuum into the living room. He deliberately planned to do it last. Angie looked up from her book as Jeff passed through. He looked so cute in his tee shirt, bermuda shorts and sandals. She made a mental note to grope him later. Jeff took the trash to the can outside and returned to the kitchen. He was pouring a second cup of java when Angelique snuck up behind him. She groped him and gave him the customary hot kiss for the completion of the chores and her appreciation of his male attributes.

Jeff relished the attack. "Are you trying to molest me?"

"You know, love, this brunch with the Whiting's has made a favorable impression on me. I have some thoughts I want to share with you later. I know that you are going back to the bomb shelter. I just want to tell you that I am struggling through the first thirty pages of Weiss and it has really been an eye opener. I didn't know the dreary, misunderstood financial world could be so exciting. It's like . . ."

"Like having your foot in a bear trap?"

"Maybe your checking account. But it is also about financial dreams. We are better off to save and plan ahead than to upgrade this brick hut with junk, just to suit our small selfish desires." Angie adeptly added enough hugging and groping to get Jeff to press a good lip lock on her. No further advances to arousal were made. **Hopefully**, that would come later. "Come see me when you are finished. I might share my thoughts with you."

Jeff smiled. "That would be wonderful. I would like to talk with you about your small selfish desires." Angie smiled lustfully into her husband's eyes. She gave him a short meaningful kiss and then turned to pick up her book along with the cup of java Jeff had poured for himself. She sashayed on down the hall and back to the living room.

Jeff returned to the strategy room and the 'wizards table,' as Angie often called it. He presented himself to the front of the desk. Again, he looked at the stack of newspaper articles on the left. Here was every smooth line or rift that you ever heard being echoed throughout the investing community. They were gleaned from decades of Associated Press articles. This is one way to keep the marching band playing and the indexes inflating. Jeff skimmed the titles. *'Just blowing off steam'*. *'The DJIA/market has climbed so fast that it is only natural for investors to take some profits and pursue some other stocks for diversification.'* *'Stocks slip'*. There were words like *'plummet'* or *'climbed'*. The Whiting's were right. Socially correct market language was used to prevent lawsuits on phrases like, *Your stock sucks!*

He continued to skim through the AP news articles in the local newspapers as quickly as he could from last July to the 500 point drop on the 4th of October, 2014.

The newspaper claimed that housing starts were up this year. Jeff snickered. Maybe they were up from yesterday. Ha! Ha! Ha! Same old, loose, irresponsible words. Compared to what? This was a question Jeff had learned to ask many times. Compared to which decade? Vague and incorrect explanation was everywhere in the AP articles and TV news media. It was all misleading. Success was claimed! Comparison was conveniently forgotten. There were a few more housing starts this year. Yet the number was still hopelessly below the number in the year before the last market blow off when construction was doing better due to high home demand. Starts might be higher than last year, but they were hopelessly lower than the high of construction boom seven years ago during the Bush era. Did any paper try to point out that over half of the housing starts were modular housing? Heck no. They don't even know. As far as Jeff was concerned, there really wasn't any housing construction going on worth mentioning. Rumors were just leaking out again to the media machine. Positive rumors to make everyone feel good and to make everyone believe in the current administration and economic recovery. Either that or the news media is just **blind stupid.** Jeff considered more and more every day *that the media **is blind stupid**.* He was beginning to understand that these rumors may well be circulated around the world. Another mortgage after shock was rumored to be scheduled for 2015 or 2016.

Accidents, unfortunate situations and disasters cause share prices to drop. And rumors! Rumors always abound to drive share prices up or **even down**. There is the copper scare rumor designed to run copper commodities up. *'China is making millions of cars and they need copper for the radiators and there is no copper to be found!'* Bull manure! There is plenty of copper. Similar rumors were spread around the world about rare earth material. Cell phones and new miniaturization in the nano world required the mining of the new rare earth metals and *'There is none to be found anywhere in the world!' 'Buy stocks in rare earth mining companies now before the prices go through the roof!' 'Manufacturers will have to pay twice as much for the metals!'* The big lies! Load up on the cheap new darlings and then lie, lie, lie until the prices are driven up to the ionosphere. Then sell out the brokerage house inventory! Sell out the stake! It is just like salting a mining claim in the old prospecting days! Throw a few nuggets in one's claim and maybe someone else will be dumb enough to buy it. The thing about this angle is, if one is sharp enough to recognize what is going on, then *one should play the rumor for a little while. Heck, **everyone else does**.*

New scams. Fake start up mining companies in the pink sheets. Lease holders were the only ones to have the mineral rights for rare metals. Blah blah. Thousands of silly lies are given to the investing public from unscrupulous partners in crime.

He perused more article headlines. *'The market advanced slightly.' 'Little activity as market waits to hear jobs report.' 'Economy showing signs of 'expansion.'* Jeff wondered what the heck **expansion** meant.

Wasn't that word more than slightly misused? Manufacturers make more widgets, but they don't expand. Jeff laughed. Media writers love expansive terminology. *'Trade embargos.' 'Market dropped with profit taking'.* The market was, *'Back up Friday'.* Heck! No one cares about Friday anyway. All the action is on Wednesday and Thursday or so the story goes.

Jeff knew for a fact that the short term investors of the day and of the week were as competitive and optimistic as daredevil race car drivers. With four years of market observation under his belt, he knew that *if the market dropped on heavy trading on Thursday,* then a quick buy during the downward trend before the closing bell could produce a two to five percent gain by the closing bell on Friday or maybe early Monday morning. Jeff witnessed that the market would bump up a couple of points in light trading with no selling resistance on Friday, especially one hour before the close. Prices rose a little as the bids and asks on companies could be moved up arbitrarily at no cost to the trader at the brokerage house. There was not much time at the end of the day to even care. Half of the workforce was on their way out of New York City at three pm Eastern time. Workers had to get out of Manhattan (New York City) early so they could get back home to New Jersey, Connecticut or out to Long Island.

The upticks were token gestures that a rebound may appear on Monday. Saturday, the media would blast the news that the market had recovered from the midweek onslaught of selling and showed *'Signs of strengthening'* just before the close. This seemed to convey the thought that one had all weekend to think about a purchase Monday morning *before the market took off for the moon! Didn't you buy shares on Friday? The market closed up. Are you afraid? Are you a loser? Where is your money?*

Jeff was wildly into the mystique of market motion and the reasons surrounding the movements. If there was idle time at the shop, he would sneak into the market. He would tap into his online account to watch the trading activity. If there was idle time in the field, then he was on the website through his cell phone. He watched the patterns of the upticks and downticks of his five favorite stocks throughout the trading day if he had a chance. He checked their volumes and their closing price. He would watch the DJIA Index as well. On a couple of occasions he watched the last half hour while he was at work. Jeff made imaginary bets with himself that the market and his five favorite stocks would close up, down or stay the same. He kept his eye on current events in the USA and around the world to see what effect the events had on the market. He noted any exceptional movements. He found patterns during the trading week that might be helpful in making a profit on short term trades. One thing he caught onto after a year of observation was that during lunch (New York, east coast time) the NYSE floor traders and the brokerage house traders in New York City dug into their brown bag lunches. The market went on the back burner for at least 30 minutes with little volume activity.

Jeff was the kind of person who could put two and two together. He could use an active imagination to try to solve the mysteries of the whys and wherefores. He began to realize that short term traders had a few opportunities every week to eek out a few bucks from the market and walk away with cash in their pockets. He quickly realized that a living, although bleak at times, could be made this way with just $5,000 or more to trade. The only problem was that short term trading often required constant monitoring.

Jeff knew the next time around that he would be playing the subtle price changes from Thursday to Monday. If he was brave enough he could buy a stock that dropped in price on a heavy downward day of trading on Wednesday or Thursday afternoon and sell it back at just 15 minutes before the close on Friday on the usual Friday afternoon upticks. With the light trading Friday just thirty minutes before the close, it was possible that you just might get your way with a 'sell limit' order *if the tape was not running more than 20 minutes late.* If he missed, he would have time to place a 'market' order. If the market order filled, then he would have time to cancel the limit order. If he missed the chance to sell Friday afternoon, then his trade could possibly be done Monday morning in the first half hour of trading before any heavy selling began. Jeff had noticed the first hour of trading on Monday was kind of neutral. After the first hour, the uptrend or downtrend from the Friday close would sometimes reverse and a new direction in the market would be set.

He knew the *limit* order entries may or may not fill. Sometimes there are investor orders stacked up in line in front of any new order entered to the exchange trading floor. Those orders in line would be honored first.

Orders are sorted and cued by size, date and price. Of course, there were *'good until cancelled orders'* as well as *'buy limit'* or *'sell limit'* orders. Jeff had been thinking that a **'fill or kill'** order could be introduced in the last hour on Wednesday or Thursday. *'Fill or kill'* orders are buy orders for the day only. *Fill or kill* did not execute immediately like a market order. It would be executed usually within an hour or two. Sometimes half a day. It would depend on the size and the price. A market order will always fill at the moment the order is placed, but the price will not be the current bid and ask quote shown on the screen. Heck! So what? The streaming quotes were usually running 30 minutes behind the actual trading being done at that very moment anyway. Sell at market or buy at market. That will put you first in line as *the very next trade attended to and executed* by the floor traders!

Jeff skimmed more headlines. There was the usual rally after the Fourth of July holiday (due specifically to the pension fund buying). Business as usual. New jobs were created just filling the old vacancies from previous layoffs. After two years of being on unemployment, the names were automatically dropped from the count whether work was found or not. Jeff knew this to be true. These folks could still be unemployed, but there is nothing like positive news even if fabricated. In this new 'great recession' the rules had been change from six months to two years for the length of time that one could draw unemployment compensation. The Fed Reserve had decided 'not to raise interest rates'. That was just a filler article. At these low interest rates half a percent up on the Fed Funds rate didn't mean shit. 'Gasoline prices were dropping'. This was great break for households running in the red. Finally, some extra cash to pay off some short term debt.

Jeff thought of the upcoming holidays. He could imagine all of the holiday touts now. *'The market will rally back next month.'* *'We should have a good year end (Santa Claus) rally after the share prices recover in November.'* *'Now is a great time to buy.'* *'Buy on the dips!'* *'Hold your stocks for the long run!'* *'It is still a bull market.'* *'The economy is fine.'* Jeff mused. Well, in a farfetched, loose definition, the GDP economy might be fine, but there were no more strong upward advances in the stock market. There were only small advances up and small drops down.

Jeff began to ponder the depths of the ocean. The bottom of the stock market lasted 6 to 9 months. Was it the same at the top of the market? Would the D area go sideways for a year? Two years? He studied the fifty year chart again and looked for comparisons. He was looking for the market to define a peak. He knew it was close at hand. He had never experienced it. He had never witnessed what the market top would look like. He made a note of that in his diary. *What we are on is a plateau in the D Area. This may be the prelude to the downturn. Earnings of half of the companies are coming in below estimates and market expectations. A few have reported no earnings for the quarter. Most all company earnings are lower than the same time last year.*

There were other signs of a slowdown. Companies were announcing stock buy backs. Companies could buy shares of their own stock that were trading in the market. The story goes that the action would increase the price value of the existing shares by decreasing the number of shares outstanding to the public. The smaller the number of shares trading, the more valuable they would be. Usually, any honest attempt to do so was dropped right after the announcement. There never was any intention to follow through. This was another empty promise used to encourage an investor to buy the stock. This was all bogus hype to pop up the share price and create a small flurry of buying activity.

Another slowdown sign was the fact that many companies have enough money at this time to pay dividends to shareholders. Instead of doing this, the Board of Directors would decide to hold on to the cash because the environment of the next twelve months was too uncertain. It would be better to save the money for payroll and expenses, should sales revenue fall off. Cost cutting announcements were another sign. This could be a layoff of employees of 10% or more. Lower earnings might lead to plant closings. Overall, *a defensive stance* for the next twelve months was being taken by the 2600 NYSE companies.

The Dead Cat Bounce paid detailed attention to the month of October, but this October, 2014, was not the same financially as the October of 2007. This October was a mixed bag of earnings. Stocks close to their 52 week highs were having trouble. These companies had earnings, but there was not enough fresh money coming into the market to keep their stocks buoyant. 30 to 40% of the 2600 NYSE companies were reporting that earnings were down. They were showing signs of weakness in their share prices, all of which were down 5 to 10%. Most all company earnings reports were less than the year before and some were even lower than the previous quarter. This was a sign that something was wrong in the *USA consumer goods economy*. *So far,* there were no companies with back to back quarters of no growth or negative growth. At least not yet.

The next article mentioned that there may be another round of foreclosures in the mortgage industry. Many families had struggled through the 2008 to 2010 mortgage meltdown and had hung on for another year or two. They were giving up here in 2014 after completely exhausting all of their meager assets and savings. They were taking foreclosure because they couldn't sell the house. Even if there was an offer to buy, the sales price would not cover the remaining balance due on the mortgage.

What was it? What was going on? Here we are in the fourth year of advance. It made Jeff a little nervous. Are we just moving along and keeping everybody happy right now? Money was available to consumers. Loans with very little interest could be used to pay off past debts, if you could get one. Was this our stimulus? Consumers were still shopping, but Jeff figured they were shopping and spending less than in 2007. There. He stuck his neck out. Things were winding down in consumer spending. He wasn't certain about construction. He needed to dig into Barron's and find these things out. Maybe he could find out with an internet search.

By coincidence the next item was **a 32 page pull out section** from the local newspaper. On the first page in large block letters were the words **Tax Lien Sale Notice**. Jeff looked at the **County Seal** on the front page and thought about this situation. Is this the direction he should go? Were tax liens the secret bonanza? Is this what investors bought with all of their cash profits from the market? Would it be more safe than investing on the downside? Jeff wondered. Maybe this is where his winnings were supposed to go.

Jeff realized that the tax lien sale was thirty two pages of property listings in the county that was lost by people who went bankrupt in the **2008- 2009 melt down.** These poor beat up people were finally letting go of everything they had and they were moving on down the highway. **Hopefully**, they would find a new vital economic community where they could find employment and raise their families. Jeff considered this new idea of thought and action. This was it! This could be a defining moment for his actions over the next two years! He could find an acre of land or a low price house that Angie could rent out as a hobby. Or whatever. This tax lien sale was true diversification!

Jeff's thoughts went back to the top of the market. You can't pick the top. Stocks hit their highs individually. They hit their highs on different days and different months. Some of them would hit their highs one year or more before the DJIA Index tanked. He looked at 1980 on the wall chart. He looked at the 1990's when Veronica and Richard began to invest. The pattern told the story. Jeff could see the course of his future if he stuck with his plan. There were four huge market crashes from 1980 to 2009. Four devastating stock market crashes that lowered the 'standard of living' for all US citizens. For the first time in his life, Jeff discovered that he was beginning to understand this 'financial road'. He and Angie could make enormous returns on their investment money, if they kept their profits intact and timed the cycles of market disasters accurately.

One of the many things Jeff had figured out was that the real character and flavor of the market was a long, slow daily grind. A little trading here, a little trading there, over a long, long boring period of time. The earnings reports were bright spots that appeared now and then over the long haul. They were golden news and they increased trading activity. The answer was stick with the plan. Buy disaster at the bottom of the market. Get your double on the way up, maybe a little bit more and get out. Don't look back. And when you diversify, don't diversify by reinvesting in the market. Buy some land. A classic car if you can store it somewhere. Or go to work for yourself. Home repair, patios, fences, stand alone garages, new front porches! Buy used cars at the auto auction. Fix them up and sell them. An unopened Barbie doll. An unopened Elmo. They could be tucked away in a garage or a closet. A two cycle small engine repair shop. Maybe even foreign currency at the airport. Maybe an ATV franchise! That would make the big bucks! Whatever Jeff did, he would never buy a time share. No time shares!

In these choppy waters of Area D, once in a while you will hear a strong rumor from the Street that so and so company is a turnaround situation. With nothing new going on, rumors abound. Occasionally, the hype and the lies work. When the 'Street' decides to run a darling stock they have picked out, **occasionally**, *the self-fulfilling prophecy makes it to reality.* Jeff realized that he didn't have to like the stock or the reason, but he did have to be on his toes to pick one up. Investors like to run stocks just as much as the brokerage houses.

He checked his wallet for cash. Angie wanted him to run to the store for some food items in the morning. He pulled out a lotto receipt that was mixed in with his cash. The words *'Expect the unexpected'* appeared on the bottom of the ticket. How absolutely trite! How asinine! That is how our government treats the taxpayer. Could that asinine quote be reference to a sunny day? How absolutely doubtful. Could it be in reference to the powerful economic hurricane that would lift your financial house to the sky and scatter it across the county? That was more likely to be the case. Jeff laughed at the horrific humor..

He picked up another local business page with the list of 60 companies. He glanced at the volume column. Whoa! Microsoft! 155 **million** shares traded and it was down $4.35 just a tad over ten percent of the share price. It was on a Wednesday. Hummmm. Gosh, ten percent on a five thousand dollar risk once every week would be an extra $25,000 for the year. It seemed like a lot of effort. He knew that every week would not present such an opportunity. Still, a five percent gain could be made once in a while if he was on his toes.

He looked back to the articles of the local paper clippings. It was a Saturday edition, a recap of the end of the market activity on Friday. *'US stocks jump on late trading.' 'Shares jump on Friday!'* Well no kidding. 'Rally back in late trading!' The word 'jump' is more exciting than 'barely advanced' or 'hardly any volume'. Words like climb or jump in Saturday's analysis in the local paper made non investors realize that they were sleeping and missed something. The word smiths played on thoughts like strings on a harp. Jeff noticed that his astrology chart was on the back of the page. It read, *'You will find vast fortune in your new endeavor'.* Ha! Horoscopes were simply thousands of years of mysticism and snake oil that flourished across the nations of the earth.

But no worries! Jeff harbored no ill feelings or disdain to the newspapers. It is just the paper doing their job. Fill a page to sell a paper. If you are a worldly sophisticated investor, then you need to be reading worldly, sophisticated business magazines or newspapers. Investors should not feel cheated or lied to by the dreary Associated Press articles in the local rag. Get the right sources to read. There are plenty of good ones.

Jeff's mind was jammed with thoughts popping in and out of his head. The market certainly was emotional and interlinked. He stretched and touched his toes to get some oxygen in his lungs. Then he decided to look at the articles in the stack on the right.

He picked up a weekly newspaper. It was Barron's. August 19, 2014 was the date. Right there on the front page was the big news. *'Profit estimates will be lower for the first fiscal quarter of the year'* *(2015 January, February and March).* There it was in black and white. **Someone knew what was going on!** What more could he ask for? Huge capital letters right smack dab on the front page. No wishy washy sugar coating. No smoke and mirrors. No misdirection. No baloney. A professional financial opinion, **seven months ahead** *of announcement time*! Jeff welcomed this truthful information. It eased his anxiety level. In addition, there was no mention or hint of a market index downturn or a market sell off. *Just the valuable conclusion* that earnings would be lower. Jeff noted no such predictions from the Associated Press articles in the local papers or the TV business news. An upcoming disaster was never put into print.

Jeff knew if the headline had read that 'estimates would be higher', then indeed current share prices would hold or rise slightly through the end of the year and into the first quarter 2015. He concluded there was going to be a slight downturn in December if investors decided to sell stocks that were dogs. The dogs that had '**underperformed**' would be sold to lock in short term loss or long term loss for the capital loss deduction on line 14 of the yearly 1040 IRS Federal Income Tax form. On the other side of the coin, if the earnings were trending downward, then so would share prices of those companies that would not achieve their estimated earnings forecast.

Jeff's views and thoughts were in agreement with the article behind the headline. This was stuff that you could sink your teeth into. It was not stuff like watching the talking heads on TV or reading the fluffy weather reports in his pile of local papers. Here was solid, reliable economic verification that earnings of some companies were going to be lower. No words were minced. He could understand that this 2014 would be just a gray October, not a black one. This thought encouraged him to relax and wait six months to a year for the market downturn. He still had a little more time as Veronica and Richard had told him during the Sunday brunch. **They were right**. The new scenario would be to wait for the drops in prices to buy shares and play the short-term rallies. Sell the shares after the price bounced up and stalled out under heavy volume and selling. Play for a rally **after the price drop** when the disappointing earnings were announced.

Jeff understood that the first quarter of 2015 would be the months of January, February and March. Company first quarter earnings would be responsibly announced by a company official fifteen days after the end of the quarter. Companies occasionally released some clues before the end of the quarter. Earnings and operations performance may be 'on target', 'disappointingly lower', 'the same or greater' or 'less than the previous quarter'. Occasionally, *the unofficial announcements* from anonymous sources that appeared in the papers *were **just plain lies**.* Responsible reporting would compare current earnings with the same quarter one year ago and the previous quarter (4th). These announcements *most certainly moved the direction of the share price* and it behooved any short-term investor to take note and plan accordingly. He thought about placing an earnings scoreboard next to the wall chart. It would be good to have some instant feedback on the trends.

The official company quarterly results would be a public statement to the associated press or other news media by the company press representative or a company officer. Often news is leaked by employees and people in the know, without any official announcement from the company. This can cause stocks to miraculously jump 5% without any news a month before any official announcement is made to the public or the papers. Sometimes front runners would buy early based on the assumption that earnings were going to be higher or better than the previous quarter or the same quarter a year ago. Jeff had witnessed this phenomena many times over the past four years. Occasionally, the statement made by a *'spokesperson'* would be an out and out lie. *'We expect earnings to be in line with our projections and perhaps slightly higher.'* The stock would rise 5 % or more and 30 days later a flat earnings report would come in. After that, the stock would sell off.

Jeff recalled that he promised himself to go over to the library. They carried Barron's along with other top rated financial magazines and newspapers. He planned to drag Angelique along. Jeff loved the Barron's weekly. It is very different in appearance and the manner of presentation of financial market statistics and facts when compared to most market newspapers. There were equity rankings of mutual fund performance and interviews of NYSE listed company officers. There were successful market analysts, mutual fund officers and founders and officials of many other things. Barron's highlighted all items traded in the market places. Everything from stock and bond indexes to commodity performance. He especially liked the pull-out section titled 'Market Week'. He considered Barron's to be vastly superior. Some of the journalism was kind of 'tongue in cheek'. Witty, one might say. Still, investors must decide on their own as Barron's often published opposing views. The viewpoints are due to different perspectives that originate from different backgrounds and environments.

One of the highlights every year were the four weekly issues in January. This was nothing less than the very big picture of what was going on. The editions were filled with rankings of mutual fund performance, consumer goods and products. Every January, one issue was devoted to analysts' predictions of the growth for the *consumer economy* (GDP) and the *stock market economy* for the upcoming year. Predictions of corporate stock and mutual fund shares were openly made by interviews with listed NYSE company CEO's, mutual fund officers and founders.

Jeff really liked the fact that if something caught his interest, then he could sit down and read about the item in depth and detail. The local newspaper AP articles were limited as to space and were not able to provide this service. What was amazing about Barron's were the discussions of items of which Jeff was totally unaware. This fed his curiosity and kept him learning more about the world of finance.

Barron's and other economic newspapers and magazines would look into the future, and make comparisons to the past. Still, things could get a little confusing due to the facts coming from the different viewpoints. Just like internet news, there could be opposing views and opinions and arguments on a subject. But, after all, half of the people in this country disagree with the other half. It was up to the astute investor to pick which view was correct. Barron's carried a hefty first subscription price, but was always fair about offering discounts especially to current subscribers.

One article was openly discussing whether or not the Federal Reserve would raise rates. But in the same breath they added that *at this juncture, it would have no real effect on the economy.* The economy was not overheating. The dollar was gaining strength internationally. This would weaken American company profits on USA goods if they sold overseas. Foreign competitor prices and currency were cheaper than the USA's. American goods would not be bought because of the higher price foreign nations had to pay.

Other thoughts crossed his mind. In relation to the severity back in 2008, one could imply the economy was recovered now. The Associated Press had an onslaught of positive articles this fall (2014) about the health of the economy and improvements all due to the miraculous efforts of the current administration. Jeff knew this was feel good fluff. There were all sorts of good positive statements floating around the media right now. Currently, the President righteously proclaimed an economic recovery and the media plastered his statement everywhere. The recovery was all due to the POTUS good work and management of the new administration's strategies. But this statement did not take into account the current downward trend of company earnings reports. Ain't that something? Positive spin six months before the official government 'bad news' would be released. Go ahead and lie to the public. Mince the words into harmless praise or spittle just before the holidays. Just another president reading a script crafted by a media manager. These lies made Jeff sick. This deceptive article of pure gloating and self-praise without merit confirmed Jeff's suspicions. *The downturn was on the way.* The present slowdown was being ignored.

Annual government reports were always six months late. Too bad! It takes six months to run the totals and publish the results to the public. Quarterly results were always three months late. Never the less, the marching band and the Street always bumped the market bid and ask upward on good news. The recent declines would not be reported for six months from now. Jeff thought the big institutions with money at risk had taken the clue and decided to 'lighten up on their positions'. This would be the reason for the 500 point drop from out of nowhere. Jeff felt that the economy was out of the big hole, but not by any means was it in a full recovery. The definition of '*a full recovery*' was, by itself, **elusive**. Jeff mused. Just wait until things start to heat up. Then the Fed will claim that the economy is performing so well that they will have to raise interest rates 'because the economy is beginning to overheat'.

The next item was one of the few *guru* investment newsletters he had subscribed to for a year. It was nothing more than pure market bull manure left by the thundering herd. None of the recommendations had moved more than 20%. The reports usually preceded quarterly financial earnings announcements. He tossed it to the circular file. He recalled the 'Dead Cat Bounce' mentioned that if you went short on some of the newsletter recommendations, then you might make a quick investment return. The reason is that the recommendations have been bid up since the first rough draft and newsletter press time. News always leaks out, and so, by the time Jeff had received his report by mail or internet, the recommended stocks would have risen 15 % in share price. Maybe Jeff could sell the recommendations short during heavily trading activity when the price peaked and stalled out. The near term investors hoping for 20% or more short term profit would pull out their winnings and the price would then fall back to the lower point from which the action began. Jeff strongly felt that he could go short and play the downside of the stocks listed in the newsletter. Maybe for as much as a 15% sell off.

The actual announcement of the quarterly earnings results are usually released ten to fifteen days after the accounting department finished crunching all of the numbers. After these numbers are crunched, all of the individual accounts are closed out. Then the Income and Expense Statements and all of the Financial Statements are prepared. Of course, the tallies are talked about in the company up and down the halls.

The plant operations are eventually talked about to friends, neighbors and relatives. In the newspaper clippings he had just read from July to September, occasionally, an anonymous person tipped a hand to the news media.

Basically, these are leaks of confidentiality. Occasionally, a company will issue a press release ahead of time if they feel that the quarter might be a disappointment. The current psychology is to announce the bad news and get it over with. Go ahead and let the cat out of the bag. Get it over with. The company is doing a favor to tip investors. Smart short term investors may take a little stake after the sell off to make a bet on a small recovery for a small, positive gain.

Then again, some scammer from a brokerage house might release some information (true or false) on good earnings for one of the stocks that the brokerage house has in inventory. The 'research' department might release a rainbow earnings report and allude that sales would smash the competition and lead to 5 to 10% growth for the year. This is a standard pitch. There would be a mad dash for the stock by the short term investors to play it for 5 to 10%. Hey! It is a war in the financial game just like anywhere else. The casualties and collateral damage are hard earned dollars in checking and savings accounts of average Americans and their standard of living.

Jeff knew heinous crimes and shenanigans existed in the investment world. Outright lies float about the surface. It is the same in the political world and just like false advertising in the retail world. New investors should not get mad at Wall Street just because they don't know the market. It is just like any other competition. **Some** first time investors will never educate themselves. They will say they were the victim. They will say they were cheated.

Wall Street has always been nonchalant about the 'shenanigans'. *No harm done! Buyer beware! Never pity the poor new investor!* How would we ever be able to make any money in the market if it were not for the new investors hopping on board and bidding the price of the shares up over three times what we paid for them? *This always happens when the media is screaming every day,* '**The market is at a new all-time high**'. Of course, short term trading keeps the DJIA Index up. Short term investors are continuously trading a small amount of money. Seasoned short term investors are smart conniving and shrewd. They refuse to be taken. Their profits have been converted to cash and are sitting in the bank. The band keeps playing as if the current DJIA Index record high *is the greatest achievement since the landing on the moon.* As an example, the market will back off 200 points and then come back with 201 points for a one point increase to '**A new all-time high**'. Or the market will trade even the next day and in the last half hour of trading, it will run up one point higher than yesterday's new all-time high and the papers will say, '**New all-time high**'. This is grandstanding. Phony grandstanding. After six months of this nonstop music, a new, gullible or unknowing investor might see a chart and become convinced that now is the time to get in the stock market just before everything goes to the moon. Actually, the marching band is always playing *new all-time high* when the stock market is churning in Area D. Area D *is the time to be in **cash**! Area D is deceptive!*

Jeff knew that after the crash in 2000 that half of the mutual funds were totally destroyed because the managers and founders (new to the securities business) were too stupid to figure out that the telecommunication, computer and internet mania was over. They held on. The portfolio managers did not sell their winners. Those **stocks were ten and twenty times higher than what the share prices were just two years before in 1998**. An incredible modern day tulip bulb mania performance! The portfolio managers were too stunned on their amazing successes. The tail was wagging the dog. They were floating high on the clouds and they were on a never ending rainbow living the dream. They were too egotistical about everything to even consider selling. These managers had never seen a market blow out. Much the same as the Japanese when their Nikkei 225 experienced a mania and subsequent blowout. USA mutual funds numbered 7500 in 1999. In the year 2000, at the crash, they shrank to 4500. **Forty percent of the funds were totally wiped out**. Almost one half of all the mutual funds in the USA.

One person offices thrived. With the advent of advanced software, personal computers could handle all of the administrative functions. Mutual funds could be set up easily. All the owner had to do was pass the required NASD exams. Of course, we need the mutual funds to persuade the novice investor to just relax and let the wise managers of operations in the mutual fund industry manufacture money for them. '*We can manager your portfolio for you and we can do it better than anyone else.'* Isn't that wonderful? For an easy sale, all a representative had to do was push the chart with the upward moving fund price across the desk. The new client would view the ascent path on the chart as *the road to his future wealth.* **This is a big, deceptive item**. The new investor interprets the chart as *a God send* of pure, no risk investing. The charts looked like stair steps to financial wealth. Invest $10,000.00 today and retire, with a million, thirty years from now no matter what. Jeff knew that was a crock. He had made more money in his first five months in the market than the mutual funds had made in the last two years. Responsible salespeople **should note** that the downturns were harmful to many investors.

*Charts are a visual clue used by instructors to represent and clarify a thought or concept to **students**.* But, by no means are pictures or charts absolutely precise. Human interpretation could drift off to the wrong conclusion very easily, especially when misled or coached incorrectly. The wrong conclusion can easily be drawn. Jeff stared at the wall chart. Underneath the six market index charts, was the Gross Domestic Production chart. The GDP chart was a steady upward climb compared to the whipsaw action of the six market index charts. Jeff focused on the condensed spaces of time that represented one year. What was wrong with it? He had been asking himself for two years now. One hundred times at least. What was it not telling him? He felt that this chart had at least one fault.

The 50 year wall chart was well crafted. It did convey the overall message on one piece of paper. But there was no way that the small space of one year on the graph could portray what actually happened for 365 days. The space of one year had to be very small so all of the years would fit on the large 24 inch by 36 inch wall chart for viewing. As a result, the downturns became less pronounced. They looked like mosquito bites. Compared to the long four, five and seven year advances, the mosquito bites were small and short in duration. The mosquito bites, however, were the most damaging recessions that the American consumer has ever experienced. They were tsunamis for 8 to 10 million families in 2007 through 2012. American lifestyles and standards of living are permanently lowered in every recession. And each time this happens, some unfortunate families are almost damaged out of existence. In short, they lose everything they own. In 2009, it was obvious that the

USA economy had taken one of the worst setbacks in the last **90 years**. Americans were bleeding out financially.

Jeff realized that there was important information that was not shown on the chart. Each tiny space that registered a downturn and a stock market crash, actually represented thousands of hours and minutes of painful waiting, painstaking drudgery, horrifying monetary family losses, long hours of family squabbles, millions of new job searches and don't forget about the foreclosures, bankruptcies and divorces. Jeff smiled. ***That*** *was what was missing! All of that in a tiny little mosquito bite!* Salesmen always smiled and told client not to worry about any small, short lived downturns. *'Hold on for the long haul!'* Jeff knew that the phrase meant that the stock was on its way to the landfill.

There were dots on the chart that represented a point in time of some important event as if it had a direct impact on market direction. There were no dots noted at the mosquito bites to represent the number of mortgage foreclosures, the number of American families filing for bankruptcies, or divorces. On average, bankruptcies usually number around 250,000 a year. The USA had 1.4 **million** bankruptcies every year from 2007 to 2012. This six year stretch of foreclosures was nine times the average number of foreclosures.

Jeff decided that the 50 year chart should be 50 feet in length. One foot for every year.

It was all clear as mud except for one thing that stood out as being crystal clear. In Jeff's opinion, it looked as if this was going to be another seven year stretch of so called **'bull market baloney'**. The Dead Cat Bounce had warned that the longer the bull, the faster and more unexpected the drop. Jeff could imagine the excuses at the brokerage house for not having sold investor shares before the crash. One of them was going to be, *'Oh. We had so much activity that all of the emails and the internet trading activity took our server down along with the computers and the PDA display screens! It was a smoking hot day! Totally burned up the server and the software! It will take a year to get it all sorted out.'* Nothing but insincerity here!

Jeff was going to stand strong. For the third time in the last three years he was going to draw his chart extension. The time period would include a two year sideways DJIA Index market slide to coincide with the analysis in *The Dead Cat Bounce*. His extension would include this recent 500 point October, 2014 drop and the new DJIA Index high for this market peak. It would outline the swell of the last wave and the choppy water that would arrive for the next two years, 2015 and 2016.

Instead of a small quarter of an inch space to represent one year, Jeff decided to make his 8.5 by 11 page extension represent two years. Two inches would equal 6 months. The path would include all of the ups and downs, and the final drop. *The low point of the DJIA Index would list divorces, foreclosures and bankruptcies. The high point would be labeled mutual fund profit taking.* Fund managers were locking in profits, but would the clients realize they should sell their shares?

Jeff pulled a clean 8.5 by 11 inch paper from the desk drawer. It was time to put a new face on the top of the 2015-2016 DJIA Index. He sketched the path and went over it with a black marker. Then he pinned his extension to the DIJA Index chart path.

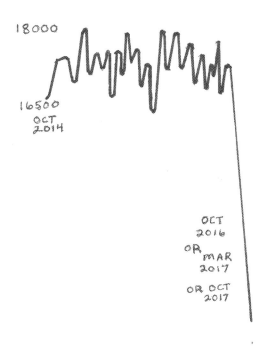

Jeff's Graph

Jeff was forming a different image of the DJIA Index and it was not the sterile, one dimensional chart image at which he was staring.

He reasoned the DJIA Index consisted of the best and the largest companies out of 2600 NYSE stocks. These stocks were used by the very short term investors to trade on an hourly, a daily and a weekly basis many, many times. These stocks maintained high prices as long as short term investors traded them.

Obviously, short term investors make over 100 trades or more each year. This would be an average of one buy and sell every week. A long term investor would make only one buy. This is one very stout reason that the DJIA Index could stay up in share price. It is simply because of the sheer volume of short term trading on the 30 DJIA stocks. Everyone around the world traded stocks in the DJIA Index and the S+P 500. If they suddenly decided to stop trading because all of the other stocks had succumbed to bad news and the economy had gone sour, the 30 company stocks on the DJIA Index would drop like a brick falling out of the sky.

There was a twinge of disappointment for Jeff, because the market had continued to go up bit by bit over four years. He knew that he could have made a few more trades and made more money. But Jeff had taken a solemn vow, a solemn oath to follow through with the main goal recommended in the Dead Cat Bounce. *Focus on the goal and stick to the plan* and get out before the market drops for whatever reason, war, famine, bad earnings reports or recession.

Jeff had to force himself to turn away from the powerful, addicting urge to throw himself into the fray in a shotgun approach to '**diversify his funds**'. These temptations were strong and they ate a hole in his head. This had all been a learning lesson for him and above all else this lesson was his golden rule. He had learned to buy disaster and stick to his plan. Once he sold his stocks, true diversification would come into play. He could buy the tax lien of a small commercial lot. Eventually, it could become a site for a franchise. He could buy an old warehouse and fill it with carpet. Or he could build a small metal building. Just gravel, a roof and framework first. He could finish the rest a little bit at a time. At least he would have a hard asset to trade. Above all else, he understood that it would take time, commitment and unswerving allegiance to play these ideas in the correct manner.

He had skimmed enough. Jeff had his fill of diligence. He wasn't really current, but he felt that it was time to cash out. Enough studying. Having satisfied himself with his rationale, he logged on to his online account and put in *sell at market* orders for TXN.O, and Citigroup. After four years he couldn't wait to say **'cash me out'**. Jeff thought about the impending crash as he closed out his positions. On Monday morning he would have $32,000 of cold hard cash added to his account. Coupled with the $30,000 proceeds from sale of 2000 shares of Bank America at $15 a share three years ago, the total amount of cold hard cash in his account would be $62,000. $46,000 of pure gross profit from his original investment of just over $15,000. He felt like an extra year's salary was dropped in his lap. He scribbled in the spiral notebook. $20,000 for the mortgage. $15,000 for the upcoming disaster day. $10,000 for savings and tax liens. He made a note to call the agent who controlled the company KEOGH plan and tell him to sell the stock in it and turn it all into hard earned cash.

Jeff's wanderings and musings were suddenly interrupted by the big brown spider that scampered across the front page of the Barron's. His whole being was captured AND frozen in the moment. Unbelievably, his thoughts left Dow Jones and focused to the threat in front of him. The brown spider crawled slowly across the cover of the Dead Cat Bounce. The nerve of that little bastard! Imagine if he made it to the bedroom! Jeff pounded the spider into a liquid spot with his bare hand. It felt good to release all of his pent up energy and mental frustration. It felt so good that he smacked the remains of the spider two more times while yelling, *"You didn't ask permission. You didn't ask permission to walk on my desk!"* An earth loving, female environmentalist no doubt would have jumped and run. Never let it be said that planning attack strategy for the stock market wouldn't get a person so wound up that they would explode! Never let it be said that there was no stress in the securities industry or the brokerage houses.

Angie stuck her head in the utility room. "You okay in here?"

"Yeah. I just crushed a big spider in a manly fashion. Sorry to disturb you."

Angelique stepped in and looked at the wet remains. "Yeeeeck! Then she turned to give her husband a lingering kiss. Jeff thought he detected some heat in the action. Maybe he would get lucky if he finished up quickly and went to bed.

"Well, why don't you bring some of that energy to our bedroom before you wear yourself out in here? I hate it when you get discouraged."

"I will and I love you for thinking of me. I want to discuss some financial propositions with you."

"For my body?" Angie giggled playfully.

For some small lingering women, Jeff lost it. "What's with you women? Before you read Weiss and talked with Richard and Veronica you wouldn't believe one word I told you about the stock market, would you? Are my words no good to you? I have no more credibility?"

"Honey! Please settle down! All of your research and the big ugly spider has caused you to snap at me! Like Ronnie said. I prematurely profiled the market as a losing proposition. I passed quick unintelligent judgement on it because I knew nothing about it. My friends know nothing about it. They don't know beans about it! *But they sure talk like they do.* So o o, I took the easy way out. I phoo pooed it. Don't you know how it is? After you live with deceitful people for as long as we have, I just could not trust anyone anymore. But now, I think I can trust you. I think you might get lucky in the market again. You might even get lucky tonight."

Jeff threw his hands in the air and gazed at the ceiling light bulb. "God! The world has gone plum loco! My marriage partner doesn't trust me!"

"JT, can I finish? I skimmed the book and now I am reading it. Weiss is a good guy who watches out for the interests of the uneducated investor. He runs a research company that rates companies and high grade bonds. He exposes companies that have tweaked their earnings reports along with the companies who willfully mislead. He is a full professor of finance and has been called to Washington, DC to testify before the Department of the Treasury on various subjects and economics. He exposed the Savings and Loan Scandal shenanigans, starting with the tip of the iceberg and he sank that titanic fraud! He has been verbally attacked publicly and privately by the evil doers. He reveals their scams and frauds. He sticks to his guns. He doesn't back down. He is a connoisseur of worldwide finance.

A moment of silence passed between them as they looked into one another's eyes. "Weiss warns about doctored financial statements. He says that the cash flow statement will quickly reveal deception. He says you have to *compare earnings statements with the actual cash flow statement.* This will give you a clue that something is amiss when there is no cash flow in existence. He says one out of three companies fudge on their financial statements and the earnings can be inflated as much as five percent or more without being obvious."

Cash Flow Statement Company XYZ FY Ended 31 Dec 2003	
all figures in USD	
Cash Flow From Operations	
Net Earnings	2,000,000
Additions to Cash	
Depreciation	10,000
Decrease in Accounts Receivable	15,000
Increase in Accounts Payable	15,000
Increase in Taxes Payable	2,000
Subtractions From Cash	
Increase in Inventory	(30,000)
Net Cash from Operations	2,012,000
Cash Flow From Investing	
Equipment	(500,000)
Cash Flow From Financing	
Notes Payable	10,000
Cash Flow for FY Ended 31 Dec 2003	1,522,000

CASH FLOW STATEMENT

She gave JT one last peck on the cheek. "Don't stay up too late, Mr. Carnegie. I'm beginning to miss you." Jeff was crazy about her. All these years and she never lost her innocent ways of messing with his mind. "I'm going to call it a night." She had one more thing to say to Jeff before she turned for the bedroom. "Don't study too much longer. I might have to go and find someone else."

Jeff was tiring. He summed up his evening with a note in his spiral. He penciled in, 'The market has begun its move into Area D. It will last another six months to a year. In the meantime 90 % of stocks will drop 15 to 20%, in share price during the first six months. Then, in the second six months, prices will be 20 to 30 % lower than they were a year ago. New investors will rationalize that it is not a bad loss and they will regurgitate the timeless salesman's pitch, '**Hang in there for the long haul**'. The DJIA Index will keep making small, miniscule advances and the drums will keep beating louder and louder while the majority of stock prices continue to decline. The last year will include sell offs with weaker rallies. The overall price declines happen just a little bit at a time and each time the new inexperienced investor will tell himself that his loss is not that bad. They will hold their position while the wind is racing past their ears. Their face will hit the pool of water at the bottom of the waterfall with enough force to snap their financial necks.

Jeff understood that there were small price drops in stocks when there was a slowdown in buying activity or the hype meter was low. But this sell off was a big one. 500 points *on heavy volume* was a very large day of selling. Something was going on. There had not been three quarters of negative earnings reports in a row *as there had been before the last market sell off in 2008*. Still, Jeff knew that this big sell off was an omen. A sign. Somebody, and *not just anybody*, but some **big institutions** who controlled **100's** of **billions** of dollars, wanted to *get their money out* at these current prices. Jeff figured it was the mutual funds, the corporations, the banks, **the big investors**.

He sat in his chair. He picked up *The Dead Cat Bounce* and skimmed the chapters on The Four Year Business Cycle and the Greater Fool Theory for about the tenth time. This was the answer. It was all right here in *The Dead Cat Bounce*. In plain words. Jeff was in Area D. Share prices were 3.5 to 4 times higher since the crash four years ago. New investors were paying the high prices. They thought the market was on fire. Even the day *before* the 500 point drop, there were articles on the newspaper business pages that declared, 'Now was the time to *get in before the Christmas rally!*' There were new highs on the DJIA Index every week before this drop. All of the encouragement in the world was still going strong in the media. 'The market will come back.' Sure it will. And my ice cream won't melt on a hot sunny day!

His butt flat and his mind over loaded, Jeff decided to call it a night. He closed up shop. He was alive again. He stuck his head into the bedroom to ask Angie if she wanted any liquid from the kitchen. Then he swaggered back through the hall to the kitchen for a big glass of V8. He would need the energy for what he was planning to do for the next two hours. Back in the bedroom he explained to Angie how the tax lien system worked so she would be able to think of the possibilities of buying a plot of land to hold as an asset that might appreciate in value. He encouraged her to venture out to the countryside to look at properties with liens on the title. Angelique kind of liked the thought of buying land, paying it off, selling it 'For Sale By Owner' and then carrying the mortgage to *play mortgage banker.* 5 to 8% interest on the loan was not unreasonable.

Angie had been waiting for the chance to bend Jeff's ear about Weiss. She played with the hair on his chest. "Honey. You have got to read the first 60 pages so you can understand his beliefs about the kind of investments you should make for capital preservation." Jeff raised an eyebrow. Angie was working on her terminology. She was using big words now. This was a good omen. "He has incredibly safe selections to match or beat inflation and, honey, this man is a scholar. He is a full-fledged PHD. He is a financial wizard. As a paid consultant, he has lectured the USA Treasury Department." She stretched and paused. She rolled on top of Jeff and put both hands on his chest. "I am soooo glad Ronnie gave me the book. The man is a genius." Angelique was quickly becoming an expert. "I remember our wedding day. Everything appeared to be the glory road before us." She looked at Jeff straight in the eyes. "We stepped out together with our dreams to build a place for us in the future. And now, here we are in our future and we have a new commitment. It will be exciting to continue to work towards our next future success. We do have a path that will take us there."

"It isn't done overnight." Jeff looked into her eyes. "We should talk about these things with Richard and Ronnie when we get together for the croquet match."

"That would be wonderful, love. Wednesday evening would be great. Or Thursday. The sooner the better. I need to talk with Veronica."

"That is a good idea, but It could snow you know."

"Who cares? We can play in the snow." Angie moved her hand down to her husband's stomach and played with his belly button. Jeff gradually became extended. "Honey, look! Your stock is going up!" Angie grabbed for Jeff's stock urgently. "We need to get a handle on this situation."

After all of the promiscuity was over, they held hands and lay side by side. Angie said with a smile, "Honey. We have always done well together and been supportive of one another. Now here is another adventure that I can share with you and we can grow some more together. Will you forgive me for being a nonbeliever? I am sorry I was against what you were trying to do." Angie rolled over to eye check her husband's answer. "Has that tension between us passed, sweetheart?"

"You know, Angie. At first it was scary being married to you. But after I lost my mind, somehow everything has been easier."

Angie rolled her eyes upward and sighed in exasperation. "What I mean is, you have forgiven me, haven't you?"

"Baby, you might have to pound me two more times before we go to sleep."

"I'll make it up to you, darling. I promise!"

"Well I am really going to have to think this over. It has caused me great emotional grief and mental anguish. I'm just not sure right now if I can give you an answer. Do you think I might get lucky again tonight, baby?"

Angie thought for a moment and replied, "I have to speak with my attorney and parents first." Angie rolled towards Jeff for the warmth of his body, and she kissed him on the cheek. "I knew once I got you into my lair that I could surround us with enough web so you could never run away from me."

"Isn't that kidnapping?"

"You are hardly a kid."

Jeff's new dream was to become a heavy hitter. A bag thrower. He would have diamond rings on every finger of his hand and diamonds on his Bic pen. He would be chauffeured around everywhere he went. He had confessed his dream to Angelique before she drifted off to sleep.

She replied once again, "The only way you are going to be in a limo is if you are the chauffer."

They fell asleep dreaming of limos, yachts, tax lien sales, mansions, green golf courses and the social clubs. Jeff dreamed that Goldman Sachs was begging him not to sell all of his shares to buy tax liens because it would precipitate a market sell off and send stock prices plummeting. Jeff replied to the President of Operations of Goldman Sachs that, "It would be healthy for the market to let off a little steam." He would send the brokers and the houses screaming for redemption. Jeff wanted to feel tremors in the earth after he unleashed his holdings and shorted the market. They would beg him not to unload all of his positions on the same day. He was watched night and day by the Fed boys, the Treasury Department and every other imaginable enforcement agency. He would have to buy a condo in a foreign country so he could have more freedom. They shadowed him everywhere. They recorded his conversations and communications be it cell phone, internet or the country club restroom.

Angelique dreamed of being the lady rancher in the old TV series Big Valley. She screened potential renter and buyer backgrounds for past inconsistencies and indiscretions. She had a large office with two secretaries. She sold tax free muni bonds and whole life to wealthy clients. She played the stock market as a hobby. Finally, they drifted off to sleep and dreamed of being land barons.

HALLOWEEN WEEK

I t was the middle of Thursday morning the 29th of October, 2014, two days before Halloween when Angie finished talking with Veronica and yelled to Jeff. "Richard said to tell you to relax. There is not going to be any Black Friday this October! Ronnie says we are late and to come on over right now."

Jeff handed the two Erdman books and 'The Dead Cat Bounce' to Angie. "Do you want to give these books to Veronica?"

"Sure, and I will thank her for the Weiss book." Jeff then picked up a cardboard box full of goodies that Angie had prepared. Angie grabbed a bag with two bottles of wine and closed the sliding glass patio door behind them. The two walked with warm smiles and hearts across the yard to the Whiting's patio. There was a fancy metal table with a glass top and four chairs. A medium sized propane barbeque grille stood next to the glass patio door. Ronnie slid the patio door open and welcomed the Thompson's into the kitchen. "Isn't this great? No snow and a warm sunny day to boot!" The Thompson's entered and set the books and snacks on the kitchen table. The table was decorated with a pint of whiskey, a pint of scotch, four liters of Seven Up, two bottles of wine, bread, cheese and cold cuts. There was hardly any room for the lettuce, veggies, crackers, salad dressings and dips.

Jeff rubbed his hands together. "This looks great girls! We are in for a good time this afternoon."

Angie answered, "We have to hold ourselves in check at the church luncheons. We can let loose a little bit here."

"And my husband can wear his trashy clothes." Veronica paused. "There is chicken in the pot on the stove!"

Richard entered and greeted his neighbors. His hair was slicked back. His plaid bermudas were hanging carelessly around his hips so the world could see his Arizona Diamondback boxer underwear. He wore a thick neck chain, a glitter belt and a giant glitter baseball hat cocked to the side of his head. "Whaaaazzzzzzuppppp Thompson?" Laughs were exchanged.

Jeff piped up. "Are you looking for a boyfriend, Richard? Is that why your pants are so low? Richard spun around pretending offense and Jeff handed him three books. "Thanks Jeff. I have a book for you too. Let's go to the living room for a minute. Ronnie and I want to give you and Angie the nickel tour."

The Whiting study took up half the living room. In the corner of the living room arranged with good taste were two desks facing one another. A desktop computer sat on one and a laptop on the other. A four drawer vertical file cabinet stood in the corner. A bookshelf was next to the file cabinet behind the desks. A huge poster of Alan Geenspan (once Chairman of Federal Reserve) decorated the wall above the bookshelf.

To the left, were two lazy boys in front of the living room window. A lamp table sat conveniently in between. The chairs were facing a large flat screen TV on the opposite wall. There were baby palms in large planters strategically placed about. It was a classy, efficient set up. The neat arrangement hit Angie like a freight train. Everyone seemed to notice. Her face flushed with guilt and her stomach churned all at once. Angie felt terrible. Jeff was relishing the moment.

Veronica broke the ice. "What do you think, Angelique?"

"Wow! You sure take your investing seriously!" Angelique was floored with guilt and awe.

"We don't do anything we like with half-hearted measures, Angie."

They chatted in the Whiting's peaceful, comfortable ambiance of success.

Jeff could not help himself. "Old Alan! That poster must be thirty years old! Ha! Ha! Ha!"

"Let's show a little bit of respect for the man," Richard insisted.

"We used to make fun of his comb over hairstyle!"

Veronica led off. "Richard and I were the same age as you two when we started. This is our fourth participating cycle. Like you and Angelique we did not participate too much in the first one. We did not have much money to throw at it. We had a little help from Richard's uncle who entered the market on a small scale once he turned 21. He opened an account when he was on leave in the military instead of buying a muscle car. He was in at the top of the market with a small amount of money and saw the downturn. When he saw the cheap stocks at the crash, he impressed a local banker with his plan to invest as much money as he could. The base bank wrote him a check for $5,000. $5,000 could easily buy two cars back then. When he left the service he studied for the NASD Series Seven exam. He took the insurance license exam on the same day. Walt got Richard and I involved when we were in our late 20's. We lived frugally. We bused or carpooled to work and parlayed the low transportation cost and thrift store savings into enough cash to buy a stock and follow the market. It is like anything else. If you don't get hooked, you are not going to be there when the time is right.

Ronnie continued. "We were working at a semiconductor chip plant company in 1997. We were in our early thirties when we really caught the stock market bug. I was working in administration and Richard was working on the twelve hour night shift in the clean room. All of the young associate tech geeks were constantly talking about their IRA's, Netscape, Yahoo, Amazon and AOL. We heard all about their forays into the market. We were sick with envy. So we conspired to take the plunge. We lived like dogs for a year and a half. We sold the car and took the bus or rode bicycles. No air conditioner for the summer heat. We used a big down comforter we bought from the thrift store and an electric blanket in the winter. We turned the hot water heater and the furnace thermostats way down. We bought everything at the thrift stores for years. We dined on canned chili and cheap TV dinners. We dropped our IRA's and plowed $15,000 into stocks before 1999. We paid nine dollars a share for Amazon. Yahoo cost us eight dollars."

Jeff interrupted. "Gosh, it is difficult to imagine that someday Angie and I will be old and senile like you two." Ronnie gave Jeff the evil eye. Richard looked at Angie. "I didn't know your husband was such a fruitcake."

Richard moved to the vertical file cabinet and opened the bottom file drawer. He removed a three inch stack of newsletters. "Here is our favorite newsletter from back in the late 90's. It is Donald Rowe's, '**The Wall Street Digest**'. There is a world of information in these letters. You are free to look through them for a week or two. There are some great explanations in here of inflation, deflation, currency fluctuations and trade deficits." Richard handed the newsletters to Jeff. "Rowe was one of the good advisers at the time. There is no telling how many investors made millions from his recommendations. He touted Qualcom and Worldcom before they were over $10 a share."

Veronica placed the Erdman books and the Dead Cat Bounce on her desk and moved to the bookcase. She pulled out a book and approached the group. "I have another book for both of you." Veronica handed the book to Angelique. Angie read the title as Jeff looked on. "'**Jesse Livermore. The World's Greatest Stock Trader.**' Wow! Thanks Ronnie! I didn't know there were books like this."

Ronnie continued. "Richard and I have stayed disciplined and focused by buying only on the severe market sell offs and '**corrections**' as the newspaper and the TV commentators call them. We usually sell out a year before the market collapses. We sold before the Dot Com bust. That was the second market correction we actively witnessed. **And, Lord have mercy**! Was it ever a blow out! We watched the devastation take place. We had turned our paper profits into *cash before the crash* and we were waiting on the sidelines while the media told us every morning and evening for six months that the DJIA Index was at its lowest point since 1994. But that did not stop us. We bought at rock bottom prices with $80,000. We realized we could secure our future and have a pile of money in a savings account. We wanted to be our own boss. It took ten years, but we made it."

Richard butted in. "After the Dot Com blow out we bought telecommunication, internet and computer stocks. Apple. Microsoft, and of course, Yahoo once again. Apple was the only computer company worth buying."

Veronica added. "Our tiny starter home was quickly paid for. Eventually we sold the house and played banker to finance the new buyers. Our second home was paid for in ten years. We have money in savings. We never had a savings account before. We take vacations at the market tops. It helps us to fight the urge to follow '*the thundering herd*' over the cliff."

Richard picked up. "Intel and the other process chip makers made it known in the 80's that the memory size would increase every two years or so. Then miniaturization in semiconductor chips and resistors led to smaller and faster cell phones, computers and laptops not to mention photocopiers, office machines, cash registers and credit verification."

"The chip speed and storage kept doubling. Software programs were faster and user friendly. That kept the consumers and companies upgrading every three or four years for speed and convenience. It kept sales revenues pouring in to these innovative companies. New online memberships from subscribers swelled the revenues year after year after year. These companies moved from less than 30 million shares up to 200 million or more in five years with all the stock splits and extra issues of common stock to purchase plant, property and equipment that you could **hope** for."

"Richard and I look back on it all now and compare it to the world that you and Jeff live in today. And let me tell you. **There is no comparison.** Back then, all of the government coffers, the county, the local, the state were full of surplus cash just from retail taxes. The federal and state governments had record income tax revenues. Just about everyone was employed and paid a decent salary."

Angie stepped beside Jeff and whispered. "We need to assume their identities." That drew chuckles from the Whiting's.

"The USA is not fully recovered today. Our economy will never be fully recovered. Taxes never go down. Local taxes are getting worse everywhere. Those government people shuffle paper and make decisions slower than a snail can cross a highway. They are totally inept. Totally! Government spends too much and it is getting bigger. So is social welfare. We are going deeper into debt at a faster rate than ever before, and when the big devaluation of the dollar arrives on the door step, which is coming soon, that will be the final tax dagger in the back of the American middle class."

"Devaluation Professor Whiting? Really?"

"Could you repeat that please? Are we supposed to horde gold?"

"That is what Ronnie and I are going to do. We have a list of one hundred mining companies. We are waiting for prices to drop a little further. We will probably make the move sometime in 2016. We will have to wait and see."

Angie wanted an explanation. "So what you are saying is that USA companies are just now getting back on their feet?"

Jeff nodded his head. "I know what you are getting at. Three or four years after the mini depression ***most*** industries are operating at the level they were before the crash."

Richard responded. "Exactly. You could say it another way. The consumer has recovered from the mini depression and is finally starting to spend again, but not as much as before."

Angelique interrupted, "Listen. We need to get a move on or we are going to miss our bright sunshiny day."

Jeff smiled at Angelique. "Let's go over to our house and get the croquet set out of the garage. We will give you Whiting's the nickel tour of our luxurious abode, but you have to promise not to harbor any ill feelings or jealousies towards us. I will show you my strategy room so you can see firsthand how my wife has made me suffer and kept me under her thumb." Angelique's face went sullen. She was filled with guilt.

She couldn't take it anymore so she blurted out, "I've been so horrible to Jeff. I was stuck on my women's lib support group! I thought I was controlling our destiny by struggling to brighten up our little house with every extra penny I could spare."

Jeff snapped, "Oh! Come on Angie! You can do better than that!"

Ronnie picked up the newsletters and the book and handed them to Jeff. "Don't despair, Angie. Now, come on everyone! Let's not ruin this great day. Let's grab some drinks and sandwiches and head for the croquet gear! For crying out loud!"

Angie shuddered. "That is what I'm about to do!" Her shoulders shook. Jeff put his arm around her and kissed her forehead. Angie turned her face to her husband. "I'm glad I vented on you." Then she punched him in the gut. "Sometimes you are really ugly."

Ronnie admonished, "Stop your arguing right now! No fighting in our house! Go outside!"

The foursome grabbed some liquid refreshment and sandwiches and headed over to the Thompson's mansion for the tour and the croquet set. Both houses were three bedroom, single story ranch style homes. They entered through the patio sliding glass door. Veronica and Richard set the newsletter and book on the kitchen table. Veronica could not repress her sudden urge to blurt out, "Oh, Richard! It looks like the old beat up kitchen we had in our first home. Remember?" Angie visibly shuddered and gave Veronica the dagger stare. They moved into the living room. It appeared as a normal living room and dining room combination with modest, but tasteful furniture and a flat screen TV.

Veronica still could not resist a little mockery. "Oh, my! So luxurious!"

Angie snapped. She frowned with hostility. She could take no more. "Shut up, Ronnie! You witch!" "I won't have you dissing my house or my arrangements."

Richard observed, "Sensitive are we?" Everyone but Angie chuckled.

Jeff added, "We have just received word from our taxidermist that our trophy heads of wild game are finished and ready to hang here in our living room."

"Any zebras?"

"Just bulls and bears." Laughter erupted. Angie dabbed a tear away with her new found kleenex and she actually laughed at her husband's joke.

"Now for the bedrooms." Jeff led the way to the bedrooms. "Several famous homeless people have slept in our bed when they visited us for handouts. They are mostly ex bankers from the big east coast states. They come to Iowa to start over and get jobs working as farm hands."

"This room is the one where Angelique keeps all of her sewing gear." Jeff smiled. "She is making millions. She is selling her designs and fashion internationally with the retailer Ross. Eat your heart out Veronica! This second bedroom holds some of our outdoor gear. We can only be penned in for so long." Jeff stopped at the utility room door in the hallway on the way to the master bedroom. "Oh! By the way! In case you are wondering, this is where the family genius hides when he is in his research sessions. Every man's home is his castle and this is where all of the heavy financial decisions are mulled over." He opened the door, walked in, and reached up to pull the light string to light up the room. "You may enter at this time." Then he stepped back so Richard and Veronica could get a view. Richard looked amused, but slightly bewildered. The Whiting's slipped inside. There was enough room for two people. Three made it crowded. Veronica looked doubtful and perplexed. "There must be some mistake. Isn't this where you do your laundry, Angie?" Angie burst into tears.

Rich and Ronnie looked at each other. Jeff, standing behind them, hollered out. "Now, Richard! I don't want any jealousies to come between our friendship. I know you are the loathsome type. Please, try to control yourself. Petty jealousy is a sin, Richard. Remember church last Sunday? I will just tell you two that I am willing to share my elaborate research facility with you. So please do not harbor any ill will or ill feelings towards us Thompson's." The Whiting's surveyed the surroundings. The exposed light bulb on the ceiling. The washer and dryer. The furnace and the gas water heater. The utility sink. The second hand desk was covered with newspaper. They studied the wall chart and the triangles. Richard stared at the chart extension that Jeff had taped to the 50 year wall chart. "You got to be kidding!"

"About what? Well? What do you think?" Jeff said sarcastically. "Don't keep me in suspense! I knew you would like it! Now remember what I just told you about jealousy!"

The Whiting's eyes were searching out the small confines and the cramped space with looks of doubt and disbelief. They began to giggle without hesitation. Angie began to sulk. She looked down at her tennies. Richard asked, "Where's the dart board?" The Whiting's began to shake with laughter. Ronnie piped up, "When is the divorce?" Rich and Ronnie held each other's arms and roared with laughter! Ronnie stepped in front of Richard and fingered the triangles. "What are these?" Richard stared at Jeff's hand drawn extension of the Dow Jones Industrial Index a second time and broke out laughing. "Wait Ronnie. Look at this!" They both stared at Jeff's prediction. "He's got it! He knows what he is doing!"

Angelique looked at Jeff. Tears welled up in her eyes and she fought to hold them back. "I'm so ashamed. I'm sorry. I'll make it up to you."

Jeff tried not to smile. "We will talk about that later."

"Yes. He has got it down." Ronnie agreed. "It could be the scenario. Angie, the market will be churning all next year and Jeff certainly has sketched out a very credible chart pattern here. It is very possible."

Jeff insisted. "Richard! Let's go to the garage and get the croquet gear. We can meet the girls on your patio."

Veronica consoled Angie on the walk back to the patio. "Angie. Just let all of this baloney go. I know it is a big shock and embarrassment, but you and I need to get on with the program. It's not too late to make up and turn things around. My, aren't we lucky? No snow at all this October. Just that dusting the first week. Everyone in the hood is in the Halloween spirit."

"Yes, they are. Ronnie, if Richard wears those clothes on Halloween, people will throw candy at him to keep him off the porch, huh?" Angie was beginning to recover. "It's about time we got a vacation here. Jeff and I have been anxious to get some time off." The girls disappeared into the Whiting's kitchen. The boys returned to the patio with the croquet set and chatted.

Jeff decided to get an early start messing with Richard. "Well, Richard, Angelique told me we would build a big field. She is always testing me Richard. Maybe you weren't aware of that. I think she is trying to break me. I don't drink anything she hands to me because it could be tainted. As in poison. Do you have any alcohol?"

"It is a little early, Jeff. It is only the end of the morning. Take it easy. Shhhh! Here they are." Both Veronica and Angelique emerged from the sliding patio doors. The boys helped move the food to the patio table. Two big trays of snacks, salsa dip, sour cream, four bottles of wine, four liters of Seven Up and various pints of alcohol were carried out to the patio table. Ronnie announced, "This should get us started."

The four neighborhood trouble makers conspired to use both back yards to set up a giant croquet course. The center wicket would be planted right between both yards. Richard and Jeff each pounded a stake at the far ends and the foursome began to set up the course. The corner wickets were not quite symmetrical due to flower gardens and bushes, but that was no problem. Everyone complemented Angie for thinking big on the field size. Richard was concerned about diplomacy. "Who is going to do the honors? Shall we toss a coin to see who goes first?" Jeff showed his care and love for seniors. "Why don't you old farts go first? You will need a good head start. Have you taken all of your meds today?" Jeff began to laugh madly. Richard and Veronica stared at Jeff.

Richard rebounded, "Quite the contrary, my friend. Old age and treachery will overcome youth and inexperience."

"Jeff!" Angie yelled. "How dare you ruin our lovely day. We haven't even started! Have you got it out of your system? You apologize right now!"

Veronica was appraising Jeff laughing away at his own mad jokes. "Richard if you will get him immobile, I will cut his throat out with the butcher knife.

Angie wanted a quick, no nonsense, simplistic solution. "Why don't we play Thompson's against the Whiting's? Go ahead, Richard. Flip the coin and let it hit the patio. We take heads." Richard fished his plaid pockets and flipped the coin in the air after deliberately placing tails up on his thumb. The coin landed tails.

Jeff offered a quick prediction. "We go second. Not a problem. Angie and I are going to clean out your savings account."

Veronica eyed Angelique. "Has something gone wrong between the two of you this morning?"

"I don't know Ronnie. He gets out of control once in awhile. Too much time in the strategy room by himself. He has developed some strange behavior over the last two years. He is quiet for a long time and then all of a sudden he just explodes!"

Ronnie admonished, "Okay, Jeff. Just to give you a heads up. If you continue your course of verbal abuse to us, then Richard and I are going to cave your skull in with your own croquet mallets! How is that for irony?" Ronnie knew that asking questions and providing choices in situations would make a person stop and think. Jeff's laughter began to soften up.

"I think he heard you Ronnie. Maybe he is coming back to earth." Angie spoke to the group. "I'm going to be first. I always get to be first. Don't I, Jeffy?" Jeff's disposition seemed to bounce back to normal.

"Yes, you do sweet one. And I apologize to you, Veronica and Richard. I have just held things in too long. I was trying to get some trash talk going. T'was just trash talk. I just got ahead of myself. I just went a little too far. I got carried away. I'm sorry."

Ronnie took a sip of her wine and said, "Angie is right. Why don't we just play singles. This is supposed to be just for fun anyway. Everyone agreed and took their last sips of refreshment.

Richard led off. "I'm going to go first for being brazenly insulted. Anymore trash talk like that and they will be carrying you to the hospital, Mr. Jeff. He tapped his first shot and made it fifteen feet out through the first two wickets and over to the first corner wicket. Angie followed and everyone ended up in the far right corner. Richard hit through the corner wicket and tapped Jeff's ball. Rich set both balls together, placed his foot on top of his ball and sent Jeff's ball flying across the yard.

Veronica assumed the role of referee and organizer. "No! No! We aren't going to do this! This course is too big to allow 'sending' your opponent all the way across the yard." Then the trash talking began.

Richard told his wife, "You are just a weenie."

"I said, *no sending* this game! Let's get this over so we can sit down and eat."

Richard playfully responded. "Who said you could bitch us around today, anyway?" Ronnie gave him a look that settled him down. He slammed his ball towards the center wicket. It was a good thirty feet away. Everyone else followed in turn.

The conversation quickly turned to stocks. "Richard, I stopped by the library yesterday to check out what Barron's had to say about the 500 point crash. The picture on the cover page is hilarious. Check it out online if you get a chance. It shows an investor in his living room. He's sitting on the couch with a soda in his hand. He is watching the 'Nightly Business News'. A bear crept into the living room behind the couch and pulled the TV plug out of the wall socket! It's funny!"

Veronica cajoled Jeff. "You can't call it a crash, Jeff! It is a 'contraction'. The market is just letting off steam."

"Okay, Miss Manners. Whatever you say." Chuckles arose from the group. Ronnie continued. "The securities community will push the **DJIA Index** higher yet, just to prove that the 500 point drop was only a hiccup. They will say that it was healthy profit taking. You all know that the holidays are coming up and all of us boys and girls, John and Mary Public, will be focused on those holiday events.

Richard cautioned Jeff. "Jeff, we are not at the point of the tsunami or the Niagara Falls yet. Between now and the waterfall the market will just be a series of downward drops and upward rallies. Just like the rapids or the turmoil that the river has as it rolls downstream and moves toward the large cliff. It will continue until the big boys are all in cash. New investors will not understand why the market is not going anywhere. And much to everyone's surprise, the DJIA Index will set records all year long. It will last *at least* a year." Richard looked deep in thought and added, "You know, Jeff, the more I think about it, the more I believe that your year and a half extension is right on the money. I couldn't understand it at first glance. It also occurred to me that if all the years were as big as the one you drew, that wall chart would be twenty five feet long! It would stretch across one wall of the living room and on to the next one."

Ronnie hit through the first corner wicket and sent her ball flying for the center wicket. "I like this long distance. We get to vent a little bit. Hey, you Thompson's! Richard is absolutely correct. The market indexes will swing up and down in a small range just like a yo yo. It will keep churning away as the big boys sell for profits. That is what they will be doing. They will be stealing the money of the newcomers who are buying stocks for the first time." She continued. "It will all happen several times over the next two years within that one thousand to two thousand point range that you drew, JT. So, congratulations on that illustration, Jeff. It is a classic! I can remember the top of every market Rich and I have experienced. They are all duplicates of your chart extension."

Jeff questioned. "So, while the big dogs are taking profits, the share prices slide back. Then everyone will turn into a short term investor playing the drop. Is that it? Buy on the drop and sell at the top of the rally?"

Richard answered, "That is right Jeff. Now let me ask Angelique a question so she won't think I am a chauvinist or that I have excluded her all day long. Angie?"

"Yes, Richard? You stinking, chauvinist pig. Do you have a question for me?"

Veronica howled. "Good girl, Angie! Sock it to him!"

Angelique nodded at Veronica. "You know, all of this is really fascinating. Just to think that people are actually betting on stocks, but that they call it investing. Jeff and I talk a lot more at bedtime now about the **undulations** in the market. Is that the right way to say it, Jeffy? I know you are such a stickler for correctness." A smile appeared on Veronica's face. She chuckled.

Jeff corrected. "**In un da** ting market, baby."

Veronica smirked. "I wish Richard would talk to me about undulations. Richard! Why don't we talk about **un du la** *tions* tonight?" The girls snickered.

"I will get you for this, Angie!" Richard leered at Angelique. "Don't you mess with our sex lives." He firmly tapped his ball to position it in front of the center wicket. It stopped close but not centered. Richard waved his arms in the air and undulated his body. "Spress u sef, baby! We are really hitting it off with the conversation here!"

Angie smiled at Ronnie. "Looks like those were the only undulations you are going to get today."

Veronica agreed. "Right. He could have thrown his back out."

Angie paused and then asked a question. "I have something I have been wanting to ask you and Richard. Why does the market **drop**?"

"Good question, Angie. Here is the answer that most average investors believe. It will have to hold you for now. Richard and I are planning a strategy get together with you and Jeff in a couple of weeks. You will get the full detailed analysis then. But for now, back in 2000, part of the reason was because the institutions bailed out. These institutions reach a point of no return where they have profits and they have to start selling to get their money out. They have to convert the paper profits to cold, hard cash. There is no looking back, Angie. There is no wishful thinking. They don't wonder if the prices are going to go higher. *They have to liquidate.* By the time the rest of the world figures this out it is too late in the game.

What really happens is that all of the big selling is over because no one is buying. When no one buys, the NYSE floor traders have to drop the bids until they find buyers. That is Securities and Exchange Commission law. This action usually precipitates more selling. Sometimes a selling frenzy. When the prices drop low enough the buyers jump back in depending what kind of shape the earnings reports and the goods economy are in."

Richard added two cents. "There are clearing houses that match every sell order with a buy order. When there are no more buy orders and millions of sell orders the floor traders for the NYSE are required by the Securities Exchange Commission laws and rules to drop the prices until there are willing buyers."

"But the prices are so low."

"That is why it is called a crash. Profit taking is over. How did you like the *Smart Money* book?"

"It really got my interest, Ronnie. I owe you a big favor on that one. I think I understand my husband's planning. I used to think he had a gambler's addiction that competed with my need for new paint for the kitchen walls, and my new wall to wall carpets." Laughter broke out.

Jeff responded. "Yeah. **Her** new everything! I still wear the same underwear I was wearing four years ago."

"That is so disgusting, Jeff." Angie tapped her ball through the first corner wicket and smashed it over to Richard's ball at the center wicket.

Ronnie smiled at Jeff. "Good for you, Jeff. It builds character."

The foursome was sharing a gorgeous day under a blue autumn sky. Their game began to slow. They began to relax and enjoy their conversation and the company.

"Angie, just keep reading. Just keep learning. Wait until you read about Livermore!" Ronnie was animated and waving her hands in the air. "The real aspect of the peak of the market is how the winners cash out. It is just a little bit at a time so the market does not slide back all at once. They use the news media. Wall Street primes and pumps the media while the big boys sneak out their cash fortunes. Everyone trades the big DJIA Index and Standard and Poor's stocks. You have to remember that the news media will never go away no matter what happens. They use positive strokes to appease all of the jittery, easily excited, USA citizens. Blind optimism fills the air!"

Richard jumped in. "Every day for two years the media will scream, '*The market has finished another record high day.*' Angie, you have to realize that it may only be a point higher than yesterday, but the marching band gets louder when the record highs are hitting every day. One point every business day would be an extra 245 points on the index for the year. That, dear Angelique, is no big deal. But the band is relentless! The new investors finally give in to the message pounded into their heads every day by the financial community. '*The economy looks bright!*' '*Get on the wagon now!*' '*Don't be left behind!*' '*Don't miss this bull market!*' The boys on the Street keep the bull manure flying!"

"I didn't know bull manure could fly. Hey, everybody. If manure could fly, Richard would be a 747!"

Richard interjected some wisdom. "During the Dot Com Boom, the common expression was, 'If you are not into Dot Com stocks you are stupid. You are the dumbest person in the world if you are not in this bull market. This fairly common statement was used to let all the dumbasses know that they missed the boat. People were shamed into the market. The financial media and the talking heads on the television business news were going berserk! They had the first time investors stirred into a tizzy. New investors were jammed into the mania for three years during the run to the NASDAQ high. And what you have to understand, Angie, is that the new money keeps the rallies going until no one has another penny to give.

"I think I got it now, Richard. All this goes on while the smart investors are sneaking out billions of profit a little at a time."

Ronnie continued her rant. "Right. Everyone hears the word **market** and they automatically think 2600 NYSE stocks are the subject of discussion. That is not so! Only the DJIA Index and half of the S+P 500 Indexes are the culprits that stay up in price. They are the most actively traded. The other 2300 stocks are languishing and sliding backwards."

Everyone had caught up with Richard. It was his turn again and Jeff wanted to agitate the leader just a little bit before Richard's tough shot to the center wicket. Jeff expressed a thoughtful question. "Richard, I read that Fed Chairman Greenspan gave some speeches on irrational exuberance back in the day. Is that right?" Richard's shot bounced off both sides of the wicket but made it through. Richard breathed a sigh of relief and sent his ball zinging to the second corner wicket. He then looked to the clouds in the sky to search for his answer. "Yes. Investors were borrowing money any way they could. They put up any kind of collateral they had on hand. They sold things they could do without. They even borrowed at the brokerage houses using their portfolio balances as collateral. The Fed knew the crash was coming. Greenspan tried to get the broker houses to let the air out of the bubble gradually. But, true to form, the media went for the gusto and kept the drums beating. I will never forget it. We were all on the edge of our seats." Jeff walked over to Richard's ball during the rant. Nobody noticed the big red and green wine hocker drip from his mouth on to Richard's ball while Richard was busy blabbing about the mysteries of the stock market.

Ronnie finished the answer for Richard. "Everything took second place to the NASDAQ stock market. The Fed raised interest rates five times starting in 1999 and again in 2000 right up to the crash. Greenspan attended many international meetings to try to influence everyone to calm down and let some air out of the bubble. Many Gen Ex young folk were buying the internet like there was no tomorrow. They thought their generation was going to save the world. Just like these millennial cell phone people. Non investors were totally disgusted. They had missed the boat, but eventually, the NASDAQ Index and the DJIA gave up the charade about a year later."

Ronnie and Angie passed through the center wicket and sent their balls flying over to the second corner wicket. As the group walked to the wicket together, to join Jeff, Angie inquired, "Well, Richard. What happened? Don't keep me in suspense."

"Finally, there were no more buyers. The market had soared so high that no one could afford to buy a share of Dot Com stock. Everything was expensive at the end. No one wanted to pump anymore money into expensive stocks and the big boys were waiting for the inevitable crash. It was devastating."

Angie was anxious to prove she was learning. "There you go using that '*market*' word again!"

Veronica told Angie. "Just wait. After Halloween, you will get an earful about the 500 point drop. All of the financial pundits will be out in droves crying, '*Hold your stocks for the long haul.*' '*The Christmas and January rallies will soon be here!*' 'Now is a great time to buy while prices are lower.' 'There are undervalued, and *reasonably priced shares* to add to your portfolio'."

The group paused at the corner wicket to continue their interesting discussion. Richard had a new thought. "Let me say something about this 500 point drop. The financial community is going to brush off this setback. What an astute investor has to do now, at this juncture, is adjust their temperament and attitude. A couple of news articles this week quote brokers as saying that we are still in a bull market. Understand here, JT, that your chart is correct and we should take notice. Ronnie and

I are in agreement with your chart, Jeff, but you also have to understand that the financial community is going to *totally ignore* this signal of impending danger. We will see a strong rally."

Ronnie interrupted again. "You won't believe it. The Index will rebound before Thanksgiving! The securities community will bump up the bids and they will push the DJIA Index higher. They will prove to John and Mary Public that what happened was only a hiccup, a burp of indigestion from the gluttonous investing of the last four years. Wall Street will say that it was healthy profit taking. They know the holidays are coming up and John and Mary Public will be totally distracted from the market. All of us girls and boys will be focused on the holidays. And once the Christmas rally and the holidays are over, the drums will keep beating for the promise that market advances will be made well into the new year. *'XYZ stock is oversold and good for a possible 20% rebound.'*"

Ronnie put her hands in the air and did the funky chicken with Richard.

Richard asked Jeff, "Did you read the article that said, 'The **global** economy is in good shape and set to expand this quarter'? Boy! Is that ever a crock of bull manure! It is a total, flagrant lie to pacify the public. The public does not know squat about the global economy." There was laughter across the backyard. Richard predicted. "You know, this balloon is going to let itself out. It ain't gonna be the interest rate. It ain't gonna be gold. It ain't gonna be oil. Bad earnings and no growth are going to sink the 2600 stocks. The short term investors will quit buying and the market will fizzle out. Period!"

Jeff confirmed Richard's thoughts. "This economy that we have now just isn't as good as all the politicians and news media make it out to be. They are lying! None of them are educated enough to know what they are talking about. And that is God's truth! They couldn't explain the situation in the market to save their lives. So how could they possibly explain what is going on to the public? This economy is no better off than it was six years ago."

Richard emphasized, "Heck! We haven't had an economy since 1998." Richard walked over to fetch his ball. He saw Jeff's transgression. He spun around and sounded off. "Jeff! You would be better off to shave the hair off a tiger's ass than to mess with me or my croquet ball!" Soft chuckles broke out across the back yard.

Jeff expressed his thoughts. "And the price drop is going to be just like 1987. I swear it will. One bright Wednesday morning the market will drop abruptly. The market will be shut down. Thursday and Friday will be shut down. A weekend break in the '*plummet*' will not calm anyone's nerves. And no one, **no one** will have anything to put into the market. So, on Monday, the market will drop again to an automatic close. *It will need 10days of 400 point drops to get it down to 12,000. **As I am** God's* **witness!**"

Ronnie caught the suggestion quickly and cautioned, "Careful now! We don't need any lightning here. I think one Sunday night while we are sleeping, all the Asian markets will tank. Their market opens on Monday twelve hours before ours. When the Europe Exchanges open, Germany, Spain, France and England will all tank. All of them will be looking at huge losses. Overseas investors who have accounts in USA will flood online orders to sell billions of shares into the NYSE before Monday at the 8am bell. Then, panic selling in USA will close the NYSE market before the first hour is over. You guys are absolutely right. This market is going to drop like the proverbial rock. And no rock has fallen this far before. You only have to push a keyboard button to sell or buy NYSE stock from any country around the world."

Richard added two cents. "The SEC will be shuffling around in the cloud of dust trying to make new regulations to keep such a fiasco from happening again." He tapped his ball through the second corner wicket and then sent it whizzing over to the two wickets in front of the second stake.

Ronnie worked her ball through the corner wicket. "You are right. And we are going to get some new regulations from the Securities Exchange Commission. They love to step in and offer their little band aid solutions. Maybe foreign investors will not be allowed to dump more than half of their holdings in a single year. It might be the same for mutual funds."

Angie followed Ronnie. "Maybe the restriction would be more like twenty or thirty percent. How would they regulate it? I don't think they could."

Jeff threw in. "The *Occupy Wall Streeters* will be demanding the money that Wall Street owes them because the protestors were born in America." Laughter was exchanged. "Interpol will be hunting for the derivatives crowd that siphoned the money out of the banks." Jeff threw his hands in the air. "I think it would be hilarious if the financial community let it all go tomorrow! Just dump it in Osama Bin Obama's lap! He deserves it!"

"I wish they would!" Angie looked at Ronnie. "Would that be a terrorist plot?"

Jeff looked at Angie. "No. It would be a radical right wing conservative extremist plot."

Richard looked at Angie. "No, Angie. It would all be George Bush's fault!" Laughter erupted.

Jeff scanned the smiling faces. "You know, the USA is not just our financial community any more. I think the world is going to let the USA crash right into the POTUS lap! Osama Bin Obama has pissed off a lot of people around the world of all nations and race!"

Richard piped up. "You know, Jeff, at the top of every market, there has **never** been one Associated Press article that advises investors to sell everything and head for the hills. That would be like *yelling 'fire' in a dark movie theater.* They might print one or two small articles that tease you with the question, '*Is the market nearing the top?*' This issues a warning to the experienced, knowledgeable investor. But, there is never one article or one newspaper that ever advises investors to *sell everything and **bask in your cash**.*"

Angie spoke up. "There are no warnings to new investors not to buy at the top. If Weiss had his own national press, '*Sell Now*' would be plastered all over the front page."

"Good girl Angie! You are catching on fast," Ronnie exclaimed. "Let me mess with you. And pretend to be the financial media. I am going to give you one of the newer bull manure sayings to dissuade your negative suspicions. It is a global economy now and I am going to use global reasoning to give you a positive spin of exuberance. Okay Ready? *We are living in the best of times. The tail is wagging the dog! It is a huge rolling global economy now that cannot be denied. Things just keep getting better and better. People just don't realize that the world is a better place. There is no drought. There are no floods and no famines. There is nothing but pie in the sky!"* Angie stared, dumbfounded. "Angie. What I am trying to say is that the marchin' band never stops playing. The hype and the music must continue 24/7, rain, snow or sunshine, every day of the year. It goes on all the way to the bottom of the trough, the low tide, and back up again with the rising tide and the crest of the new wave. It never stops."

Richard explained, "We are going to go sideways here at the top for a while. Next year the market will be moving like a yo yo. There will be a lot of back peddling after first quarter results are posted, especially for all of the outrageous statements analysts will make between now and Christmas. The only time the truth will come out and show itself will be when losses appear on the new earnings reports for the fourth quarter and the first quarter. Mark my words, *that will be the only time that the proof of losses will be presented and printed in black and white*. And three months later it will all be forgotten."

Ronnie finished for Richard. "But fear not! The band will strike up again! They will play the **So What** song! Analysts will drum up any excuse to cover up their lies that they promised just before Christmas. Thirty days after Christmas you will find out that the *tiny New Year rally is over and you have been screwed!"*

Richard held his mallet with both hands in front of his chest. He twisted his hands on the handle to flex his arms. He was tensing. "Mark my words, Angie and Jeff. Come March when the guestimates leak out before April on the quarterly earnings for the first three months of the year, there is going to be quite a bit of back peddling. Analysts who made all of the rosy, pie in the sky predictions before Christmas for an up year in 2015 *will be eating crow and dumpster diving for a living*." Laughter flowed across the yard. "They will search the want ads looking for a new line of work. They might even be dumb enough to move to Europe or China where the global economy looks so good!" More laughter rose on the playing field. The first quarter reports will be way below expectations. Some results will be a loss or just breakeven on earnings. But the DOW Index will not tank! Heavens no! Prices will decline slightly from January to April. Only a few of us will remember the faces of political spokesmen and women who were brimming over with confidence, smiling the whole time they lied to the public."

Ronnie spoke up. "The funny thing about this phenomena, is that no one will be able to remember who said what or when. The talking heads will say. '*Who cares what we said before the holidays? That was last year! Disappointing earnings are all due to the snow storms that kept the shoppers at home.*' That is one of their favorite excuses. The bad weather and the snowstorms kept the holiday shoppers and the bargain hunters at home. The analysts' angle will merely shift and focus on their new predictions. There will be all kinds of excuses given. Back peddling as Richard called it."

Jeff confirmed Ronnie's speech. "Thank you, professor. You will be happy to know that two months ago Barron's had an article that confirms what you just said."

"I'd like to see it. Richard, let's get over to the library with the Thompson's and invade the finance section after the holidays."

Richard added, "Here is something else, Angie. During the quarterly earnings announcements Wall Street will address any bad earnings or any negative earnings, just like it was a fluke! They won't even care because one month later it will all be forgotten. Brokers will say, '*Oh! Too bad that happened. Life goes on!*' Then they will flip the misdirection on you. '*Well, what do you expect after six years of a robust bull market?*' And then, they will predict that April, May and June will show profits. It is a double edged sword. It is always used! That is how they cover their lies to the public and launch new false hopes and higher prices." All at one time! All in one breath for the stupid Americans to assimilate! Just like Bill Clinton said about Obamacare. '**Too bad that didn't work out.**' All of the misery and the higher taxes and the efforts to stop Obamacare. All dismissed with slick Willy's snot nosed, teen age, juvenile delinquent, smart ass statement."

"Gosh, Richard! You feel pretty strong about that. Are you sure?" Angie understood the consumer economy in April. "I get the April sales bonanza, Ronnie. It is because of the big sales on all of the Easter bunny eggs, the straw baskets, the artificial basket grass and the egg coloring kits." Everyone broke out in a laugh at Angie's joke.

All the players were in various spots around the two wickets in front of the first post. Veronica was lining up to pass through the two wickets and hit the stake when her husband deliberately began to crowd her. "Richard I'm concentrating. Stand back and let me hit." As Ronnie drew her mallet back for the stroke, Richard poked her in the ass with the end of his mallet handle. Angie poked Richard. "Don't you poke my neighbor in the ass."

"Hey! No more illegal contact of any form or you will be expelled from the game! And Richard, if you do that one more time, I'll shove that mallet up your ass next to your cellphone." Ronnie clarified the aggressive assertion to the Thompsons. "It's the only place he can remember where his cellphone is." Ronnie smacked her ball through the two wickets to tap the stake. Everyone followed suit.

Richard, pig that he is, led off for the last half of the game. "Stand back and observe. I will show you how it is done." Richard smacked his ball through the two wickets by ten feet. He then lined up for the corner wicket and sent his ball flying. All the time Richard talked non stop.

"Listen to me Jeff! Here is a new perspective of what the market is going to do next year. The bulk of the trading activity is directed at short term trades on a daily and weekly basis. Hold this thought whatever you do. Now. I would say at least 80 % of trades every day are the very short term investors. Especially now through the rest of next year, 2015. Short term investors know the market like the skin on their hands. They know potential losses are lurking about and that consumer spending is over. Think about that. This will be the true creature of the market in 2015."

Jeff threw his arms up in the air and yelled, "It is a gazillion dollar race to the finish line! If they sold all at once, the market would crash in one day. And there is only enough cash floating around to pay off a few winners. The Fed will have to open up the vault to keep the Street from going bust."

Jeff mocked Richard and repeated his speech. "The same strategy is used at the bottom of the market. There is little volume. The market is going sideways with less and less volume as everyone is scared. The prices drop again. Then, at the bottom of the market the institutions begin to buy. They buy a little at a time so the share prices don't jump up higher. And they build a support level." Jeff mimicked Richard and held his mallet across his chest He twisted it with his hands. "The market languishes on the bottom for quite a while. They drag it out for at least six months. Of course, not all sectors or all stocks hit the lowest price on the same day. Every day the talking heads say, '*This is the worst market we have seen in seven years.*' '*The market has hit all time lows.*' These statements keep the new investors scared and afraid to put money in the market. The public gets an impression that it is a bad time to invest. No one in their right mind wants to buy when the market is at an all time low day after day after day for six months. Do you want to buy on the worst day in the market?"

Ronnie looked at Angie. "Your husband is right on the money, Angie. No wonder he did so good." They exchanged smiles. "I have a new analogy for you, Angie. Listen to this. It is the top of the market. The global economy, according to the Street bull shit and the politicians, is running smoothly. You have nothing to worry about. So, you decide to take a luxurious bath."

"Now, girls. Don't kick the sacred cow."

"The bath tub is completely empty so you fill up the tub with hot water and pour in some Mr. Bubble. Now I'm going to help you out here, Angie. *Mr. Bubble is the Wall Street and the world media marching band.* Got it? So, you fill up the tub with medium hot water and add a little Mr. Bubble.

"Sounds good so far. Drive on, Ronnie. I'm with you."

"You toss in a bar of soap before you get in. Now, are you ready for the tough questions, Angie?

"Fire away, Ronnie. Let's make a deal."

"What does the water signify?"

"I'm going to take a wild guess and say stocks and stock prices."

"Fine, Angie! Absolutely wonderful. Now what does the bar of soap represent?"

"I'm just totally stumped, Ronnie. What ever could it be? Don't keep me in suspense. I have no clue."

"Relax. Angie. I'm playing guess what to try to help you remember. The bar of soap is the DJIA Index and half of the S+P 500 stocks!" This brought laughter. "Now, here is how the market works. The tub is full and the water is just hot enough. But you can't see the water because of the bubbles. Now, the water is the total value of the stock market on the NYSE. The total market capitalization. The bubbles are the media marching band and the smoke and mirrors of the Associated Press, the world financial community, the political community, the Wall Street of the World, the TV talking heads and *everyone else* **who's opinion is of no consequence** *at the top of the market*." Ronnie looked at Angie swinging her mallet back and forth from hand to hand. "You can't see the surface of the water because of Mr. Bubble. Guess what happens now."

"Are we playing 'guess what' or croquet? I don't know. How should I know? But I am going to hit you with my mallet if you try to keep me guessing." At this comment, Jeff became intrigued. "I don't know. I give up. I guess somebody pulls the plug. Right?"

"You picked up on that pretty quick for a 28 or 30 year old, Angie. The plug is slightly bumped and the water begins to leak unnoticeably, a couple of drops at a time. Out of the tub and down the drain, but you don't notice it because of Mr. Bubble."

"So the band and the media keep on playing as they usually do."

"Correct. Now, Angie. What about the soap? The bar of soap *stays on top of the water the* **whole time**. We are talking about 300 stocks here listed on the S+P 500 and the DJIA Index. The Dow is hitting a new all time high every day. Every minute. Every second. Now why does the bar of soap float on top?"

"Because it is Area D, and the DJIA is up one point every day, all year long for a whopping 200 points. You can't count the 104 days of weekends and the ten or fifteen vacation days."

"Okay. Good work. You put your foot in the water to test the heat. Then you get in and sit down to lounge and relax. You cause some waves, some small declines and rallies when you get in and the plug pops off the drain opening. What does this mean, Angie?"

"I tested the water and invested in the market, but it is area D and the water is getting cold and slowly going down the drain. The only thing left is the bar of soap and the Mr. Bubble." The men were laughing. "I would say that the prices are going down the drain. This is the waterfall and we are heading for disaster. It means I have taken a bath as a new investor in the top of the stock market, and now I am standing out in the cold with goose bumps and quivering flesh. Thank you, Ronnie. That was one heck of a story but there was no cold hard cash at the ending."

Jeff was beaming. He walked to his wife and gave her a hug and a kiss. "I love you so much more now as compared to this time last year or two years ago, Angie. I am only kidding snookums. Are you okay? How about I freshen your wine cooler?"

Ronnie and Rich look at each other with the same questioning look. Snookums?

LUNCH

The game finally ended in a four way tie. Richard and Jeff put the burgers on while Veronica got the chicken from the pot sliced up and on to a plate. They sat around the patio table munching food and swilling liquid refreshments talking with their mouths full and interrupting one another.

Angie asked, "Richard, why can't the prices go any higher?"

Veronica noticed Richard had just taken a big bite of his burger so she answered. "It is simple Angie. Investors have made three times their money. Would you buy a car or a dress that costs three times as much as it did four years ago? Investors want their profits. They are selling just a little bit at a time so prices don't drop overnight. *If the brokerage houses raise bids and try to get the market to run up right now,* **they would get deluged by sellers from around the world**. There will be a few stocks that will rise in price and climb on their own merit. Experienced investors will play the game and jump on board with small bets as that may the only stock that climbs to the moon before things get nasty."

Richard swallowed and interrupted. "We need a good old fashioned IPO. Something like police cameras! Drone toys. Any fifty dollar product that a household desperately needs will be fine."

"A new gizmo like the stun gun! One of those things that no one in the USA can live without. We need a home alert system that will notify your cell phone. Some gizmo for every fireman or policeman. Some new fad for the teenagers."

Angie butted in. "A little five dollar gadget that people can't live without that wears out fast." Angie sipped her iced tea. "What are IPO's?"

Jeff contributed. "A small company that has a new gizmo like Twitter. They have no cash, so the inventors start to look for money so they can grow and expand. They may wind up at an investment banker office. Now, this is not the traditional bank operation where your checking account is. If everyone likes the product and the odds, then they will put the officers of the new company under contract and the company is bound to the banker according to those legal terms. The banker agrees to raise money for the company. They can do this by raising cash or they can go to the public and sell shares of stock in the company. The prospectus has to be reviewed by the Securities and Exchange commission. Legally, certain terms and conditions must be in agreement with the rules, regulations and the law. Payment in the form of stock instead of cash is the way the new company will pay for the services."

Richard took over. ""Thank you for your little tidbit, Jeff. Then what the banker does is call some rich folk with deep pockets. If they can provide all the start up cash then they do so themselves. This is called a syndication of individuals and maybe some potential business partners who could manufacture the new gizmo. The investment bankers draw up a red herring if the sale of stocks is between private parties. Go ahead Ronnie."

"If their group does not have enough money, then the investment bankers solicit the brokerage houses until they find some accomplices who will agree to the underwriting and then the bankers write up a prospectus with the name of all parties included and the distribution of commissions for the sale. The brokerage house management teams review the prospectus and they may, for a cut of the proceeds agree to help with the sale of stock to the public. Once the prospectus is drawn up it is reviewed by the SEC and if approved, then a date is set for the sale of the IPO to the public."

Angie was inundated with information. "Okay. Fine. Richard, what makes them so popular? Jeff has been trying to pick one up. He says the share price just takes off like a rocket!"

"Well. Let me start with the dynamics of the new product going into the market place. I'm not talking about the test market for new toothpaste or soap. I'm talking about . . ."

Ronnie finished up for Richard. Ronnie took the conversation back while she munched on her chicken sandwich.

"See, Angie, the number of **counties** in all the states in the USA is *three thousand one hundred and forty two*. The number of cities is sixteen thousand. The number of towns is about the same and they all have a couple of precincts that include fire districts, police districts, school districts, water districts and so on. *So, you have some 32,000 municipalities* that need to supply their realm with the new widget. All of these fabulous markets exist for new gizmos. And the competition is fierce." Ronnie sipped her wine. "And don't forget the 140 million households. You learn about this in your marketing classes."

Angie said. "I think my head is going to explode."

"And then there is the effect of a hot new company producing 100,000 gizmos the first year. 300,000 the second. More sales every year. More new clients and amazing growth. Not the kind of cheap words or phrases you hear the politicians or the nightly business news talking about. This is not quite exponential growth, but it is more and more every year. The word gets out. The stock price moves up. The earnings reports are better and better every year. The company announces a stock split. Then it announces an expansion into a new leased building. It buys commercial property and plans to build their own plant in 2 more years. The stock takes off. It may slip in price if the market turns down but it will not fall far in price. Usually, this type of situation will produce a stock doubling of price within two years, if not sooner. If the product is widely sought after, then more buildings are acquired and 'round the clock shifts are added."

Jeff stood up with a wine bottle in his hand. "Here, here! I propose a toast. A toast to Thursday the 29th of October. Just think. This is Black October. Black Thursday! Can you feel the tide receding?" They raised their glasses for a toast. "Here, here. Black Thursday! Think of all of the foreclosures! There are usually 250,000 foreclosures a year, but from January 2006, to 2011 there have been six million."

Ronnie contributed, "That is where Ross Perot's famous line '*You will hear a large sucking sound!*' came from (Ross Perot was a successful businessman with a small beginning. He started with a small business and expanded internationally. He ran as an independent for president in 1992).

"Never fear, Jeff. It is only a Gray Thursday. We have to wait a year or two for the next Black Thursday." Angie spoke up and said, "And not to be confused with Black Friday the shopping holiday! But just the same, all of the prices drop!" Richard stood and raised his glass. "Here, here! Pity the poor new investor! If it was not for them, we would not be able to sell our massive stock accumulations at high prices and pull our winning cash profits out of the market." Glasses around the table were raised and the phrase, in unison, was spoken. "Pity the poor new investor!"

Jeff was certain that the 30 Dow stocks were getting some special attention. He decided to ask Ronnie. He waited until she was about to take another bite out of her sandwich. "Ronnie, tell the truth. Is it collusion in the financial community to keep the DJIA Index moving up a point a day to a new all time high? It sure seems that way to me. The financial community acting in concert. Isn't it?"

Woah, Jeff! We have been through this before," declared Ronnie. "We all have to make a living. The newspapers, the retail store sales people, the franchises, the big companies, the schools the teachers, the government, the list is endless. Even newspaper reporters and media hounds have to make a living somehow. They are not going to stop writing bogus articles even if the DJIA went down. They are writing for a paycheck. They have to fill up empty pages with articles for people to read and enjoy.

Angie questioned the obvious. "Weiss says that Standard and Poors took bribes and doctored and embellished financial positions of companies in S and P ratings. How much proof do you need?"

"Angie you are right, but you have to remember the whole world takes bribes. Take off your two goodie goodie shoes.

"Well is it collusion???

"Not when everyone has the same goal and desire! It is a symptom of the human condition. Yes, it is so vast. It is like everyone running for the 'Blue Light Sale' at Kmart."

"Well, if they are holding up the indexes and raising the bids, isn't that collusion?

"No, because the whole world trades the Dow Index."

Richard's face soured. "It is more of a set up, Jeff. The whole world is a set up and a double standard. Even Alan Greenspan called it irrational exuberance. His college dissertation referenced a previous chairman who used that saying in the 60's." Richard finished his second sandwich and sipped the liquid refreshment. "Let's go back to my retail analogy, which incidentally, is part of the actual *hard goods economy* and not the *intangible stock market economy.* I mentioned this before, but I did not elaborate greatly." Three pair of eyes rolled to the ceiling.

Ronnie interrupted with her favorite one liner. "I will say this again. Collusion requires jail time and an investigation by the Securities Exchange Commission and government agencies. *The Department of Corrections simply does not have enough space.*"

Richard continued. "Look at all of the hard goods, the durable goods sector. Goods that last 5 years. from refrigerators, to cars, to air conditioners to boats and houses. And then consider the soft goods. Clothing for all seasons, food, travel. These people have the same situation. These people act in unison as much as anybody, only it is in sales discounts, not in the DJIA Index. No matter how you slice it, everyone is after your money."

"Even the insurance and mortuary business beat the drums and broadcast loud and often to stay alive. The competition is fierce and overlapping and overwhelming. Look at clothing. They have been known to stretch the truth. This may not be a very good comparison, but here we are in a seasonal environment where we live. Spring, summer, fall and winter. You throw all of these duds on the rack at inflated prices so the store can cover its fixed overhead and employee payroll. They mark up a high first round price so the price can be marked down at sales time."

Angie contributed. "Yes. And in every local paper, in the middle of the week, all the stores have their coupons, discount notices and sales notices. Sunday's paper is loaded with announcements to get you shopping at one particular store and steal you away from the competition."

Jeff pitched in his two cents. "The best product that money can buy! The best car, truck, turkey, or furniture. The best grass seed fertilizer. It never ends and sales people yell, 'Sale, Sale, Sale! Buy, Buy, Buy! The sale is on now!' You will never see an advertisement that says, '*The worst in the nation*' or '*One hundred other brands are better than ours.*' Chuckles could be heard. '*Our products placed last in production quality*'. Do you see any trucks on the highway with advertising that claims, '*Our company is the worst one in the transportation industry?*'"

Ronnie continues. "This is how they pay the bills, cover the employee paychecks, and keep the company in business. These companies and corporations are trying to survive and make a living. And these are the good people! They have scheming competitors. Our goods are excellent quality, but our competition has low quality knock offs from Asia. This is a world wide method of operation. Wall Street is no different. The stock exchange provides a legitimate way to raise money. They sell bonds and secondary offerings for established companies and new companies that put new gizmo's, widgets and services on the market." Ronnie confirmed, "And this goes on all around the world. And it has been going on for many centuries. There are stock exchanges in well over one hundred countries. There are twenty major exchanges. Common Americans can't name more than three or four."

Ronnie continued. "And in this devil may care world, competition in every industry runs the full gambit. We have the full scope. Everything from fair deals and prices to bad deals and prices. From bad crook to angel. From cook the books to clean ledgers. I mean come on. It's not just the broker houses, there are crooked executives at companies like Enron, or execs at the Savings and Loans Scandal (see Appendix). And there is John Madden with the pile of pyramid money he conned and the few pennies that he gave back to investors he fleeced. He printed falsified statements that the pennies were a dividend from their investment."

Angie threw in, "And, just like the circus, they don't fold up the tents and roll on down the tracks until everyone in town is out of money."

Richard jumped in. "Let me add something. The government and Wall Street bump heads once in a while to figure out how to best handle obstacles in the road. Together, they sometimes depend on each other to for suggestions on how best to handle crisis. How best to work things out. Half of our population thinks that it is collaboration or collusion. When failures occur, it is usually the result of inaction from both sides. Regulators lack of knowledge requires experts to pick up the pieces and provide at least a temporary solution. These are basic 'work together' agendas."

"Things get fuzzy and out of proportion when stock prices are inflated more than they should be. The stock market and investors take care of that by themselves. Sure it seems the brokerage houses might operate in collusion to move the 30 stocks of the DJIA Index and two hundred and fifty others. But, in reality, the short term traders are trying to make a buck every day. *The truth of the matter is that every expert investor, everybody in the world who trades short term in the NYSE market, is **in the know on this set up**.* They play the stocks knowingly and willingly. And, I might add they do make money on the chances and the risks they take. **They know the set up and they stay with the big stocks**."

"Everything just seems to get ridiculous in the year before the selloff. It truly is a cruel world out there. All of the retail stores who buy products wholesale to sell to the public say they are the best. They are number one. They may not be one hundred percent truthful. They may stretch the truth. They may even lie a little or maybe they lie a lot. They have big sales and they have them often. They do not wait for the holidays. Everyone is in this game."

"What about oil Richard?"

Richard jumped straight out of his chair. "Let me go get the coupon. I have a collector's item. It's a gas ration coupon. Those royal arabs tried to break the western hemisphere and Europe as well as Scandinavia. They held the whole world hostage!"

Richard returned with the coupon and handed it to Jeff.

1974 USA GAS RATION COUPON

"Where did you get this, Richard?" Richard answered, "I can't tell you that, Jeff. It is classified. My uncle was a broker in the late seventies and early 80's. He says back then oil was a runaway due to the OPEC Cartel boycott and deliberate OPEC production cutbacks. People don't remember or talk about the fist fights at the local service station gas pumps here in the good old USA. A couple of gunshots were fired at stations around the nation over line position at the gas pumps. Arguments broke out over who needed the gasoline more than the other fella. Take a good look at that coupon again. Where could you get it? How many could you have? What is the value? A full tank or just 5 gallons? Can you imagine the counterfeiting? Your transportation would be your feet or the bicycle. Citizens would seize the buses." That comment drew laughter.

Angie remarked, "I can see my Jeffy driving a stolen bus. He's *Italian*, you know. "What about oil, Richard? It keeps dropping in price. Won't that effect the profits and inventory valuations?"

"That spigot will stay on full blast." Everyone who is somebody has been building their oil inventories at the lower prices, *including the USA Department of Defense*. They need fuel for their **ships, tanks and jets**. Oil companies will cut back on drilling new wells but the producing wells will keep flowing. The companies that help the drillers, the well servicing companies, they might have to lay off workers. *But I just love it*, Angie. You know the amazing thing is that all of the drilling, all of the new exploration in North Dakota has put the OPEC world and all the American **naysayers** to shame."

Ronnie commented. "Too bad for the middle east. They started the price wars to begin with. Now it is their turn to suffer. They had forty five years to enrich their countries and their citizens and their cities. If they did not get the job done, then that is just too bad. People don't realize that the middle east countries are all under 6 million people per nation except Iran and Iraq. 200 million people in six countries in the middle east. A few countries in Africa, Egypt, Syria, and Yemen have larger populations. And there are the large countries, Brazil, Mexico, Russia, and Venezuela. They were brought on board to OPEC eventually. The price of a 44 gallon barrel went from 10 dollars to 40 in just ten years.

That was the first step in destroying the middle class in the free nations of the world. And know this one fact, all of you. They are still pissed at us."

Ronnie embellished the discussion. "They had some help from the Jimmy Carter administration. Congress passed the Windfall Profits Tax. Basically, the government would ensure that the selfish oil companies would not profit from the jacked up price. All oil recovered from drilling activities in the USA and the Gulf were subject to taxation. Thousands of small companies would have to hand over a large chunk of their profits from sales to the government in the form of the windfall profits tax. Texans and Oklahomans just plugged their wells and said, '**Screw you!**'" They had no interest in the stupidity of a **windfall profits tax**. People have *no idea of what it takes to find oil, let alone put in a producing well.*

Angie questioned, "Whose idea was it? Wasn't Carter the Habitat for Humanity guy? Didn't he live off government grants and build small houses for poor people?"

"Carter denied responsibility. He claimed it was actually Congress."

Ronnie continued her rant. "Jimmy is just a regular humanitarian, huh? If they make it to the presidency, then all of a sudden these flaming egotists think that their mere presence, their mere personality will enable them to negotiate peace with any country in the world. They sign a peace treaty or trade agreement that would not mean a thing if tensions were to flare. But the government will always announce that it was a milestone achievement. That is their way of throwing the USA citizen a chicken wing. I remember when General Schwarzkopf had just run Saddam out of Kuwait, a country of 1.4 million people with half of the oil reserves in the middle east (**100 billion** bbls a one hundred year supply). It was the President Bush senior who held Schwarzkopf at the Iraqi border. Schwarzkopf could have followed Hussein's troops and corralled them in Baghdad. But old President Bush senior gave the General and the USA citizen this line, 'Saddam is beat. He won't bother us anymore.' Have another chicken wing USA citizen. Bush was a US Air Force pilot in WW2. He should have known better, but he underestimated Hussein's resolve. Just like Obama underestimated the ISIS resolve. Just think. In two more years that worthless Pres will be history."

"Jimmy Carter just wanted to be loved and admired and go down in history as the best president ever. The Shah of Iran just mesmerized the little peanut farmer. Now he is being loved by muslims everywhere. Such a humanitarian. He's involved with educating muslims now. He tries to raise money for them through the Carter Foundation. He probably immigrates them to America.

Angie expressed her feelings. "Politicians suck when they learn how to rip off the tax payers money for their own pockets."

"Let's not go there. Carter dropped sanctions to Iran. Jimmy Carter is a very vain man. They all want to be the best president in history and many of them end up stepping on their baloney. Jimmy thought he was head and shoulders above President Regan. That was Jimmy's personal opinion."

It was Richard's turn. "But the Brits and the Norwegians saved our asses. They finally opened some working wells in large fields under the cold unforgiving North Sea. It was an incredible engineering feat. A mile to the sea floor, then two more miles inside the sea floor. OPEC vowed to keep production up and prices up. In the end this would hurt them as the inherent laws of the market place of supply and demand would flood the arab nations states with unsold inventory and lower sales figures. I guess the arab children schooled in foreign countries forgot to sign up for an elementary economics course. The arabs and their own children educated in the west were unaware of economic theory. But of course, they all had rights as citizens and they had learned to be disruptive. The hard truth was, Venezuala, the arab nations, Mexico and Russia would suffer big time as oil was not going to climb right back up to $40 dollars a barrel. The days of marvelous oil revenues was over for another decade or so. Go ahead and blame the Devil USA. Everybody needs someone or something to hate. Right?"

Angie snickered. "Apparently, their college educated children in schools in Europe and the USA did not sign up for good old fashioned Economics 101. Ha ha ha, that's funny!" Angie asked Richard, "Why can't the cost of drilling be as cheap as before? Isn't everything in place?"

"Well equipment wears out just like the human body. It rusts. If it does not rust, then it weakens and wears out. My cousin says that oil had run up in 1980 and that the precious metals, gold, silver and platinum had run up too as a hedge against inflation." Richard inhaled as he was running his mouth and trying to get a tiny sip of wine at the same time. Tiny droplets of the wet stuff lodged in his wind pipe and he began to cough reflexively. He began to shudder and spasm. The trio watched him stand up and walk around in tiny circles trying to clear his throat with a big intake of air and a huge cough. It only inflamed his condition. He began to hack and wheeze in earnest. Jeff and Angie stared.

"Don't be alarmed," Ronnie cautioned. "He does that for attention." The plastic glass of wine slipped out of Richard's hand and spilled on the concrete. Ronnie commented, "See what I have to deal with Jeff? That is why I don't let him use real glassware." Richard stepped sideways to avoid the plastic cup. His right foot moved backward and settled precariously on the on the edge of the patio. His ankle twisted from his unsupported body weight. "Eeeee yowwww!" Richard gracefully tumbled off the patio. Ronnie commented, "I give him an 8.5. I've seen better. You would think these patios would be flush to the ground, but the workers were too cheap to make it so." Ronnie, a little wobbly, managed to stand up along with Angie and Jeff. They danced and clapped their hands as her poor, injured husband hopped and limped around the patio gritting his teeth.

"Oh, Richard! This is so romantic. Just like when we first started dating!" Richard hopped around like his foot was on fire. Finally, after thoroughly enjoying their torment towards the man they helped him to a chair. Ronnie and Jeff went into the house for first aid equipment while Angie and Richard inspected his ankle. It began to swell immediately.

Ronnie and Jeff returned with two buckets and set them in front of Richard's feet. One bucket was filled with ice water and the other one was hot. Richard intoned to Angelique, "Rub a little higher please."

"Don't do it Angie. My husband is a lecherous pervert!"

"Aren't they all?"

Richard alternately moved his foot from the hot bucket to the cold one as he sipped another glass of wine and observed the beautiful day and the action. "Well, thanks for helpin' me, everyone." Ronnie replied. "Are we going to play another game and watch Richard suffer?"

Jeff spoke up, "Nah, let's practice our shots. You better get some ice on that ankle Richard. Use the clothing iron if you need some heat."

Chuckles arose on the patio as the trio went to the yard to practice wicket shots. Ronnie decided to tell the Thompson's about a book she finished reading last week. "You all need to read a book I just finished. It is called the Harbinger. What I really do like about this book is the way it links ancient history and our Judeao-Christaian background to what is going on today with all of the cultural divergence, the death of God and the assault on Christianity and all of our cherished beliefs. The book compares past biblical history with what is going on in today's world. It talks about the early history of the USA. The book happens to mention that in 1876, there were thirty merchants who grouped to gather to help fellow citizens share in their business. They displayed their wares along a one hundred foot wall that was about three feet in height and two feet in width. They decided to sell shares in their companies that all local merchants might share in their prosperity. And you will never guess where that wall was." Dead silence except for the munching of snacks.

Angie spoke first. "Oh, we give up, Ronnie."

"All this was in what today is Manhattan and it was very close to the building that holds the New York Stock Exchange. That is how the street was given the name Wall Street. There is a time traveler who keeps talking and making all of the comparisons of past and present with a New York resident. Anyway, the comparison is very interesting. It mentions the Shemitah, a sign of judgement. All of this stems from the custom of allowing the fields to recover every seventh year. There is no crop planting so nutrients and minerals in the soil can replenish themselves. Otherwise judgement was brought upon the planters. I suppose the crop yields would be lower for one thing. And so it was with the remission and cancellation of debts." Ronnie hit her ball through the center wicket. "Let me set the stage for 2008. According to what Johnathan Chan wrote in *The Harbinger*, the crash of 2008 took place on the 29th day of the Elul. This is the crowning day of the Hebrew Shemitah. *This happened on the* **anniversary** *of 911 in* **2008**. And exactly seven years before this was the World Trade Center bombing on September 11, 2001. 911 also took place on the 29th day of the Elul, the crowning day of the Hebrew Shemitah."

Ronnie hit her ball through the center wicket again. "September 7, 2008 was the collapse of Fannie Mae and Freddie Mac. On September 9, 2008 Lehman brothers collapsed and on September 11 AIG announced they would collapse if they did not receive financial help. There is more. Bear Stearns raised 3.2 billion to bail out two of their hedge funds that were packed with sub prime mortgages. One was named **High Grade Structured Credit Strategies Enhanced Leverage Fund**. Barclay's Bank (British) had loaded up on American sub-prime mortgages. They sued Bear Stearns because Bear Stearns hid large losses in a fund that collapsed and swallowed up a mere 400 million of Barclay's money. Barclay's declared the fund that collapsed to be *a willfully reckless vehicle which allowed Bear Stearns to have leverage returns for its clients."* Bear Stearns had previously posted a small loss of 854 million (close to 1 trillion dollars) in December 2007. It was the first loss in 85 years). Anyway 2008 turned into a **Global Shemitah."**

Angie questioned, "So you think that this seven year market stretch is related to the ancient 2000 year old custom? I kind of like that. Work like mad for six years and take the seventh one off."

LIVERMORE

I t was 9am Friday morning after the slaughter on the croquet field. The first thing Angelique did after she screwed her husband's brains out was to head for the kitchen and load up a pot of coffee. She ran back to the bedroom to roust Jeff out of bed. She found him staggering about. She shoved a cup of coffee into his paw and she steered him to the shower. Jeff had been on the bottom during the promiscuity and a sheet was stuck to his backside. As he turned to go, Angie pulled the sheet off his body. "Is everything okay? How did I do, baby? I told you I would make it up to you." Jeff felt good. He felt manly. He was the man of the house.

That done she returned to the kitchen and counted the bills in the cookie jar and smiled. She stashed the entire ninety-three dollars in her purse. She moved to the garage and backed the SUV to the driveway as Jeff locked the front door and joined her. After a quick drive through breakfast at Mickey D's they made a dash to the Amish Thrift Shop. It was half price day on all Yellow Tags. Their agenda was to try to match the Whiting's office set up. There were several desks in the furniture area, but they opted for a large oak kitchen table. The Thompson's found two adjustable swivel chairs hidden among the furniture for $12 apiece. The two drawer file cabinet for $15 would fit underneath the table. There were several beige and blue lazy boys in the $50 area and an attractive sofa for $65. "Jeff, we can come back after those. We need to pick up a bookcase too." Jeff nodded his head and pulled out his credit card. "Let's go ahead and get it all. Angie." A smile on her face, Angie put ninety-three dollars back into her purse.

In the living room their arrangement was similar to the Whiting's. Angie had the oak table close to the corner and Jeff's desk faced her table. There was room to walk between the two. Jeff tacked up his 50 year chart on the wall between the windows and the corner. They would both have access to view the chart closely. Jeff tacked one triangle to the wall behind Angie's chair. He used one small nail at the apex to hold the second triangle to the first. He wondered how soon Angie would be spinning them. The two lazy boys were in front of the living room window, between his desk and the front door. The flat screen went on the wall across from the living room window and the lazy boys. Angie moved her husband's plastic weight set out to the patio. The bookcase stood in the corner. On the book case they had *The Ultimate Safe Money Guide* by Weiss. *Livermore, The World's Greatest Trade.* **The Securities Research Company Blue Book** and a space for *The Dead Cat Bounce,* Erdman's *Crash of 79* and *Crash of 89.* The file cabinet was under the end of Angie's oak table and the printer was on the table top just above the file cabinet. Jeff put the news clippings on the left side of his desk. The professional news and magazines went on the right. He had two cardboard boxes of special articles on notorious goofs by businesses and crooks in the equities industry, from Milliken to politicians, the Savings and Loan scandals and Whitewater among numerous others. They went under Angie's desk.

"Jeff, this table is better than the one we have in the kitchen."

"The thrift stores have good deals, don't they?"

"Baby. It is because we are special. We are discerning, cost conscious scammers."

"This is fabulous Angie. I might let you off the hook. By the way, Did I tell you that your new desk has to go in the utility room?" Angie gave him an ugly face.

"I think we got lucky this time. Jeff, we should head to the auto auction next week and find a new beater for me!"

"That will be a special day."

"Everyday we have together is special."

Jeff returned to his thoughts. He stared at the 50 year wall chart and compared the market top of 2007 to 2014. In six months or sooner everyone who did not sell at this time before the end of 2015 will be shaking their heads and saying, "My, golly! I have lost fifteen to twenty percent! I can't sell now. I will be a loser!" Gradually, the sell offs will begin to see a larger DJIA Index in point loss than usual **if** the bleak earnings reports continue to shrink. Six months after this point in time investors will have losses of twenty to thirty percent. Within a year, the earnings reports will turn into no growth, no earnings and small losses back to back. All of the layoffs and downsizing will have occurred and companies will be slim and trim. In two years, just before the plane falls out of the sky, investors will be saying, 'Oh! My God! The market is not coming back. It is going to crash! These financial people have been lying to me! What a fool I have been!' The financial gurus and financial street people will say. *'Hang on the rally is here!' 'Hold on. Don't sell yet!' 'There is a rally just around the corner!'* The financial pundits will fill your ear with glowing appraisals of the worth of a pebble in a stream. They will have you believing that the pebble franchise is going coast to coast in the first quarter next year. That is when the investors, will *realize that their* **financial success boat has been transformed into a life raft**. They are whirling about in the rapids and heading toward the waterfall.

The 500 point November rally was here. The paper was quick to point out that the market rallied back! But it wasn't all of the 2500 NYSE stocks. It was only the DJIA Index and the big S+P 500 companies that recovered. The DJIA rallied back to 16500 and later moved up to 17000 like nothing ever happened. This burned a hole in Jeff's brain. *'We told you so'*, said several brokerage house touts. The yellow brick road was back, but the tornado and the wicked witch were certain to return soon. He looked through the stack of November clippings. The articles were all that Jeff had heard over the last four years. 'The market plays it cool after the GOP wins.' '230,000 jobs added.' Jeff thought to himself, *'Whoopee doo! Compare that to millions lost over the last six years. Big deal.'*

"You know, Angie. All of our lives we become conditioned to words. Say the DJIA Index. We think that represents the market. Supposedly, the DJIA Index represents the market, but it really doesn't. It is only thirty stocks with a mathematical index that is only relevant to those thirty stocks. It is not relevant to the 2500 other NYSE stocks. The public relates the DOW Index to the entire market. It is convenient that way. That way we don't have to think too much."

"You mean like when I ask you to go to the store and bring back some food and you don't get what I want?" Angie was looking at the clippings in Jeff's box of political shenanigan article. "This box is so funny. You have a whole bunch of crooks in here and some bad companies stealing money. Oh, oh! Here is George Bush at the Enron party. He was caught with a bad joke in a private conversation. Gosh! Whitewater linked to a Savings and Loan Scandal! Madoff. Lucent (Please see Appendix). Germany's Helmut Kohl with secret money and a missile deal."

"You can read about those crooks later, Angie. It is time to learn more about charts. Jeff pulled the Securities Research Company Blue Book off the bookcase. They sat together at Angie's table and reviewed the book. The price was not important to Jeff. The new version of the Securities Research Company Blue Book contains the most actively traded and the best performing stocks on the DJIA and the NASDAQ. The book is three inches thick! USA's 3000 best stocks all in 700 pages. Four charts on each page! In addition, 350 charts of international companies and ADRs are included. Jeff bought this new one in July 2014 so he could review what had happened in the last twelve years to 1500 of the most actively traded NYSE stocks.

They sat side by side and tore into the Securities Research Company Blue Book charts. Angie flipped through the pages. "These charts are really neat because you can see the trading range over 12 years. The charts cover the high and low prices over the last full cycle, plus half of the current cycle. Hey! This looks like a cyclical stock. Ronnie was talking about them. But why buy a company that trades in the same price range cycle after cycle? Down the road, you will not have made any money at all. The sales pitch of *'hang in for the long haul'* just can't be true."

"Right, Angie. That is the reason the charts are so helpful. They help you get the low price and they give you an idea when it might be time to cash out. These cyclical stocks are mature companies that sell or make the same goods year after year and they have basically the same financials and sales and operations year after year. They successfully maintain their position in their industry. And you can profit from them every market cycle if your timing is right."

Jeff explained the aspects of the charts and how to interpret them. Angie turned to the first chart. "Holy cow, Jeff! Look at this! It is a rocket! From $1.5 in 2009 to $95 a share at the end of 2013." The symbol was DDD, 3D Systems Corporation. Jeff instantly made a note to use 3D as a possible stock to sell short. He explained to Angie that 3D was a new revolutionary, hi tech manufacturing process and that the stock price had experienced wide popularity bordering on a mania. He pointed out the PE ratio.

"Wow! 70?"

"Yes. It is way up there! A rocket! With a low number of outstanding shares it is easy to move the bid up."

"What is the price rise based on? Is it mostly betting on future income?"

"Remember when Ronnie was talking about IPO's yesterday? In 2009 3D was an IPO."

"How does it go so high."

"Well, Angie, in this case there are not too many shares. Say 50 million trading in public hands. That is one share for every investor in the USA. When the number of shares in existence is small, the price can rise faster, especially if there is a big demand for the shares. The asking price is easier to move a little higher because the shares are somewhat scarce. No one is selling because the holders of stock think there may be a much higher price in a year or so. Or maybe even a stock split." Jeff paused and sipped his tea. "More shares might be issued to the public to raise money for the new plants and new markets. The shares can be used as collateral for loans from lenders to finance the expansion. These are the big possibilities that get investors hot to trot over IPOs."

"Then it is a new stock and a new company with a new idea and a new gizmo?"

"Yes. 3DSystems is a new manufacturing process, if you will. A computer, through a robot, applies one layer of plastic on top of another, according to the design pattern in the computer software. Something like that. The software and the robot build the design. 3D is one of two companies experimenting with the process and applications for use. I don't know who the material suppliers are or really anything about the situation except to say that it is a new gizmo." Jeff paused. "This new technology will have many uses. It will take a couple of years to get them all in place and make some needed engineering adaptions. And then there are the rumors of stocks splits, or a competitor buying up 3D for a partnership."

3D Systems
Chart provided by Securities Research Company
(SRC). Please visit www.srcstockcharts.com

"The big gains in revenue on the income statement will not be seen for a year or two. Maybe three. Sometimes you just never know when the good news announcements are going to start. You never know when the big orders are going to filter in. But there are people who do. So just call up the company and ask them. You never know if a mutual fund might start to buy some shares. Or after you buy shares you could just call a couple of brokerage houses and give them that anonymous tip. Go ahead and start that mutual fund rumor yourself. Ten new niches or new applications may open up." Jeff continued. "It is simply expansion based on phenomenal success of the product. Start with an experimental project and grow to one plant. Then to several plants and from there to production around the world.

"I think I would rather buy a plot of land than wait three years. Is it worth it to hang on for three years?

"Good girl, Angie. That would be more fun than trying to figure out what color to paint the kitchen. Buying stocks is all a judgmental exercise until emotion and greed enter in. You have to have patience. Patience paid off big time for me. Here. Let me show you two companies that have grown steadily over the years."

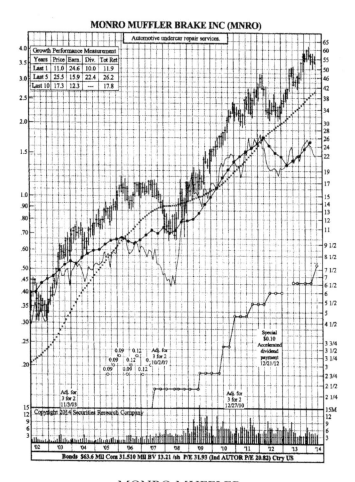

MONRO MUFFLER

Chart provided by Securities Research Company
(SRC). Please visit www.srcstockcharts.com

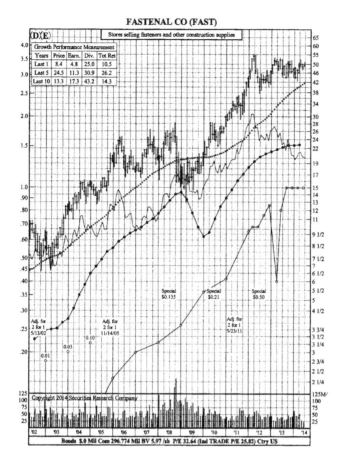

FASTENAL

Chart provided by Securities Research Company

(SRC). Please visit www.srcstockcharts.com

"Wow! I didn't know there was any money in car mufflers. Let me check out some cosmetic companies. Women will skimp on food before they give up cosmetics. Cosmetics should be recession proof." Angie looked for Estee Lauder. It was not in the book. She searched it on the net. "Jeff. This stock should be in the Blue Book. Look at this graph." Jeff agreed. Angie, it is a good play. It just is not as actively traded as the top 1500. Angie made a quick search for the best performing stocks in women's beauty products. She stopped for now and photocopied Revlon and Tiffany's. She slipped the copies into a manila folder. "I want to see Starbucks and Monster drinks."

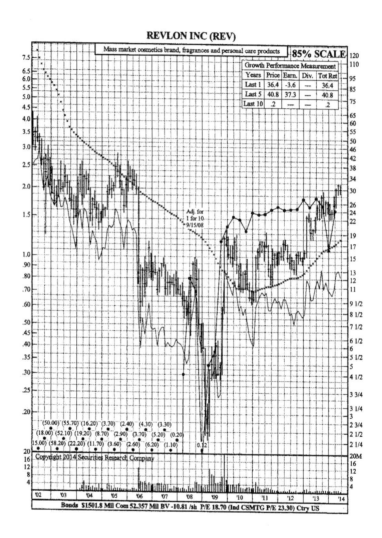

REVLON
Chart provided by Securities Research Company
(SRC). Please visit www.srcstockcharts.com

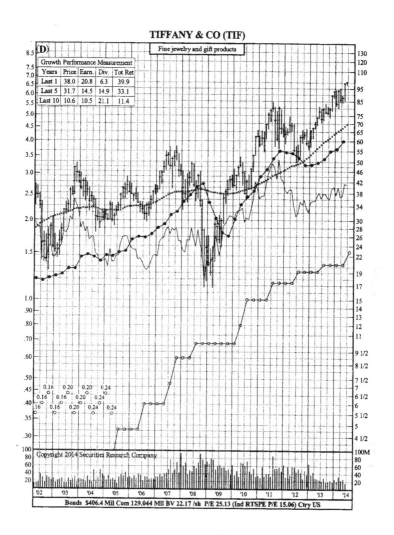

TIFFANY & CO (TIF)

Fine jewelry and gift products

Growth Performance Measurement				
Years	Price	Earn.	Div.	Tot Ret
Last 1	38.0	20.8	6.3	39.9
Last 5	31.7	14.5	14.9	33.1
Last 10	10.6	10.5	21.1	11.4

Copyright 2014 Securities Research Company

Bonds $406.4 Mil Com 129.044 Mil BV 22.17 /sh P/E 25.13 (Ind RTSPE P/E 15.06) Ctry US

TIFFANY'S
Chart provided by Securities Research Company
(SRC). Please visit www.srcstockcharts.com

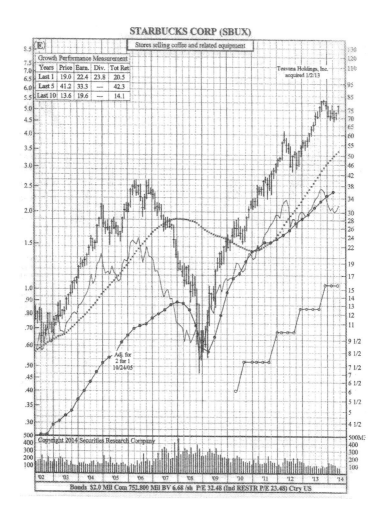

STARBUCKS CORP (SBUX)

Stores selling coffee and related equipment

Growth Performance Measurement				
Years	Price	Earn.	Div.	Tot Ret
Last 1	19.0	22.4	23.8	20.5
Last 5	41.2	33.3	—	42.3
Last 10	13.6	19.6	—	14.1

Teavana Holdings, Inc.
acquired 1/2/13

Adj. for
2 for 1
10/24/05

Copyright 2014 Securities Research Company

Bonds $2.0 Mil Com 752,800 Mil BV 6.68 /sh P/E 32.48 (Ind RESTR P/E 23.48) Ctry US

STARBUCKS
Chart provided by Securities Research Company
(SRC). Please visit www.srcstockcharts.com

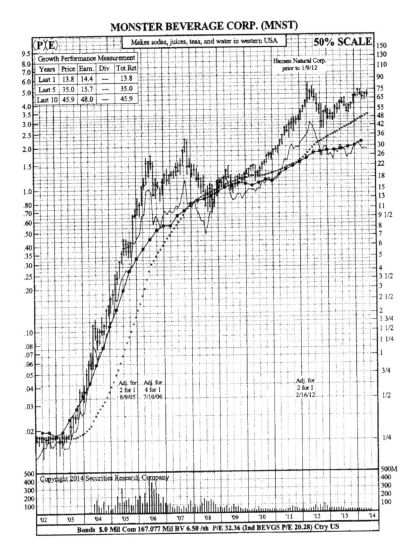

MONSTER BEVERAGE CORP. (MNST)

Makes sodas, juices, teas, and water in western USA

50% SCALE

Hansen Natural Corp.
prior to 1/9/12

Growth Performance Measurement				
Years	Price	Earn.	Div.	Tot Ret
Last 1	13.8	14.4	—	13.8
Last 5	35.0	15.7	—	35.0
Last 10	45.9	48.0	—	45.9

Adj. for
2 for 1
8/9/05

Adj. for
4 for 1
7/10/06

Adj. for
2 for 1
2/16/12

Copyright 2014 Securities Research Company

Bonds $.0 Mil Com 167.077 Mil BV 6.50 /sh P/E 32.36 (Ind BEVGS P/E 20.28) Ctry US

MONSTER

Chart provided by Securities Research Company

(SRC). Please visit www.srcstockcharts.com

"Let's check out the wall chart for a minute, Angie. You should see the Dot Com Crash chart line." They crowded in front of the chart. "First let's check this crash point on the DJIA Index chart. From this crash point in 2009, the DOW Index was 6400 or so. How long did it take for the DJIA Index *to make it back to 13,500, where it was in 2007 just before the crash?"*

"Gosh. It looks like three years."

"Good answer, Angie. Now, here is a story for you. You have a stock market crash. In this new cycle up and out from the crash, it takes three and a half years for the DJIA Index to make it back up to where it was before the crash. Three and a half years. This will be three years that the unaware, but potential investor might not buy stock because they think the DOW is worthless. The non investor hears the news media proclaim day after day that the last time the market was in such sad shape was 12 years ago. These statements tell the non investor that it is a bad time to buy stock. And during this time, the big boys are loading up." Jeff paused. "Then, after three years, the word will be out in the media that the DJIA index has finally made it back to the high point in the previous cycle and the media will declare that the market has recovered."

"Now, after three years have passed, the market will be in the high C Area on the triangles. The marching band and media drums will beat louder. The media proclaims that the market is in position to strike a new historic, all time DJIA Index high. So the uneducated investor will say to himself, *'Maybe I should get in the market now. It sounds like things are good.'* So the new investor jumps in with fresh cash in the high C or D Area. Two or three years later, after a market downturn, their investments will be 50% lower. Does that make sense?"

"It certainly does. Jeff. They will miss out on the first half of the upswing."

"Here is something else you should see. The mania in the Dot Com Boom." Jeff pointed out the years 1999 to 2001. "Okay, Angie. Check out the high point in the NASDAQ Composite chart line and then check where it is a year later. Does anything jump out at you?"

"Holy moly! It looks like the NASDAQ fell into a cave!"

"Here is something else I want to point out. September 2001. Notice the large **volume** spike right here on the bottom of the chart. That is the NYSE volume for one month. Can you add that one up, baby?"

Angie read the chart. "It looks like 60 billion shares in September 2001."

"Correct. After 911, there are only 14 days left, but the market was closed for six days which leaves 8. Eight from 60 is 52. The average number of shares traded in a normal month is 24 billion which would be a little over one billion shares a day. Divide 8 into 52 and you have 6.5. this means the market traded 6.5 billion shares every day for the rest of September to reach 52 billion. At $100 dollars a share this would be a whopping 6 *trillion, 500 million dollars.* At $50 dollars a share it would be 3 trillion, 500 million. How about that for chump change?"

"That is simply unbelievable."

It was time for a break. They made sandwiches and beverages and returned to their desks to chat and admire the new look in their living room. They laid out a plan and took an oath that they would skim the Livermore book and the Wall Street Digest newsletters together. They sat side by side and skimmed *Jesse Livermore. The World's Greatest Stock Trader.* by Richard Smitten. Their conversations went something like this.

"Now remember, Angie. These statements from 1929 are pretty much about the 1920's. The market was much smaller in the 1920's. The average daily trading was less than *1% of the total daily trading we have today.* Investors would read the ticker tape. The tape told you where the buying was going if you kept your eye on it. So the story goes. The gadgets they used were radios, telephones and telegraphs. There were no computers or TV. There were none of the electronic saving devices we have today."

Jeff continued with his history lesson. "There were no investors from all over the world that there are today. Mail was delivered across the ocean by ship in ten days if the seas were calm. In 1927 the Trans Atlantic telephone service was radio based. 1954 saw the first transatlantic telephone cable system between Scotland and Newfoundland. It carried 36 telephone channels. In the first 24 hours there were 588 calls from London to the USA. There were 119 calls from London to Canada. The caller had to wait for the call connections to be arranged and that might take 15 minutes if the lines were not busy or tied up. Now you can send out an email to 100 different addresses in the world and you can get a response from those addresses within 5 minutes. That is, if the other side of the world is not sleeping."

"Most stock exchanges were very localized in the nations of the world. By that I mean that the facilities were very close together. The brokerage offices in the USA were in buildings right next to the NYSE trading floor. 80 to 90% of the trading on the New York Exchange was in the individual brokerage offices. Runners delivered the buy and sell orders along with other documents. Other states in the USA had their own local stock exchanges for their own business needs. Mining. Railroads, stuff like that." Jeff continued. "The industrial revolution began in the late 1700's. Steam engines. Railroads. Trains. Electric generators. It hit its stride in the 1800's and peaked in the first half of the 1900's. In the 1900's, the average number of shares that traded each day varied from 200,000 up to 700,000 shares a day. In October 1929 the total number of shares traded for the **month** hit 16 million. And the largest trading **day** of the year was on Black Friday, the 29th of October. 3.5 million shares traded. Runners, ticker tape, telegraph, chalk boards, paper and pencils were on fire! The environment was different 100 years ago. In 1900 there were 1 million people in California. Communications were slow compared to the high tech world we live in today. Word did not spread fast. Now, 100 years later in California there are 34 million people."

"How many of them traded stock Jeff?"

"That is just the point. The market has changed from just the locals investing in local exchanges to the whole world investing in all the exchanges around the world. From one million shares a day to one billion. Communication went from copper wire to instant world wide satellite communications."

"Okay. Thank you, professor. That pretty much sets the stage for our reading assignment. I am impressed with your knowledge, but let's move on." Jeff cast a crooked eye at Angie. "There is one more very important thing, Angie. There are similarities that still exist in today's exchanges." Angie replied, "And what would that be?" Jeff looked at Angie's eyes. *"That would be human nature. That is the reason that Livermore's rules are timeless."*

MONEY MANAGEMENT

Never, lose more than 10%.

If stock goes opposite direction, Sell! Never sustain a loss of more than 10 %.

The big money is made by the sitting (not the thinking). The hardest thing to do is wait. Be patient. Wait for the move to play out.

There are times when you should be completely out of the market. No one wins all the time.

Play only when all factors are in your favor. "I really like this one, Jeff."

Take your position with the utmost caution. Twenty percent at a time. This could take as long as three to six months. This means confirm your judgement before you take a full position. Prices must be going up. If stock drops then close all positions.

Do not spend time trying to figure out what moves the price of a stock.

Beware when stocks get heavy and churn after a long upward trend. The end of the move is near. This means that stocks are going from strong hands to weak hands. From the pros to the uneducated public. The public has been lead to believe, by the industry, that this is a healthy sign. A vibrant healing.

Angie recalled, "This is what you and Richard and Veronica were talking about during the croquet game. The churning will last all next year. There will be no significant advance in the indexes. A few individual stocks will take off on their merit alone. And the short term investors can buy the price drops to play the rally back for five or ten percent, if you stay in the big stocks."

"Excellent. That is correct."

*Behind **all major moves** in the stock market there is an **irresistible force**.*

You can't or should not try to anticipate.

You should be able to identify a pivotal point.

"He means that one day in trading the stock price sets up to reverse direction of movement. That day the highest price is higher than the previous day's high and the lowest price is lower than the previous day's low."

"Why is that?"

Jeff got up from the sofa and returned with a legal pad. He sketched a rectangular box. "Here is what the box brokerage house trader refers to as the 'box'. On the left side is the bid and the number of shares available. On the right side is the ask and the number of shares available. The bid and the ask. The box is carefully moved higher and then lower to find out where buyers and sellers are willing to trade the stock again."

"They bump the bid up to see if there are any more sellers at the higher price. And they drop the ask to see of anyone is ready to buy at a lower price. When the bid and ask are far apart, the stock is not actively trading.

Watch for wild capitalization in good stocks selling at 40, 50 or 60 times earnings. These will be the companies that will have lower lows and the same high every cycle.

Big positions are crept up on, added to a little at a time, and this is to keep the price from jumping up suddenly and having to pay a higher share price.

Never average down.

EMOTIONAL CONTROL

Clear concise strategy and stick to it. Reason, logic and pure economics do not drive the stock market. It is driven by human nature. Human nature being **greed, cheating, lying and stealing.** *Emotions carry the extremes. The manias. The feeding frenzies.*

Stick to your plan. During the lulls or at the top or bottom you should be completely in cash

Don't anticipate. Wait until the market gives you a clue. Pivotal point.

Forget tips. Don't take them. Stay focused on your five stocks.

Jeff offered a thought. "Now, here is something to keep in mind, Angie. Do not focus on the DJIA Index. You keep an eye on it only to figure out what part of the cycle the market is in. Your main focus is on your five stocks."

There is no such thing as **hope.**

When the market goes sideways and you are confused. Take some time off.

Angie said, "I like that idea. A vacation. That is what the Whiting's are going to do."

Some stocks hit a wall and cannot go any higher. It is because there are too many people who are getting out who have waited for this day to happen. And they are selling.

"Angie, this would be the mutual fund and the corporate dump. When the big boys and girls are selling out."

Turn paper profits into money and cash out.

"Yes, Angie. It means get those paper winners in your stock portfolio account sold and the winning cash goes into your savings account." Angelique responded, "Turn your brokerage account to hard cash She gave her husband a tender kiss. "And you did that, baby. You sold your stocks when you made a profit."

Time is not money. There is no reward to buy a stock before it starts moving. You have to wait for the direction of the stock or the market to reveal itself. Therefore be out of stock.

Beware when today's high is higher than yesterday's high and today's low is lower than yesterdays low. This is a one day reversal.

The line of least resistance is the trend, the direction the market is moving.

If a stock drops suddenly and does not rebound, it will fall further. It is inherently weak. The reason will be revealed at a later date.

Pivotal point - If you catch it, it pays big rewards.

The second pivotal point is called the continuation. It confirms the new direction. This is accomplished by a heavy increase in volume. The new direction (if downward) tells you to exit. Or if you are not in position, then it tells you to enter.

End of the bull market. Watch for stocks with PE's of 30 40 50 60 times annual earnings. These stocks traded at much lower multiples in the last crash.

Group action. If one stock in a sectors climbs, sooner or later a similar company in the same sector will. Or likewise, if one leading company drops then so will similar companies.

Buy the market leaders in the sectors or industries.

The Market operates in future time. It has already factored in current trends.

"Jeff this is saying that our market right now, is trending in the June area to July of next year 2015. And we know Barron's predicted reduced earnings next year. **The big boys and girls are getting out six months ahead of time.**"

EMOTIONAL CONTROL RULES

Let your profits 'ride' if there is no reason to close out the position.

The action is with the leading stocks which changes with every new market.

Keep the number of stocks you follow limited so that you may focus.

Cheap stocks tend to appear to be bargains and safe to buy after a large drop. They often continue to fall or have little potential to rise in price. Leave them alone.

Use pivotal points to identify changes in trends.

The market is a study in cycles. When it changes direction. It remains in that direction until it weakens.

Shares that are thinly traded (low volume) are not good for trading. The share price is held by few investors.

The stock market is never obvious. It is designed to fool most of the people most of the time.

Do not like a stock. Cut losses immediately. Do not lose more than 10%.

SHORT THE MARKET

J eff wanted to learn to play the downside. He knew that the direction of the market in the next two years or sooner was going to be down the rapids to the waterfall. He knew that he and Angie would battle inflation in their senior years and he was not looking forward to a life of repainting second hand furniture or theft and burglary just to pay the utility bills. Nor did he want to live in a tent close to an uninhabited ravine by a stream. At that moment he knew that an experiment was at hand. He was going to short one or two stocks with just a little bit of his money to see if his scheme would work. He might lose, but then he would no longer suffer these fits of fever. Just the thought got all of his cylinders firing again. His excitement was immediately followed by some fear in his gut that he might fail.

He briefly pictured himself as the big headed monster straining at the straps as Dr. Frankenstein turned up the electrical current that brought him to life and awareness. He was totally unleashed. No longer was he restricted to invisible ties of his mundane life, his job or the union. Maybe he would become a stockbroker. Maybe he would manage a brokerage house. He imagined that most of the new brokers simply abandoned the industry after a good old fashioned market crash. On the other hand, maybe they didn't care and they learned to mutter the catch all phrase, *'You can always average down.'* This was the anthem to financial death and obscurity. Other phrases were *'Things will get better.'* *'The market is burping.'* *'The run up was too fast.'* *'Short term investors like to lock in their quick profits.'* That was a new one. He felt that by March of 2017 the tour boat would be at the edge of the waterfall. That would be a little over seven years of the market stretching out from the last correction. In Jeff's opinion it was way too long. There was a floating sea of paper profit out there in the investing world.

Together, with Angie, they were out of Area D in fashion and style. Together, they would record everything about how to short stocks in their spiral notebooks. Jeff was on the right track. He could feel it with every fiber in his body. The thrill of participation. The gamble. The sense of the hunt and bagging the big game. The weather was right and the direction was right and his attitude was right. He would find out how to complete the transaction safely. Somewhere in the universe, Jeff knew the stars were aligned in his favor. Somewhere in the universe there were really decent possibilities.

He put his head on the desk and rested. The blood was surging through his body. Maybe he should have his blood pressure checked. Angie had been reading the internet print outs of margin accounts and shorting. She put her hand on Jeff's shoulder. "This is really weird. It explains nothing. I just don't understand why people would do this. The brokerage house loans you money to buy stock and if the stock goes down 30% then your account is adjusted for the loan money *that you lost? You owe this money that you lost?* "Wow!" *And that is right then and there? You have five days to bring more cash to your account?* That sounds like a set up to me, Jeff. How stupid! They should have to eat it if they were dumb enough to loan it to you."

Jeff mused. At times Angie had the thought processes of a devout Catholic Priest and a Logics professor.

Jeff called in for sick time due to severe stomach and intestinal flu from the Halloween weekend. He knew that it might jeopardize his job. His boss would have a chance to assess some demerits against him and possibly take some type of punitive action. The simple truth was that he really didn't care anymore. Let the unions suffer! Angie had excused herself from work for the same reasons.

After a full lazy breakfast and the morning news, they prepared to sit at their desks to learn how to short the market. Today, Jeff and Angie were going to call some brokerage houses and talk with those in the know. Jeff wanted desperately to get the answers to the big question that had burned a hole in his head for the last two months. *How in the world do you short stock? Does anybody know?*

The home phone was hooked to an answering machine. They could hear and record conversation. They began to call the local brokerage houses. The first hour was very tiresome. They called wholesale houses first. Both were laughing after the fifth call. The routines were all so similar.

Most of their calls were answered by voice robots. The robots welcomed the caller and presented a list of concerns and a corresponding number for the person in charge. '*For trading, press one. To talk to a broker, press two. To hear your account balance, press three. For bookkeeping, press four or stay on the line to speak to the next available representative.*' When a live person answered, Jeff and Angie were surprised.

"Hi. This is Shelly. How may I help you? No. I do not know how to short stocks. If you give me your number I can have someone call you after the market is closed"

"All the brokers are talking with their clients. I have checked around the office and no one here knows how to do that. Everyone is on the phone right now. Let me get your name and number."

Jeff and Angie soon discovered that all of the answers and excuses were similar. 'Sorry we are busy. We would need to set up an account first. We are busy with the customers right now. If you call back after the market closes today, we will open an account for you. Let me transfer you to an assistant and get your account opened so you can be off and running. What did you need? Short the market? The market is great right now! Why would you want to short the market? No. We don't do that. We don't short stock. Everyone is busy right now. I asked around and no one here knows how to short. Can you call back in an hour? Everyone is at lunch. Everyone is busy. Let me see if I can transfer you. Why don't you drop by this afternoon and open a margin account? We can talk about it then. You have to come in and sign a margin agreement. You need $500 to open a margin account. Let me transfer you. If you don't have an account then I cannot talk to you. Open an account with a rep and then I can talk to you."

Angie and Jeff just stared at the message machine and they broke out laughing. Angie laughed to Jeff. "Isn't this just incredible? They can't handle calls when there is no heavy downturn in the market. You can't get through. What are investors going to do if there is a sharp downturn?"

Jeff responded evenly. "Play golf."

When they did get connected to a broker, most of the answers they received were redirection. "No! You don't want to sell short! I believe in the American economy. It the best in the world. Just buy and hang on for the long haul." Jeff Explained again. "I just want to learn how to sell short. I just want to know how to sell stocks short." The reply to his request was, "Are you crazy? The market is at an all-time high!"

Jeff would ask them, "Can you just answer my question please?"

"No. I won't do that. You will have to get someone else. Hold on. I am going to transfer you to Bernie." Whenever they did get transferred, it was 30 seconds to one minute before anyone picked up the line. A few brokers responded with the statement, "Oh, no! You don't want to sell short! You will just be caught between the price swings and you won't be able to get out of it without a loss. Call me back after trading hours are over. I'm very busy with client business."

"How much money do you have? I only do business with investors who have over $10,000 in their accounts." Both Angie and Jeff broke out laughing. The representative hung up.

Jeff stood up to stretch. "For cripes sake! The guy didn't even answer the question. None of the people answered the question. Instead they just rattled off some other meaningless line as if they knew what they were talking about."

"I don't know about you Jeff. I feel very, very lost. That last guy. He was just trying to get you to call back. He isn't doing anything. He just needs time to think up a line of bullshit to feed you."

"I think you hit the nail on the head. I agree with you, Angie."

Even Jeff's wholesale broker discouraged him. "Jeff, if you go short. You will just be bouncing back and forth between a little bit of a win and a little bit of a loss. It will be a totally unproductive situation. You may as well take a butterfly option position." Jeff wasn't sure what a butterfly option was, but it did remind him of his R and R days in the Pacific. "I think you are Jonesing. You just need to play a little bit with some options. That will dispel your fever. After a couple of losses you will wake up and lose your urge to gamble. You just need to do some short term investing. God, Jeff! You've been sitting on your winnings for three years. You should diversify!"

The answer pissed Jeff off. "Mark. Let me ask my question again. **Do you know how to short?**" The conversation ended abruptly. Jeff slammed the phone down. Angie saw the look in Jeff's eyes when his stomach turned sour. Jeff thought he was going to heave. "Do you feel insulted, dear? Weiss would have shot the guy. We need to find you a good broker, Jeff."

Somewhere in the world there must be a good broker.

Jeff vented. "Brokers don't know shit. They just write orders and pass the hype. All he does is wear fancy clothes. He dresses up and pretends he knows more than everyone else. All he does is sit behind his desk and bullshit on the phone." Jeff stood and walked around the living room. "They are spineless order takers. Oh, yeah! I'm a broker. Oh, yeah! I make everyone rich!"

Angie watched in wonder. "That was a pretty good vent, Jeff, but I have seen you do better. Ain't no Martin Weiss at any of these dumps. Why don't we head for the kitchen and some snacks?"

Angie spoke as she made sandwiches from chicken salad. "I think it is funny that we got so many similar answers and when I really think about it, no one told us how to short! Everyone put us off like we were the zika virus! Isn't it funny? All of these account executives, financial representatives and financial assistants have no idea how to short. *I wonder if they really know anything about the market*?"

The break was good and they were soon back at the desk dialing the last phone numbers and listening to the same answers they had heard before. They noted that no one had returned the earlier calls.

Angie was rapidly losing interest. Her old doubts floated to the surface, but she immediately suppressed them. She kept passing phone numbers to Jeff until they had exhausted all of the large print and the retail ads. She went to the list of brokers in the small print list. "Just a couple of more are left, honey." Jeff dialed another number. Their hopes picked up when a human voice answered the call. Jeff managed to turn his courage up a notch for the conversation.

"B. C. Christopher and Company," replied the female voice. "This is Liz. I am Greg Potzer's assistant. May I help you?"

"Hi. My name is Jeff. I have an unusual request. I am trying to find out how to short the market. I have read several articles I found on the internet about how to short the market. I can't make any sense of them. They are talking about unlimited liabilities and stuff. Can you tell me how to short the market and walk me through the process from point A to point Z?"

"Jeff, you can call me Liz. Tell me briefly. What is your investment experience? How have your investments worked out and what stocks do you have?"

"I just happened to buy three stocks four years ago. I had $16,000 to invest. I bought Citi Corp, Texas Instruments, and Bank America. This was my first plunge and it happened to be during the last market crash."

Liz waved her hand at Greg who was on another phone line. Their desks were shoved together head to head. They sat facing each other. Potzer was a young, sharp kid. His cherubic face made him the typical Dutch Boy. His brown hair was six inches in length. It was trimmed around the hairline on the sides and the back of his neck. Today, he wore his standard office outfit. Blue blazer. White shirt. Red and navy diagonal striped tie with a narrow stripe of gold between the two colors. He wore a brown belt with his khaki pants. Greg was a mature, clean cut individual *and very savvy.*

Liz was five and a half feet tall with short black hair. She had not changed her hair style since she completed her tour in the Air Force. She was very competent. She wore little make up and held a decent appearance coupled with a wholesome personality. Liz preferred black business outfits with white blouse during work hours. Once in a while she wore a black velour blazer. She whispered to Greg. "You're gonna want to talk with this one!" Greg patiently held up his index finger. "Jeff, you called the right place. I understand the process, but Greg is excellent in the explanation and communication department. He is just finishing up another call. Would you wait a half minute for him, please?"

"Sure." Jeff and Angie stared at the answering machine. Their eyes were wide open. A twinge of exhilaration hit the air. They both felt an excitement rise within, just like six year olds opening a birthday present. Jeff's pulse quickened. He wrote down the names, the location and phone number in his new *green for money* spiral notebook. Jeff planned to tape a $100 Ben Franklin to the cover. Right now, he was ready to record the truth. A drop of drool escaped the corner of his mouth. A desk speaker phone was turned on. A male voice echoed down the tube.

"Potzer! May I help you?"

"Greg, my name is Jeff Thompson. Some people call me JT. I think the market is going to tank. Maybe not this year, but possibly 2015 or sometime in 2016. I want to learn how to short stocks and make a profit as the stock market drops. I want to learn how to play the downside, but I don't know how. I printed out these explanations from the internet, but to tell you the truth, it is like Spanish to me. These articles say I have unlimited liability and that I have to borrow stock from the brokerage house and that they charge me interest. Does the interest apply to all of my worldly possessions?" Greg and Liz laughed.

"Good for you, Jeff. Liz seems to think you got in on the ground floor. Was that beginner's luck or do you have a thorough knowledge and understanding on the low points in market cycles?"

"I read *The crash of 79* and *The Crash of 89* by Paul Erdman. And I have a book called *The Dead Cat Bounce.*

A smile appeared on Greg's face. His brown eyes brightened. "Excellent! I know Erdman. I have read all of his books. *The Dead Cat Bounce* I am not familiar with. Liz, order The Dead Cat Bounce today so we can get a handle on what Jeff has read.

"Do you have a cash account and know how to use it?"

"Yes, with an online wholesale house."

"Okay then. You mentioned unlimited liability, Jeff. These words are used by the brokerage house and the sales reps to ensure that client (who wants to borrow money in a margin account) thoroughly understands what will happen to the account, *if the new client's stock selections lose money.* An unbelievable amount of time is spent trying to define and explain this scenario to new investors." Greg picked up the account folder he was working with and handed it to Liz. "So we are not going to do that. Tell me, Jeff. Are you ready to take some notes?"

Liz jumped in with a brief explanation. "Jeff, there are fancy words used in the margin accounts and in the short sale transactions. They are a combination of banking, accounting, legal terms and broker house terms. It is all contractual and binding. So pay attention."

"Okay. Ready to copy, Greg."

"Good. Give me a minute to try to explain a few things and then we will answer your question about selling short. If you need time for your notes, just say *'give me a second or two'* and I will wait. Let's do this initial round quickly."

"Alright."

"First I am going to give you a quick explanation of how a margin account is used to buy stocks so you can become a millionaire. I will emphasize the key dangers associated with a margin account. Then after that, you and I will talk about selling short. Greg glanced at his watch and loosened his tie.

"First of all, there are some simple chores you have to do. You might be able to do this over the phone or on the company web site. If you have to go to the brokerage house and open a margin account, take two or three ID's. Driver license, social security card and maybe a credit or debit card. Take your check book. Most houses require at least $500.00 deposit or more to open the margin account initially.

"The brokerage house will lend you money to buy securities based on the present market value of stocks in your account. The house will loan you up to 50% of the total value of the securities and cash that you have in your account. They charge you interest on the loan. Sounds like a great way to expand the small amount of money you have in the stock market so you can make a big killing and retire. Right? So, you borrow as much as you can and you buy more of the beautiful stock that is going to make you a million dollars. Am I right?"

Not forgetting his wife, Jeff answered. "Angie and I need a million apiece." Chuckles could be heard.

"Okay, fine. Now let's say the market drops significantly and your total account value is down 35%. Your balance is now 65% of what it was when you borrowed the money and entered the margin account. This is not good. You will get a margin call. *Whenever the balance drops below 30%, the brokerage house will contact you by text, email, regular mail and you will get a phone call. You will be ordered to pay up **right now** and you will be told that your account is in arrears.*"

Greg continued. "A margin account is a big legal deal, Jeff. It is a legal contract between you and the brokerage house. This margin agreement spells out very specifically what the brokerage house is going to do to you and to the stocks and bonds and any other securities in your account, *if* the account balance drops or declines in value by more than 30%."

"You will have five business days to bring in cash or securities to cover the loss and bring your account back to good standing. According to the agreement you made, if you fail to do this, then the margin agreement is broken **in favor of the house**. *The house will sell securities in your account* until they recoup the amount of money that you borrowed in the original margin agreement. At that point you will be back in a cash account. *The amount of your portfolio value will now be something like* **37% or 40%** *of what it was when you started your margin account.*"

Liz jumped in. "This is a real shock to all of the new investors who are trying to get ahead too fast."

"Let me explain it this way. I will use small numbers to make the math easy to explain. You have $700.00. The house will let you margin a full 50%. So, say you borrow $300. You now have $1000. The share price falls 35%. The house wants all, I say again, **all of the money they loaned** to you because they just lost their $300. Let me tell you what is going to happen. If you have not restored the loss by the end of the fifth business day, they are going to sell at least $300 worth of what you have left and collect the amount of the interest you owe on the loan. Well, you only have $700 left in total stock value after the drop in the share price. **The $300 loss is yours**. After the house takes their $300 out plus interest. The shares you have left will have less than $350 in value. You started with $700, borrowed $300.00. And now, after the ink is dry, you have less than $350."

Liz jumped in again. "This is what is known as a margin call. It is instantaneous. There is no stalling. No recourse. You are bound by contract. There is no grace period and no mercy. The house wins."

Angie exclaimed, "Wow!"

Greg interrupted. "Now. This money that you pay back is not credited to your account. The money is used to pay off the amount of the loan that you margined. It belongs to the house. The margin agreement can only be an ongoing game *only if you immediately replace the amount of money that is lost* from your transaction. Otherwise the account is closed and you have to start all over. This is why experienced investors do not borrow more than 10% of their portfolio value."

Liz jumped again. "The bet and the market *went away from you, Jeff.* The share price went down, not up as you had planned. It went *the other direction.* Your trade was a looser, Jeff." There was more laughter. "You are in a contract and you are responsible to repay your debt."

Greg continued. "Now. I hope I can scare you to death with this scenario. After a couple of months, you see your stock drop to a 23 % loss. No big deal. You decide to hang on. Thirty days later the market gets hammered and your account balance drops to a 50% loss. What do you think will happen?"

"I sense that you are trying to drive home an important point that I won't forget. It is hard for me to say this, but I guess that the account will be closed out and there will be nothing left in it."

Liz inquired, "Is that your final answer Jeff?" Everyone laughed. "This is the big item in the contract that usually wipes out the new risk taker's hard earned money. And it happens when you are in *a market that is already overpriced and overvalued like the one we are dealing with today.* The DIJA Index is at a historical high. It would seem logical that new investors would jump in with their money so they could retire in ten years. This is why the new investors are hungry for this get rich quick scheme to work. The problem is they never have any extra cash to pay for the loss. So, in short order they are under 40% of what they started with or even less. Basically, their new venture into stocks has been a disaster."

Greg made a point. "Jeff and Angie, successful investors will use the margin account only when they have a pick that is moving up. The margin accounts are only used for a well timed move and the time frame is a short period of time. Usually no more than six months. After the move the margin position and account is closed."

Liz added, "Most new investors think the market will hold and continue to move up. They have no idea that *stocks move up and down.* They believe that the market is healthy and that 30% is plenty of room for a small drop."

"Give me a minute." Jeff scribbled notes furiously. "Okay. I'm ready."

Greg summed things up. "Jeff, I am a believer that every investor should go through a full market cycle and witness the mass confusion at the top of the cycle. I really believe that new investors **should not** have a margin account."

Liz jumped in. "He sugar coats everything Jeff. New investors have no business in a margin account. Period. You got that?"

Angie repeated once again. "It sounds like a set up to me."

Greg continued. "Let me say this to both of you. It seems at first glance that it is a fifty-fifty proposition, a fifty-fifty chance to make your money multiply faster. But in reality, it is not. Especially if you acted on a bad rumor."

"Okay, Jeff. Let's get to your question. I am going to explain the foolproof way to you first. This method involves very little risk. In my opinion this is the best way to short. But you have to be cash rich. You have to have back up cash on hand. Now. Your short sale will be subject to the same rules and the 30% loss margin call. If you make a short sale and the stock goes up 35%, then you get a margin call because you lost over 30% again."

Liz emphasized. "This method will work for you so pay attention. Here is the answer to your question, Jeff."

"This is an easy way to play the downside of a stock price when you are waiting for the drop in the stock market and timing is not critical. There is very little risk."

"Okay, Greg. Give me just a second. I have to go to the bathroom." There was a burst of laughter. Liz told Angie. "Angie. You don't know it honey! Your man is golden!"

Greg took a long breath. "Good one, Jeff. You win the prize. Now listen up. This is the way to short a stock. It is easy. Once you understand the mechanics behind the two trades. It does require two trades."

"First of all there is some trading terminology you will have to memorize. Here is the first transaction. You buy 100 shares of stock X or perhaps stock x is already in your cash account. You paid for all of it with your own money. That is the first trade. Don't buy it on margin or in a margin account. You buy it in your cash account. Do not let the house loan you any money to buy the stock or loan the stock to you. That way you are '*free and clear*' of any financial responsibility to the house. You don't owe the house a dime. You are '**covered**'. You paid for it yourself. You have 'no liability' and there is **no 'unlimited liability'.** You have not borrowed a dime. You are now what is referred to in broker talk as '*a buyer of stock*', '*a holder of stock*' and you are '*long*' on the stock. You are 'covered'. It all means the same thing. The shares are wholly owned by you, 100%. You paid for it and you are '**Buyer.' 'Holder.' 'Long.' You** are 'Covered.' All four words are similar in meaning. You paid for stock X one hundred per cent.".

Jeff scribbled some more. "Okay. Got it."

"Good. Now, here is the meaning of the word short. Short means that you do not have the stock. So, *you are not covered*, you are **'naked'** and you are *'short' the stock*. You are not 'long' the stock. Short means *you do not own the stock, but you plan to buy it back at a later date*. In reality, we know that you are 'long' and that you are 'covered' because you have 100 shares of X in your cash account. Got that?"

"Okay. Go ahead."

"Now here is the second trade. Here is the short sale transaction. The short sale has to be done in the margin account. All short trade transactions are required to be executed and originate in the margin account. Here is how you complete the transaction. On all sell tickets, there is a box that reads **'short'**. It is very important that you check this box. Check the sell ticket *'short'*. And you want it known that the short sale is 'sold from a long position'. You must not fail to do this. This is broker house trader talk. The trader is the person who actually and physically completes the order for the brokerage house. He is not your sales rep or broker. This is trader talk and it means that the short sale is backed by stock that Jeff owns. Personally, this is why I make the 'long' position purchase of stock X in the cash account and not in the margin account. I don't want any *back office screw ups*. I do not make short sales online. I always do them over the phone."

Liz added, "Let the house and the trader know that you are a *'holder'* and *'covered'* and that you paid for it all yourself. *'Sold from a long position'* means the same thing as *'sell short from a long position'*."

"So you sold stock X 'short' from a long position. Now, stock X falls from $100 to $50. Would that make you happy, Jeff?"

"Well, Greg. Angie and I were hoping for $10 a share."

Liz's voice could be heard above the laughter. "You are greedy man, Jeff!"

"Alright, Jeff. Let's say stock X is $10 a share and that you have just returned from the bathroom. Now you need to know how to cash out and get your winnings tucked away into your cash account. Right?"

Angie stared at Jeff as he nodded. "Don't worry, Greg. I'll make sure that he does."..

"One way to cover your short position is to buy the same number of shares of stock that you sold short. This would be buy order for 100 shares X stock for the startling new low price of $1,000 instead of $10,000 when the stock was $100 a share. The important point here is that now you have 2000 shares of X at a cost of $11,000 a share and you made $9000 on the short sale. This will close out your short sale position."

"Your gain with the short sale will go to the margin account. You must call the brokerage house on this to make certain that the gains from the short sale are in your account. Take nothing for granted. The price difference of $9,000 will be credited to your margin account."

"Established investors who have sizable accounts use this method. Here is the reasoning. They want more shares of their favorite stock at a lower price. They realize the market will sell off soon and after the crash they cover their short sale from a long position with cash. They pick up more of their favorite stock at a lower price. And they make money on the short sale too. In your margin account you are credited with the profit you made on the short sale. Be sure to transfer your new money to your cash account."

"After the stock has dropped and you want to cash out, tell the broker or the sales rep, that you want to cover your short position. He may look at your account and not know what to do. You might have to wander around the sales reps until you find a knowledgeable one. If you can't then you have to ask for the house trading department and ask for the trader or a trader's assistant. Now if you do not wish to buy the stock, you simply tell the broker that you want to 'flatten the box'. Technically, you have created a box around the bid and the ask in your account. You use the 100 shares from the cash account to cover the short sale. The only difference is that you do not have 100 shares of x stock, but you do have the profit of $9000 for selling short from a long position."

"Are you ready for the second way to sell short?" Jeff was ready to copy. "The second way is to go with the margin account and borrow stock from the brokerage account. You better be certain stock X is ready to drop because *this is the point where you are open to* **unlimited liability** if the share price jumps up to the moon. If the bet goes against you, then *you are **responsible for that total amount of the price move***, as well as the amount of money that was loaned to you. You have to pay back the loan, **the amount of loss generated by the share price** (the increase in the share price over 30%) and the interest."

Liz laughed. "Angie, if Jeff's pockets are empty, it will be awhile before you get another credit card."

"Now, there is one more problem area to talk about. A couple of things can happen that you may not be aware of. Say you have a short position. The stock drops from $30 down to $7. If the company X is in dire financial straits and cannot make monthly payments on short term debt, production materials or expense payments they may be in real trouble. The NYSE can determine that the company is insolvent. Then the Exchange, by itself, can halt or suspend the trading of company stock X. The Securities and Exchange Commission can suspend company X too."

"If you have a suspension, you will be stuck with the short position. You will not be able to get the shares to cover the short. **And**, it is too late to sell or make any transactions at this point."

Liz explained. "So, you have to be careful around that $5 and $10 area. You have to be certain that the company is going to stay in business and not go bankrupt. Remember, it will be difficult to trust official statements. Officers and directors will lie for money. Another outcome would be that a competitor might buy up the company, but that would be a long shot and possibly a rumor."

Liz spoke to Angie. "In any case, Angie, it is best to stay on the safe side here. Keep an eye on Jeff and don't wait for the bottom dollar. Surprisingly, some companies may issue a notice to the financial community that it is going to go through bankruptcy court. The court will divide up whatever is left and pay off all of the creditors which will amount to so many pennies on the dollar."

"Jeff responded. "So close out the position under $10 but above $5 and get my cash?"

Liz continued her thoughts. "Absolutely! On over the counter stocks all shorts must be covered before they go under five dollars a share. If company X goes under $5, you will have to forfeit your position without reimbursement. Chances are there won't be many shares trading once the share price drops under $10.00 anyway. OTC and the Pink Sheets are pretty much boom or bust. There is an OTC Exchange rule that all short transactions must be covered above $5."

"Now. A little semantics lesson. Do not confuse these words. *Selloff, collapse, crash, tank, disaster, drop, and drastic*. These words have been misused by the media. Please note that the words have no quantitative measurement. They are meaningless."

"Say no more. We get it."

"What do you think, Jeff? Are you going to sell short from a long position."

"You know, I understand what you have told me, Greg. I believe I can win this way."

"You can and you will Jeff. Liz and I are working up some ideas right now. We are trying to choose the overpriced DJIA and S and P companies that are actively traded. They can fall in value and still be in business after the crash."

"Do you play options or index or currency futures."

"Good question. Options, index futures, and spyders are the big gambling play. There is very little money at risk and the rewards can be large comparatively speaking. But you have to get in and out within the time limit. They are called wasting assets because the rules impose a time limit on these trades. Three months, six months, what have you. Otherwise orders would be piled high beyond the ceiling. They are a different vehicle and you should only play with a very small amount of money until you find out how the market seems to deny your bet. Very often, after the options have expired, your bet will materialize. But time wise it is too late to win. It is almost as if they steal your winner away from you. I have had that happen several times. A week after the expiration dates the price would finally move in the direction I was betting."

Angie expressed her gratitude. "You two are a breath of fresh air. Some of the phone calls we made today were discouraging. We would get an answer, but not to the question that we asked."

"Angie, how are you handling all of your husband's babbling?"

"Angie jumped in. "I was dead set against Jeff's gambling in the stock market. He is a moron and you should see the putrid color of the kitchen that I have to sweat and slave in." Laughter rose from Greg and Liz. "And this old beater of a car that my neighbors and friends see me drive. I'm so ashamed! I am so embarrassed! It is rust! There is no shiny chrome on it."

Jeff agreed. "I told her that I prefer the cheap older auto auction models."

"Stop right there! Angie, let me tell you something. After you are a millionaire, you keep driving that old clunker. If all the scammers and the gang bangers see you driving new wheels, they will be after you to extort you and steal every penny you have. Angie, are you reading any books or do you still watch those stupid 'Survivor' reruns?"

"I knew nothing about the markets. All of my friends are those negative kind of people, who just mouth off empty, negative opinions of great earth shaking magnitudes that they hear from the local friends or what they hear on TV and radio. Riff Raff. *Actually,* our new neighbor gave me a book, *The Ultimate Safe Money Guide,* by Weiss and I hate that Survivor TV show."

Greg. "Good for you Angie. Reading Weiss is just like talking to the expert. Get the facts. Digest them. Ingrain them into your psyche. Stay with it. You two need to solidify and become a team for your future instead expressing those old selfish needs and the attitudes of 'What can I get from this marriage.' When old age finally arrives, 75% of Americans have nothing for retirement."

Angie asked, "Liz. Are you a broker?"

"Yes, I am. Greg and I have been a team for just over five years now. We both have clients." Greg cut in. "Liz and I are a good twosome, Angie. Liz is a trust fund baby and I was fortunate to be her broker. That's how we met."

"Angie, I made Greg marry me to keep him from running around in the afternoon. He and his male friends were drinking after the market closed and chasing women who wore miniskirts." Angie answered with a question. "Are you talking about those cheap contests that men have to see who could get the first date that afternoon?" More laughter.

Greg advised, "Jeff, just a little bit of money on your first trades. You know the steps now. Be very particular. Don't throw yourself in. Just get a couple of small successful trades. *That is **the most** important step.*

After some practice and some wins, then you can throw yourself into the rallies in a little stronger commitment." Greg glanced at the time. "We have to be going now. Stop by and see us if you get to town. Liz will make you buy us lunch."

"That's right, Jeff. No freebies from us. We have a microwave for gourmet dining. Call us back in a week or two and let us know what you did."

"Okay. Thank you." The phones disconnected. Jeff and Angie stared at one another. "Wow! Do you believe what just happened?"

Jeff reviewed his notes in his spiral notebook on how to short. He clarified some points while everything was fresh in his mind. He would rewrite the notes later. He had four full pages front and back. Just to be reassured, he asked Angie, "Do you want to listen to the tape to see if we got it all."

Angie made her way to the kitchen. "Yes, baby. I do. I am going to get us both a wine spritzer first."

"This will be an appropriate celebration."

Angie turned back to the living room. "Yes it will because afterwards I plan to jump your bones." It was all on the phone recorder. Everything except the wrestling match.

WALL STREET DIGEST

One bright sunny weekend in November, Angie put three years of the Wall Street Digest newsletters and a pitcher of iced tea on her table. She and Jeff were determined to use their spare time after work and on weekends to skim the newsletter together. They sat side by side and their conversations went something like this.

"Angie. Let's take one month at a time and skim the newsletters for all three years. It will not be in order by the year, but we just need to catch on to new information and the tone that Rowe sets for us. And remember, this is the time of the internet mania leading up to the crash in 2000. Okay, Angie. Here we go. There is only one January newsletter, January 1998. The title is *Asian flu infects US markets*. Here are the high points of the letter."

Money continues to poor into the United States from Asia and Europe. 80 billion per quarter in 1997. This year the total estimates are 110 billion. The Federal Funds (that is the Federal Funds Rate) was 5 and 9/16% before the Asian mess. Now it is 5 and 7/16%.

"Why, is the money coming in?"

Jeff guessed. "The answer is in here somewhere. I do not know, but 110 billion is 110,000, millions."

Liquid Assets in the United States are now over 4 trillion. 9 trillion dollars is invested in the stock market.

The equity market for stocks is now larger than the total Gross Domestic Product of the USA which is 7.7 trillion. Angie's eyes widened. "I just can't imagine that, Jeff."

Pension fund money continues to flow into the stock market. April and July are the big months and this is the main reason that the market is up in those months. "This is all new stuff to me, Angie. Here is a blurb on Japan."

When Japan has more bank failures, they will be forced to liquefy their economy. Angie looked at Jeff. "What does that mean, Jeff?"

"It means that the government will have to print money and get it to the banks so the banks can get the money into circulation to everyone. Banks have to make loans to businesses and the citizens so everyone can stay alive. The banks need extra cash in case there is a run on the bank if customers panic and decide to withdraw their accounts." Jeff furrowed his brow. "I'm not real sure what else. This is a guess on my part. In the USA, the Federal Reserve authorizes such action and the Treasury Department prints up the bills. Rowe says that Japan's leaders do not understand what caused their financial mess and he points out that they do not like advice from the USA. Japan learned how to whip inflation back in the late 80's. But Asia is not handling deflation very well. Here comes a blurb on China."

China was negative in 3rd quarter growth during 1997. There is a real estate meltdown crisis. Buildings are empty and there is a 20% across the board drop in prices. A financial quake in China will adversely affect Hong Kong and all of Asia.

The Consumer Price Index will fall below 1.5 % during 1998. The 30 year Treasury Bond yield will fall to 5% and the Fed will have to cut interest rates to avoid a recession. A recession will explode the USA Federal Government's deficit and will cause inflation.

"How does lowering the interest rate avoid a recession? And how do you explode a deficit?"

"Well, sweet one. You can post phone a recession by lowering interest rates so consumers can borrow money to pay bills, buy more goods and services and stay alive. This is the same for companies. The nation will hopefully wade through the mess." Jeff skimmed ahead. "Here is your explosion answer, Angie."

A recession reduces Federal income tax revenues. The Federal government has to print money for increased government programs, like rising unemployment. Leading economists in Europe and the USA say that the USA Government is still fighting inflation.

"Rowe disagrees. He says the problem is actually deflation. He points out that," *Economic weakness in Asia will have **a sustained adverse effect on oil and energy services sector of the economy and the technology sector as well**. He says 1998 will be a base building year for the stock market. **Any low risk profits will be harder to capture**.* "He says," *when* interest rates come down, then the stock market will be flooded with money and begin to advance. "Hold your questions for a while, Angie." Jeff continued. "He says," *the DJIA Index is still strong and there are no divergences in the NASD OR THE DJIA trends.* "Rowe says," **the Dow Jones Utility index is forecasting lower interest rates and it is always correct.**

There is 600 billion of new cash in the mutual funds which has added 70% to their total assets. The dominant reason investors are seeking stocks is due to the fact that corporate profit growth has been very favorable over the last three years compared to the last 50 years. Earnings growth has accelerated due to the all of the high tech labor saving devices. "This would reduce the number of employees and payroll expense, Angie. That is a big expense."

"Here is a blurb on government spending." *Government still borrows 100 billion a year from the Social Security account to fund (pay for) the Medicare for children account. This action adds 1 trillion dollars to the deficit every ten years.* "Rowe predicts," *The minimum federal deficit will be 300 billion by 2003. And if there is a recession, then the figure will double. If that happens the Fed will print super money to flood the banks for loans to consumers and businesses.*

"What is the Federal Deficit now, Jeff? A trillion something. Isn't it?" Jeff shook his head. "I'm not sure." Angie checked the internet. "Holy moly! It is right up there at 19 trillion."

"Rowe points out that," ***Europe prints money to pay for government worker pensions and that is slightly inflationary. France is cutting the work week to 35 hours per week with the same amount of pay as before. The truckers in France blocked the highways in protest for a 6 % pay raise and that will eventually spread to all industries.*** "And listen to this." ***Europe will high price itself out of the world goods market and will build huge walls to fend off the cheap Asian products.***

Rowe says," *The DOW averages are flashing a buy signal.* "The last eight pages are summations of ideas and advice from various guru's, mutual fund performances, and rankings of the top funds along with the Wall Street Digest's stock recommendations. There are 16 pages in all."

"Whew! Is that all?"

"That's enough for one month. Ready for **February**? Here we go. There is only one and it is **1998**." *USA GDP in 1997 was up* **4.9** *% in the 1ˢᵗ quarter and about* **3** *% for fiscal quarters 2, 3 and 4. Manufacturing accounts for less than half of the total GDP now and the service sector is the biggest sector and it is still growing.* "He expects a rough volatile first quarter in the stock market and an advance for the rest of the year." *The stocks in the technology sector will have to form a base before they advance and that will not happen until the Asia markets bottom out. Then the USA tech market will base build and advance.*

"JT, is he talking about an Asian stock market crash or what?"

"Not their stock market. The Asian companies have huge inventory of goods and they don't know where to sell them."

"Rowe says interest rates will drop in the USA. He says" *Fed policy is to pump money into the economy to keep it liquid. Back in 1997, manufacturing prices were falling and the service sector was rising. Plus there is plenty of cheap energy around. There is a leaner more efficient USA in this tech boom. Computer chip power is doubling every 18 months. The world is moving from a wired world to a wireless world through the expansion of global satellite systems. The first revolution was the print media, newspapers and magazines. Then Radio and TV. Then the computer revolution and now the internet revolution. Soon there will be face to face telephone calls on the internet.* "Rowe points out that ordinary people always underestimate the power of expanding industries, especially if new products are involved."

"He lists a page of advisors. Half of them are bullish and half are bearish. Go figure. Bulls are predicting DOW 8700 and the Bears predict DOW 6000. He spends two pages comparing 1998 to 1994. They had different situations and events but both years struggled to move forward as far as the stock market was concerned. He talks about the 30 year bond yield and the fact that crisis spells opportunity. There are 15 pages. The last two are recommended mutual funds and stocks."

Asian deflation has delayed the next move up in the tech boom and the bull market.

There are two kinds of deflation. Economic, which is economic decline the other is falling prices and falling wages. Rising unemployment is caused by the lack of USA company money to pay company bills and conduct business.

Angie shifted to catch Jeff's eye. "Is that a fancy way to say that sales are down so there will be job layoffs or what?"

"Here is March, 1998. Remember things have changed from 1997 and we are heading into the Dot Com Boom."

"Ready, Jeff. Educate us."

"The title is," *Company profit margins are shrinking while a record liquidity forces stock prices higher.* "Rowe says," *Wall Street is not worried about deflation in Asia or a potential air strike on Iraq.* **The Dow market cap has swelled to 3 trillion.** "That does not include the NASDAQ market cap. And remember, baby, the marching band never stops. The drum never stops beating. This is really a good example."

"Which is he talking about? The DJIA Index or all of the 2600 companies on the NYSE?" Jeff answered, "The Dow usually means the DJIA Index." Angie commented, "It sounds like he repeats some important things in every newsletter." Jeff answered, "I will try to skip the repeated information."

The USA has 65 computers to every 100 workers. Japan has 17 computers to every 100 workers. 90 billion enters the USA this quarter from foreign markets. Asia must export her way out of disaster.

Jeff looked at Angie. "They have over produced and to avoid recession they have to get their lower priced products into other countries for sale. So USA exports to Asia will decrease by 13% this year, but it is not really a big deal for USA companies. It amounts to about 5% of total profit on their income statements."

"This is interesting. Besides the usual stock and mutual fund recommendations, he has a chart that shows the path of the baby boomers. He says their spending power should peak about the year 2008. He calls it a broad view of spending, earnings, savings, and stock momentum."

Bull stock markets can't continue without economic growth and rising earnings. The stock market's function is to value the future earnings of stock. Corporate profits have averaged 19% over the last three years and now they are beginning to shrink.

"Remember, corporate profits roared ahead with all of the high tech efficiency such as new software programs, labor saving devices such as robots and computers. The end result was that fewer employees were needed to do the work and the payroll expense decreased dramatically."

Exports are 12 % of USA GDP. 1/3 of that goes to Asia and that computes to about 5% of GDP.

"Now the deal is, Asia will only pay lower prices due to their currency deflation. I think he is talking about the currency exchange transaction and that the Asian dollars are less than before or they just will not pay as much as they used to pay for the USA goods. The Asian goods don't cost as much."

"Anyway, Rowe maintains that this is one of the reasons that profit margins are shrinking in American corporations. He sees total profits shrinking eventually to the usual 5% profit level in a few years."

US corporate earnings growth has dropped from 21% to 14%.

Investors in Asian Stocks have turned those paper profits into cash. The 10 year Japanese bond yield remains below 2%. Japan government bond yields are below 2%. The USA 30 year bond is 5.6.

Angie was on this one. "Maybe the Asians are investing in the USA T Bills and that is why 80 billion was coming in each quarter."

Jeff reached over and held Angie's hand. "I owe you a kiss, Princess. I bet you are right. We are still in **March 1998**. Asia has bottomed out and Rowe is wondering if and when the Chinese will devalue the Yuan. The last devaluation was 1994."

"He mentions USA housing problem. There is a shortage of homes as well as office space, so higher real estate prices are on the move here in the USA."

Inventory of unsold homes is at a 26 year all time low. New home sales are at 11% so there is not enough available housing to go around. You have the makings of the most explosive housing prosperity since the late 70's.

Angie laughed. "I guess that is a little bit different than 9 million people walking away from their homes like the 2008 foreclosure fiasco." Jeff laughed. "You are doggone right, Angie."

Most USA citizens are out of stocks and into bonds. "Angie, I bet Rowe is in cash right now."

China, the world's second largest economy is experiencing deflation. If they devalue the Yuan, then South East Asia will slip into recession again. **Cheap imports force US companies to lower prices in the USA. Computers, software and electronics are the best sectors to be in.** *Corporate earnings growth was due to* **increased profit margins due to high technology efficiencies brought into the working environment. Fewer workers required to get the job done.** *Revenue growth remains at a subdued 4%. In 15 months companies will move from cost cutting to plans of expansion. Rising costs are on the way.* Jeff looked at Angie, "The cost cutting was due to all of the new telecommunications devices, the computer software programs and the ability to use scanners and bar codes among other things. Individual employee productivity increased with all of the labor and time saving technology."

"He hints at the Y2K dilemma." **Banks, financial companies, logistical suppliers making deliveries throughout the world, fear that older computers still in operation will interpret the computer day, time, and year figure of 00 as 1900 instead of 2000 when the year moves from 1999 to 2000.**

"Okay, here we are in **March 1999** now. Keep in mind we are getting close to the year 2000 market crash." **PE ratios** *have soared to a record level 31 for the S+P 500 Index. It has never been much higher than 20 except for the 22 area in 1929.* "Here is more info on the **semiannual pension fund payments**. They are in **April and July**. They buoy the market temporarily with cash in retirement accounts which goes into securities purchases. After July, he expects the stock market to decline, but doesn't say how much. He states September and October are typically slow months and that beginning in November things begin to pick up all the way through to April. He says that the stock market is overvalued and suggests that there could possibly be a mini crash this year in late summer or fall."

PRICE EARNINGS RATIO   S&P 500 INDEX

Chart Courtesy of Hussman Econometrics

"Rowe says," *You can pick any number of reasons to* **blame the next downturn** *on. It may depend on how events play out in China, with the possible devaluation of its Yuan or in Iran in the middle east or* **whichever surprise that Wall Street wants to use to drop prices.**

"How about that! Angie, did you pick up on that?

"Yes. It sounds like the Street and the media will use any old reason or excuse that they want to use for a market crash."

"He emphasizes," *If the market manages to squeak through the end of this year intact, then there will be a severe market crash in 2000."*

China is bankrupt with 15% unemployment. At the close or 1998, it is estimated that 248 million computers are in use in the USA in homes, businesses, schools and government.

Jeff turned the pages and skimmed. "Here is one just for you, Angie." *The computer industry predicts that 100 million computers were sold in 1998 to avoid the Y2K problem and satisfy the rush of users to the worldwide web with the new models.*

"Good grief! In just the USA? 100 million! I guess it is because there are 65 computers to every 100 workers in the USA. But there will be plenty of sales around the world too, won't there?"

Italy, France and Germany are slipping into deflation and recession. Commodity prices are falling to recession levels including oil, gold and silver.

"He points out, *The tech industry is deflationary as overproduction, especially in Asia, leads to layoffs and unemployment.*"

Angie questioned, "Now that would be economic goods deflation, right?"

"There is more. This is a big newsletter. A chart shows the DOW on a log scale at 18000 by the year 2010."

Angie questioned, "Is that for real?" Jeff replied, "No. It is a sterile, rosy outlook and projection. There are no variables allowed. All other things in the universe must remain as is. It does not take into consideration unforeseen events. Anything could happen."

From 1992 to today (March1999) USA companies' share of global market profit has grown from 25% to 38%. "Look at the 50 year wall chart, Jeff. That explains the 10 year expansion in the 90's."

"That could have been expansion of our Gen X generation goods and services too. Here is the next Dot Com pitch." *The USA is leading the world in telecommunications, the internet through phone wires, satellite, cable and computer and cell phone sales worldwide.*

"Think about this next statement, Angie. Kick this one around." *Kiplinger's Letter published an article outlining 15 leading internet stocks. AOL is the largest with a **41 billion** dollar market capitalization on its number of shares and stock price.* That is stock price times the number of outstanding shares of AOL common stock." *Yet, all **15** internet companies together had only 4 billion dollars in sales and revenues. The market cap for all fifteen stock prices was 100 billion dollars.*"

"Now if you divide that 100 billion by the 4 billion then you get a valuation that is 25 times over the actual valuation." Angie began to write. "Just a minute, Jeff. I need to make a note on market caps so I can study them later."

"Think about this one Angie. *Does short term trading exist in a big way?* Listen to this!"

On any given day 1/3 of Amazon's outstanding common shares change hands.
"Jeff, it sounds like the total amount of Amazons outstanding shares was traded every week." Jeff nodded his head. "That is correct, Angie. There is more."

"This is amazing!" *Amazon (issued to public in May, 1997) went from $9 to $138 in twelve months (15 times return on investment). Market capitalization was $22 billion for Amazon and sales were $12 billion.* Here is more of the same. ***Books A Million,*** *an online book and greeting card retailer, jumped 196% in one day. Two days later, it tripled in value after the company announced significant improvements to their sales channel on their web site.* "The market was on fire then."

EBay has ***four million shares outstanding*** *to the public for trading.* ***Yet 10 million shares trade every day.***
"This would be the short term investor buying and selling in the same day. How about that, Angie? I guess it is safe to say that most of the daily trading volume is due to the short term investor day trading." Angie added, "And it would be safe to say that it still takes place today, say in something like Three D Systems."

Oil in emerging nations accounts for almost 50% of world usage. In ***industrialized countries*** *it is growing at less than 1% per year and* ***could turn negative.*** *Oil revenues* ***in Russia, Brazil and Mexico have been cut in half*** *since oil dropped from* ***$28 a barrel to $12.***

Jeff set the newsletters down. "Let's take a break." They both got up to stretch and fix sandwiches and they were soon back together with a new pitcher of ice tea on the table. Angie picked up the next newsletter. "It is my turn to read to you, Jeff. This information is confusing to me, so don't get upset."

"Just like school work, sweet one. If you read it enough times and think about it, you might become a highly paid think tank associate."

"I should have kept my mouth shut. Here is **April**. I'm going to skip 1997. Not much is there. **1998** has some hot stuff. The title of this newsletter is," ***Record liquidity pushes market valuations higher.***

An average of 1.2 billion shares are trading every day. This is ***more shares than the number of shares that traded in an entire year*** *until*

1990. 1990 was the first year to trade more than 1.2billion shares. "Think about that, Jeff! **One day of trading in 1998** *is worth **a whole year*** *of trading any year before 1990.*"

*1.2 billion shares trade every day. After the 1987 crash only **140,000 shares** were traded every day.*

"Hey, Jeff. What is liquidity?"

"Cash. Hordes of cash, Angie. It is the total amount of cash available to the public and corporations that is in their savings, cash and checking accounts. I think this is referred to as M2"

Unemployment is at a 25 year low. "Three million unemployed in USA."

China will begin deflation in the 2nd quarter this year. Product prices are below a year ago in China. USA corporation profit margins are below a year ago in China. USA company profit margins are squeezed by Asian companies lower prices and that is reducing USA goods sold overseas. PE ratio of the S&P 500 Index is 25.

"Jeff, remember. This is 1998 again. We just read a little while ago in **March, 1999** the ratio was 31 just a year before the crash in 2000. "*The price dividend (PD) ratio or what price would be if the dividend was $1 per share is calculated to be $64.* So much for that. Now here is more of April 98."

There is a record horde of cash. Ten of the top 15 cash rich companies pay no dividend. More companies claim to be buying their own stock. Mergers and acquisitions are on the rise. USA was a manufacturing nation in the 60's and 70's. Now USA is a technology and information based service economy. The bear market in Japan did not materialize, but the worst is not over for Asia. Economic crisis areas exist in Brazil, Japan, Pakistan, Russia, South Africa and Turkey. The European Monetary Union is optimistic for their markets this year. We are in the eighth year of an economic bull market without more than a 10% correction (in stock market prices). Japanese investors borrow money in Japan at the 1% interest rate and then they move money to the USA to buy stocks and bonds. The USA 90 day T bill is paying 5% while Japan's 90 day T bill is just one half of 1%.

The NASD is stronger than the DOW. "Rowe claims that Wall Street is declaring that big NYSE and NASD companies are overpriced and that it is time to consider buying stocks in midsized companies." Angie looked at Jeff and he replied, "Those are companies that only have 200 million to 300 million shares out to the public."

NASD has room to move higher. Housing is about 1.5 million new homes a year. In 1991 it was 1 million new homes a year. In the late 80's it was 2 million new homes a year.

"There is a graph here that shows the amount of declining shares and the amount of advancing shares." **Since 1965** *the* **TRIN** *has exceeded panic selling levels 21 times. There was a selloff in 1997. On that day, October, 27, 1997, the DOW fell 550 points.* **2587 companies declined on 700 million shares. 182 companies advanced on just a pitiful 4 million shares**.

Angie looked at the chart. "Jeff, let me check the internet. There has to be a better chart." Angie searched the net and found the TRIN RATIO. "The real name is the ARMS Index. It is named after Richard Arms. It is a little complicated. Divide the Advance Decline ratio by the Advance Decline **Volume** ratio. It reveals the *short term overbought and over sold conditions*. Readings below 1 show strength in volume and readings above one show weakness in volume. It can be used with arithmetic scale or with log scale. The chart shows that the market has been oversold for three years. Wow! Just think about that JT! Only a pitiful 4 million shares to advance 182 companies! Is that deception in Area D or what?"

"Yes, Angie. The broad market advance in that move was **a huge drop** across the board in share prices. Okay. Let's move on." Angie printed out the article.

By comparison on January 9, 1998, the DOW fell 222 points. 2541 DOW companies declined on 700 million shares. 554 rose on 4 million shares. "Rowe has a word of wisdom here with regard to the statistics. He says," *The market is lagging because people have been worried about a* **bear** *stock market on the horizon. The market will perk up here in 99. People are only watching investments in the market right now, but they are not paying attention to how much money is on the sidelines and going to be coming into the stock market this year.*

"Angie. Richard told me this is a big argument that the street uses. They argue that the recovery will be immediate because there is so much cash around. You remember that Ronnie said the Fed always makes cash available 24/7 during any anticipated financial blowout."

"Let's get over to Whiting's soon and talk about all of this."

The US economy is good for a number of reasons. Mainly due to all of the new jobs the new telecommunications companies, the internet and the computer companies have provided. Local state and federal coffers from retail and income tax collections are overflowing. "He points out that, *deflation may happen in China. Prices are lower there than they were last year. The S+P 500 PE ratio is at 25 and the earnings yield is 4%.*

"Rowe says seven faucets of money will push stock prices higher. Reason number one." *Corporations are sitting on a record horde of cash and although the dividend yield is close to an all time low, the corporations have enough cash to double dividends and still have money for operations.*

"Reason two." *Corporations are using cash for stock buyback programs. This means less shares trade in the public market and that makes the stock more responsive (supposedly). Less shares make the financial statement ratios and the price earnings ratio more attractive to investors (supposedly). They are also using their shares to make mergers and acquisitions which totaled* **one trillion** *dollars in 1997.*

Jeff clarified. "Sometimes the Board of Directors approves a creation of common shares (to be used instead of cash) to buy out another company to help expand business or to buy out a competitor. They call it an acquisition. This is in addition to the current shares trading in the public hands. The shares approved for acquisitions are called '*Shares Approved for an Acquisition*,' but these shares are never issued unless the acquisition is completed. The corporate board and management approve that the shares be printed up and held in reserve. The shares are not released to the public. They are transferred to the company that is bought as part of the payment arrangement. There could be some cash involved too. Corporations have the ability to print shares of common stock rather than use cash if it is agreed by both parties. If stock price has doubled, then it would only take half as many shares to buy a competitor as it would have before the share price doubled. The lower the number of shares trading in public hands the more responsive a stock price can be."

"Jeff. We need to become a corporation and sell stock to the Whiting's!" Angie nodded and continued to read. *The average book* *value of assets per share of common stock, of all the companies that trade on the New York Exchange, is at $5 a share, which is low, but that is attributed to technology and information service economy. Supposedly, those companies do not have the large numbers of heavy assets that the old manufacturers have invested in their plant and equipment.* Angie looked at Jeff for an explanation.

"Book value is plant, property, and equipment."

Reason number 3 is liquidity. **Mutual funds are fully vested and only holding 6% cash.** *Other cash levels are at record highs. 4.1 trillion in liquid assets This is amazing when we are in the 8th year of a bull market with less than a 10% correction for the USA stock market.* **4 trillion in cash sitting on the sidelines waiting for a market correction, waiting for the share prices to fall down to the cellar.**

Reason 4 is interest rates. The lowest in 20 years. 90 billion is flowing into the 90 day T bills. 360 billion annually.

"How does that work?"

"Well, sweet one. The Fed will sell USA Bonds and T Bills to USA citizens and countries it routinely does business with, unless there are sanctions against a country like Iran or Somalia or if there are currency transaction problems." Jeff explained. "Japanese investors borrow money in their country at 1% and then they buy T bills in the USA that pay a higher rate than they can get from government bond investments in Japan. All due to higher USA interest rates and a stable dollar at that particular time. If the Fed raises rates to slow an inflationary economy (always the reason!), then the faucet will open wider, and the dollar will rise against the yen and the German mark."

"Okay. Here we are, still in April, 1998. The Fed reserve has been printing 342 billion annually to finance deficit spending by congress. But congress still borrows from the social security funds to show a lower deficit on their books. That is nothing new. It's been going on for 6 decades. Jeff, does the Congress just borrow money from the Treasury Department and the Federal Reserve? What collateral does the Congress use?"

"It is just a little bit different than you might imagine. The Federal Reserve is our nation's Central Bank. They sell USA bonds, T bills, what have you to raise money for the USA Government (Congress). The IOU notes you may have heard about is what happens when congress takes money out of a budget area and uses that borrowed money for a different purpose. That usually happens in any state or local government when the general fund is out of money."

"So the Federal Reserve is not a USA government department ?"

"Correct. It is a central bank and a separate entity that is in charge of Federal Notes and Interest rates. The Treasury Department is IRS, ATF and the paper currency printing presses."

Reason number 6 is the banking system. Mr. Greenspan (Federal Reserve Committee Chairman) and the banks want you to borrow. And spend.

"Remember, Angie. This is still two years before the crash and before the Fed raised the interest rates five times in the year 1999 and 2000. Hey! What was reason five?"

"I guess four and five were together."

"Get this, Jeff." **Banks mailed out over 2 billion credit card applications just last year and they are preparing another 2 billion for this year.** "That is 4 billion and that is ten or eleven times the number of people over eighteen in the USA."

"Well, a lot of corporations have credit cards for employees. Then there are the USA Territories. And the banks, believe it or not, operate all over the globe in foreign countries and issue credit cards to citizens of other nations." Angie stated, "I wonder if it is the same people updating expired cards?"

"And reason seven. Here it is, Jeff. Think about this one." *The growing nations pension fund assets. In 1980, pension assets were only a paltry $500 billion.* "In 1998, **2.8 trillion** was the total amount invested. Jeff, is this just the local county, city, state and federal government employees or does it include companies and small business in the private sector?"

Jeff added, "Don't forget the armed services." Angie explained, "Well, I said Federal."

*It was 2 .8 trillion, call it **3 trillion** (999 billion dollars plus one more billion is a trillion) **in 1998**. **Five times** more than **1980**.* "And get this," *The total value invested in stocks is 10.2 trillion.* "Rowe says," *There is an* **estimated 25 trillion dollars** *in cash* **worldwide** *looking for a low risk bull market to invest in at the touch of a computer key.* "He says," *The* *world is floating in a sea of paper money without inflation and interest rates are still not rising.* "In April of 1998 he is hinting that a down turn is coming. Maybe as early as 1999."

"Rowe says," *The NASD is stronger than the DJIA as it is* **the primary focus of the institution investing.**

"What or who are the institutional investors? Is that like mentally ill people who invest?"

Jeff smiled at Angie. "Baby. Have I ever told you why I love you?" Angie smiled back. "Yes, you have and you better never stop. It is because I like to mess with you. And sometimes I like to grope you during the day."

"That is pretty much it for April, 1998. He has a chart of M3 and WLAC weekly liquid assets counter."

Jeff decided to read for a while. He picked up **April, 1999.** "I have in my hand April, 1999. JT skimmed it silently for two minutes while Angie played with her hair. "There are only a couple of items here. Most of this newsletter compares the different internet stocks. Here are the most important points."

Greenspan is doing well with interest rates and keeping the world out of recession. So there is continued strong economic growth in the USA. He is threatening to raise rates if the market begins to reach an absurd level. In 1987, after the market crash, the Fed announced to Wall Street that the lending desk would remain open 24 hours a day to prevent a run of cash withdrawal from investor accounts at brokerage houses and banks.

"This is amazing." *The Fed cannot raise US interest rates while asking Japan and Europe to lower theirs. There is plenty of liquidity right now with the flood of pension money. No need to raise rates. **Asia, Russia and Japan are recovering from the worst recession since WW2.**"

"Now Rowe is comparing the market capitalization value for the internet companies only." *13.4 billion market capitalization for the Dow Jones and for the NASDAQ internet companies AOL is 67 billion, and Amazon 22 billion. These two companies alone beat the Dow 30 in total market capitalization. Stock price PE ratios are in the 200, 300 and even 500 range.* "Would you say it was a mania, Angie?"

"Rowe estimates that," **With so much money to be made there are a few (50,000) people making money by day trading** every day. Rowe says, *Wall Street is in the process of devising a way to value the internet stocks. And **no one** agrees on the parameters of the valuations. Many market analysts are saying that the internet is not here to stay.*

Only 148 million people are using the internet now, mostly in the UK, Australia, US, and Canada. Microsoft is heading to China as they hope to tap the big market there. The internet is the greatest investment opportunity since the automobile revolution. It is the newest revolution and it will have profound effects.

Nine countries, Australia, Philippines, Malaysia, Indonesia, South and North Korea, Thailand, China, Singapore, and Japan are suffering from the slowing growth in south east Asia, and it was followed by slower growth in Europe, France, Germany and Italy. "He says," There is weakness in China in the first quarter. When growth slows, prices weaken. Stock prices anticipate events by 6 months.

"Here is another one for you, Angie." *Wall Street just about passed out from the news that AT&T paid 124 **billion** for Media One. It is all about fiber optic cable providing the high speed digital transmission needed for the future high tech internet.* "Fiber optics replaced the copper wire phone line system."

"Angie. Your Mr. Weiss would like this one. Rowe quotes Mr. Bands from *Profitable Investing.*" ***Don't let the brokerage house research analysts bother you when they decide to upgrade or downgrade such and such a stock.*** "He emphasizes that," ***most of these analyst forecasts are almost as accurate as monkeys playing checkers.***

"I need to photocopy that one for Veronica. She will love it!"

"Okay, Angie. Here is **May, 1999**. It is two years after those TRIN sell off statistics for 1997 that you read to me and one year before the Dot Com crash."

Laptops are not a problem but the programing in the older computers may read 000 as 1900 instead of 2000 as the New Year rings in the new millennia.

Y2K Federal computers are antiquated and people are worried about their food stamps, Medicare payments, not to mention the worries for the Federal Aviation Administration and Defense Department. Russia and USA will house a meeting at the North American Radar Defense Operations (NORAD) in the USA Air Force Cheyenne Mountain.

Cable is 20 times faster than AOL with a phone line. AT&T bought Media one. A cable company. Slowing global growth is deflationary.

"Rowe once again states," *The market is mediocre as far as values with the exception of the technology companies, the telecom companies and the internet. The next semi annual pension fund deposits will be in July.*

"He goes on," *The mutual funds and the brokerage houses are trying to steer investors away from internet stocks by touting that the sector activity is switching to the chemical, energy services and the paper and forest products industry because they are undervalued. It might be time to accumulate positions in them instead of pouring any more money into the tech, telecommunications and internet companies.* "He is using the Fidelity Mutual Fund statistics and he has little charts that show active investing upticks in all of these sectors during the 1st quarter."

John Chambers, the President of Cisco Systems says the internet will reshape personal communications and balance the power between all companies in the nation.

"JT, would you comment, please!"

Jeff responded. "I think he is talking about a level playing field here with respect to equal access to markets, materials availability, statistics of the consuming public and also information at all levels of business and society and the instant communications available to everyone."

"Boy! You can really sling the do-do when you feel like it." Angie paused and moved the newsletters they had read to the far end of the table. "Okay. We are almost halfway through this pile. Here is **June 1999**. I am going to skip 1997 and 1998. We have skimmed all of the subjects before. I am going to read now. Have some iced tea, Jeff. Pour yourself a big one!"

The next step in the Internet Revolution will be digital wireless access. This will cause an internet revolution in Asia where one third of the world's population lives without phone wires or cable TV. 25 more nations will have 10 % of their populations on the internet by 2000.

"Rowe is encouraging investors with stocks that have high PE ratios to," *Sell them now. A selloff or mini crash is imminent. Hold that cash and wait for the best buying opportunity of the new year.* "He talks about the difference between stock market liquidity and economic liquidity. His example is the pension fund cash in April 15 and July 15 as stock market liquidity and then he says," *Economic liquidity occurs in November, December and January.* "Would that be the shopping holidays and all the cash spent during the sales? And then that cash is passed back to the employees as paychecks and vacations and stuff?"

Jeff corrected. "Stuff is not a market term, dear. You are right and not only coast to coast, but around the entire world. It is one huge money machine. The only differences are the paper currencies."

AOL stock slid 23% on the acquisition announcement by AT&T. AT&T is trying to make sure they hold a place in the new revolution and don't go the way of the horse and buggy. Wall Street pitches cyclical stocks to mutual funds. Mutual funds began to invest in paper chemical and oil sectors. The heavy cash buying boosted prices of all of those share prices. Wall Street is trying to convince investors to lighten up on the internet stocks as they are only a passing fancy. Internet stocks jumped back up after the cyclicals announcement.

"Jeff. Why did AOL slide?"

"The AOL share price was *based on the investors greedy perceptions of its future value.* It was too high. AT and T would only pay a reasonable price for the acquisition and so the AOL share price immediately dropped back to the price of the buyout deal."

Angie noted, "Can you imagine that Wall Street was making every effort to try to get people to invest in anything besides the internet stocks before the big crash arrives. Isn't that the same thing as 'diversifying' that you talked about with Ronnie and Rich?"

"You should be a carpenter, Angie. You just hit the nail on the head. Investors should have been out of the market, but the mania news and the maniac desire to let their paper profits grow overwhelmed them and they let it all ride until they got to see their first good slaughter."

"They had never seen the charts in the Securities Research Company Blue Book." Angie continued to read.

*By 2002 there will be 600 million cell phones in the world. Three times as many people will use the internet by the end of 2000. AT&T spent **124 billion** to purchase Media One. AT&T's earnings are net 6 billion a year from 53 billion in sales and revenues.*

"Jeff, if the Fed raises interest rates, then shrinking liquidity causes the stock market to take a powder?" Jeff responded. "You are right. Just as lowering interest rates gets lending and investing and business moving again."

"Maybe it is time to take a breather. We could get some sandwiches. Yeah. Want to crack a bottle of wine and celebrate?"

"You know I would like to do that. Jeff picked up all three years of July. "Hang on. I will read some more. You just warmed me up. Let's skip July, 97. We have read the highlights before. Here is July, 1998." *Every bull market comes to an end when the Federal Reserve raises interest rates to bring the overheated market or economy or inflation under control.*

"So. Since inflation is not an issue in the USA in July '98, he is saying the market will continue to climb. And he says," *The market ran out of steam in May after the pension deposits were made in April. July pension fund deposits could produce a bounce up in July if corporate profits and earnings are slightly above expectations. Historically, July is one of the best months of the year because of this. August, September and October are the worst. After that the market will be in the doldrums until the Christmas rally.*

The Asia deflation going on may get a break of consideration from the Fed and that the Fed might raise interest rates to stall the dollar rise which would help Asian currency. Asia and Japan are deflating.

The seventh year of the decade has historically been a down year for the USA stock market. "I don't know if I believe that one. Maybe since 1980. Maybe things have changed or he means all markets together. "Rowe says 1927 and 1967 are the exceptions."

"Jeff. Think about that for a moment. What was it Ronnie was talking about during the croquet match. That book, *The Harbinger*. It brought to light the deep connections of USA to past civilizations, religions and, what was it? The Shemitah. The mystery of seven's. It is a biblical custom of something like taking a break after the harvest. Every seventh year they would not plant so that the nutrients in the soil could rejuvenate. And something else. All debts were forgiven. They let go of greed and usurious payments of debt. Everyone took a break for a year. Maybe they were letting the air out of any bubble they had. Maybe they were settling debts. Maybe they were throwing out the bad ones and converting paper profits to cold hard cash or renegotiating contracts. I finally finished *The Dead Cat Bounce*. So many new topics and concepts. I need to read it again. Hopefully, that will clear things up and help my recall."

"Good. I have read it four times. Okay. Rowe says real consumer spending is falling." Jeff paused to take a breath and run his hand through his hair. "Let's see. Then he goes on to talk about market breadth. He has a market breadth index. This is what we have been talking about with the Whiting's in the discussions about **churning**. Rowe calls this breadth idea a summation index. 80% 60% 40%. This summation index tops out before the drop of the stock market. Basically, it is testament to the weakness in the rallies at the top of the market when a lot of churning takes place. In the *first rally back* after the first big selloff in the market, the number of companies on the NYSE that bounce back up *is 80%, according to Rowe*. In the subsequent selloffs and rallies, the number of companies that bounce back actually decrease by 20% every time. So, from 2600 companies on the NYSE recovering or rallying the first time, only 2300 rally back. After the second sell off, only 1800 rally back. Then 1300 and finally the last rally is only 500 or so. This probably takes place over a year or two. The air is still in the balloon and the walls are stretched so thin that the texture rips open and the balloon pops."

Angie nodded. "You know I bet your thoughts are close. And don't forget the TRIN and the *plummeting* at the very end where only Mr. Bubbles is left in the tub."

"Well said. I love you more every day now. Especially compared to this time last year." They shared a kiss. "How sweet. Have some ice tea, Jeffy. You are pretty tense."

Microsoft and Intel accounted for 18% of the NASD Index.

NASD is heavy with the Dot Com Boom companies. They keep the NASD Index up high up while the other companies are actually languishing.

"That would interrupt the usual market cycle."

*Property in Hong Kong down **40%**. Treasury Secretary Rubin pressured Asian countries to allow American Bankers and USA companies to invest in Asia in the debt ridden Asia institutions.*

"Rowe says," *Specialists (traders on the exchange floor of the NYSE) are already **shorting the market as this July issue goes to press**. The* *market specialists, go short on the market and cover their positions in late October for about 20% in profits.*

"He is calling for a," *Sell off in the last quarter (Oct Nov Dec) for this fall.* "He is split on the timing. Yet, he sees the market," *advancing in the first 4 months of 2000 with a **Breath Taking Correction** to unfold in the latter half of 2000.*

Angie made a guess. "So he is saying, if no sell off in October of 99, then it will be in the fall of 2000. He feels pretty strong about the first four months of 2000. So how do you quantify *breath taking*, Jeff?"

"I will tell you later. Here are some interesting tidbits. The richest man sold 7 million shares of Microsoft." Angie asked, "How many shares does Gates have?"

"He used to own 60% way back when. I think it is less than 30% now. I am certain he has gifted some shares."

"The second richest man took profits and is sitting on 14 billion in cash."

"Is that what you want to do, Jeff?"

"Have you been infiltrating my dreams?"

The top investment bankers sold 70 million shares this year. "Hummm. If it was $100 a share that would be 7 billion dollars worth of stock."

The Federal Reserve will be forced to raise the Fed Funds Rate by ¼ to ½ percent at the FOMC (the Federal Open Market Committee Meeting) June 29. The Fed does not set interest rates. The Fed follows the bond market and raises the Fed Funds Rate in response to rising interest rates in the bond market. It will probably raise the Fed Funds rate by enough to keep the Fed Funds rate .5% ahead of the 90 day T bill rate.

"Here is something else he has included about Y2K. There was a website Y@KNewsMonitor." ***Banks in 19 countries*** *simulated the first day of business in 2000 and passed computer tests.* ***It involved 190 banks in total****. They are described as the backbone of banks worldwide. The New York Clearing House and major overseas banks have passed the tests. The FAA also completed operational tests with flying colors.*

"That must have been an internet website to keep everyone up to date as the drama unfolded. A group effort. Should I use the word global?"

"You should. Think about the **190 banks** number. One of the Japanese banks **is two times as big** as Citigroup. Our international banks run portfolios in at least 50 countries. The number of foreign country exchanges that they make trades in might surprise you."

China is no longer the fastest growing economy. It does buy USA T Bills for the interest. It is the easiest money they make. "Remember, this is 1999."

"Are you ready for **August, 1997**? Here we go with liquid asset update again." *Liquid assets at 4 trillion in the nation.*

"This Rowe guy is something else. Really good reading. I searched the net and found a current blurb on him that he was sued by a couple of investors in 2002. But this guy ties it all together just like Richard was saying. The guy is worldly. He bundles up a wealth of information and puts it on a level of conversation that a non-investor can almost understand. Currencies and economies. Not just the stock market and the indexes."

"Yes baby. This is something that your politicians cannot impart to the world. It cannot be explained or discussed with the voters because the voters and especially the non voters do not understand the words, the definitions or even the intricacies of the financial community on a global or even a national level. They have no earthly idea of what a deficit or deflation is."

"This August newsletter addresses the aspects of conservative investments, for instance, bonds that Martin Weiss would like." *Save $2000 a year in an IRA and you will have 1 million dollars in that IRA at age 65. Funds at 8% double every 9 years **if they are opened at the age of 18**.* The old life insurance pitch. The entire issue is devoted to this principle of saving 8% a year for retirement."

Angie applauded. "Martin Weiss would like this letter. He would approve." Jeff smiled. "I agree, Angie. Are you ready for **September, 1997?**"

"Jeff. Do you think Associated Press would print that there was a 500 point drop coming up in October, 1997 or 2014?" Jeff gave his wife a quick, appreciative kiss. "Here we are in **September 1997.**"

*S+P 500 PE ratio is now at 29.5. USA exports declined by 25% which hurt the quarterly earnings. **China does not know how to figure break even points.***

"What are break even points?"

"Well, I know that the manufacturing break even point takes into consideration every dime you spend on materials, electricity, water, production line, fixed and variable overhead costs, wages and taxes. You add all of those figures, maybe even the current portion of long term debt (due this month) and you divide the result by the sales price of the units you are making. That figure will give you the number of units you will have to produce to recover your costs and expenses."

"Rowe says," *Historically, September is the worst month of the year for the stock market.* **Traders return from vacation and sell stocks short through to the end of October.** "Yes. Summer vacation is over. The kids are going back to school. Parents experience more expenses and there is no more money for the stock market."

"You know, Angie, I know they can sell short in their personal accounts. I don't know for sure if they short the stocks in their house inventory. They probably do. Barron's runs some statistics on the number of short sale positions. They have a section of a page devoted to the largest positions. I don't know if it includes the floor traders. I don't know if it includes every single clearing house. Some institutions do their own clearing. Banks have their own overseas mutual fund portfolios. I bet they do their own clearing. Jeff Paused. "Now that I think about it, I know they can short any stocks in anyone's margin account because that is part of the margin agreement with the house. Stocks in margin accounts can be intermingled with other customers for shorting purposes, so the house can probably take advantage of that as the legalities are all in favor to the brokerage house."

"Rowe points out that there are many people who doubt the internet potential for being a wholesale logistics/supply clearing house. He said that Warren Buffet has no internet stocks. *His researchers consider the new internet stocks to be* **fundamentally baseless.**"

Angie bleated. "I bet they are a bunch of stuffy old goats."

E commerce sales or internet commerce sales are operating at a loss. These internet retailers who claim to be wholesalers just need some time to get their operations smoothed out as far as material flow and warehousing. Then their expenses will diminish. You have to have the optimum productivity set up. Their sales will eventually skyrocket.

"Rowe says that these new wholesalers like Ariba are selling banner advertising space on their web sites and that provides some extra revenue. Listen to this blurb about market valuations," ***It has been said that just 20 of the NASD's 4066 stocks have accounted for 50% of the NASDAQ Index rise. And just five stocks have been responsible for 35 % of the NASDAQ rise.*** "Let that one sink in. That is absolutely astounding. The Dot Com Boom was a mania unleashed! Angie, what do you think about the misrepresentation of the NASDAQ 100 composite index?"

"So 20 out of 4000. That pretty much tells me that these indexes have nothing to do with the real assessment of the direction of all stocks. All it tells me is that the favorite stocks are traded for the short term. That is where the action is just like Livermore said. In the big stocks.

"In scientific study, one object is varied while the others are held constant. The effects of the variances of one object are studied for any effect on the others that are held constant. This is done with each object. Your gathering of information at the end of the research is absolute, unbiased information that is somewhat trustworthy. You can draw conclusions objectively based on sound factual evidence."

"So it is easy to see that an index from observing only 30 stocks out of 2600 can hardly be expected to be representative for the actions of 2600 others. That would not be very objective."

"Here is some more info about the Asian deflation. Japan and China are trying to hide their trade problems. It is so severe that Alan Greenspan Left NY at 1 am to go to Japan and tell the Prime Minister that that the USA will buy the USA Treasury debt paper that the Japanese Government and investors hold. This would be USA Bonds and 90 day T Bills. What happens here is that this will put a huge amount of USA currency in Japan and China that was not there before and actually, never in circulation. This will be fast growth in the American money supply to the tune of an **18 BILLION DOLLAR SURGE** in the M3.

"Consequently, it was no surprise that the Bilderberger's scheduled their annual meeting shortly after this happened. They agreed to sell enough gold into the gold market to prevent a false run up in the price of gold on the commodities exchange."

"So. Obviously, we helped to bail out Japan and China from their depression. The politicians won't tell you this. The USA President can't tell you what the Treasury Department is doing because it is a secret. This might make the POTUS a little unpopular and cause a little social disagreement. But, there are some concerned people around the world who keep an eye on markets and figure out answers to problems. That is why new investors have to read the professional magazines. Nobody wants the American people to know that the USA citizen is paying for these bailouts. The USA citizen tax payments are being dumped into the Treasury Department for the expense of printing bills and buying back its own debt from China and Japan. All to forestall a depression in Asia."

"Now that is not a bad deal is it, Jeff?"

"No, it is not a bad thing. I don't mean to sound negative here. It would be the best thing to do in everyone's interest. It just happens to lower our 'standard of living' and decrease the value of the dollar."

Angie found some cheap, quick humor. "Gosh, Jeff. The Federal Government needs our bankrupt citizens to recover and buy homes again to jump start our new path forward for the next seven years." Jeff threw his head back and laughed. "Our new global path forward. It wasn't just USA banks and homes. **It was banks and homes all over the world**. Lots of people would not have homes if the banks would not take the risk. So, we just put the global *Life goes on* band aid on it?"

"The average USA citizen, who has no knowledge of world affairs or currency matters has no idea about this. Your USA Government Politicians are afraid to fight wars because 90% of the USA citizens are afraid of dying. But politicians are not afraid to sell USA citizens into financial income tax slavery. This is the standard method of operation. They are trying to hide the inflation while they pray that incoming taxes from citizens and corporations will eventually repay the loan the Fed made."

"You know Jeff. The federal Government bails out the banks, but they let the homebuyers go into foreclosure."

"You are right it is a three or four edged sword. It is the only system we have in place and it works. Maybe not 100% to everyone's liking, but it works. If you let these great big world banks fail it would be like taking the working horse and wagon away from the working world in the 1600's."

"Angie, here is the **September 1998** letter. Are you ready? *Currency traders (individuals and institutions) shorted the Asian Currency and bought the USA dollar. To produce greater demand for the Chinese goods, China cut the Chinese Yuan in half (devalue) to cut Chinese prices in half. Thus, half priced Chinse goods were in greater worldwide demand which caused the Japanese production (GDP) to decline.* It's a war out there, Angie!"

Asia at this time is 1/3 of world output and Japan is the leader to stimulate growth. China needed some extra money to feed the 50 million unemployed Chinese people who have no jobs and flock to the big cities in search of food and jobs and clothing, and China still has **1.2 billion** *other people who live in the cities to worry about.* All of this was on October 27, 1997, when the DJIA took a breather and, *dropped 554 points after hearing of the collapse of Asia currencies which are Indonesia, South Korea, Singapore, Japan, Malaysia, Thailand, Australia. Asian banks had been in trouble due to bankrupt businesses who could not repay loans. At that time both China and Japan blocked incoming USA goods (China didn't need competition of American cell phones, Dell Computers, etc.). This led to lower numbers of goods sold or made from USA. It could lead to recession and lower corporate profits in USA (recession and lower stock prices). Asia has slowed world growth and USA growth as well.*

"I didn't know Australia was Asian!" Jeff studied Angie's facial expression. "Geographically only. Remember the Aborigines and the red shell crabs were there first."

The USA GDP figure is presented 6 months late.

"What is up with that?"

"It just takes time to compile the figures and announce them because nobody in Washington DC can add or subtract." Laughter broke out between them. "My daddy always said that the government doesn't know how to do math. They have more important things to do like collect and spend your tax money."

"Here we are in September, 1999, about one year before the crash."

Business to business transactions will soar over the internet from **150 million** *this year to* **1.5 trillion** *by 2003. Large manufacturing buyers and suppliers are placing orders over two web sites www.ariba.com and www. commerceone.com.*

"Jeff, is there anything in our economy today that is expanding ten times like this Dot Com Boom?"

Jeff shook his head and stretched. "Rowe says it is the greatest expansion in creation of wealth since the 1800's when Queen Victoria's reign expanded the British Empire. Nobama's sick economy pales in comparison to the Dot Com Boom."

"Rowe says," *The internet will redefine every business, test every relationship, and produce discoveries at hyperbolic rates. Efforts to control the internet will not last long because it represents the human mind unleashed.*

"And some nay sayers thought the internet and computers were a waste of time."

So called blue chip stocks that were valued by the last generation are really not moving at all. The only ones moving up in share value and seeing large growth are the telecoms, internets, computer, cable and cellphones. These companies are growing at great rates and that is where investors are putting their bets.

What is propelling the upward price moves? New subscribers, record number of sales and record number of revenues. Large expenses and costs resulted in losses in the first years of cash outlays for operation start ups. Now earnings and record growth are realized year after year after year. "Rowe lists 35 stocks that will change the world. And they were companies that investors of the older generations had never heard of just 10 or 15 years ago. Industrial age stocks are not getting any attention. All the attention is going to the companies that are going to change the world."

"Okay here we go to **October, 1999**. Greenspan is warning the hedge fund managers of tough times ahead. Congress says no more hedge fund bailouts."

"Why is that a big deal?"

"Back in 1990's, some financial institutions like banks and savings and loans loaned money to finance companies that invest in securities and run mutual funds. These finance companies may be running a hedge fund on the side. If the hedge fund positions go bad and the fund goes broke, they have no cash to repay the banks for the initial loan. I suppose they fool banks with false financial statements or false statements of collateral to obtain the loan so they can dump the money in the hedge fund. They may falsify the portfolio value of the securities they have. If they even own any." Jeff sipped his tea. "Any bank or international bank can lose big time if they loan money to unscrupulous investors. In 2008 for instance, Lehman brothers was financially backing a derivatives hedge fund which caused their collapse."

Increased *asset valuation (adjustments) especially of the leveraged kind to financial statements can wash out overnight. They can decline significantly if leveraged contracts have been used and losses in the contracts are experienced .* "This is the blatant lie of over stating asset account values."

"Rowe says." *The internet will spawn the greatest revolution the world has ever seen. In 1800 it was the industrial revolution with the steam engine. 1900 was the train and the rails spreading coast to coast and north to south. 2000 will be the computer, the internet and telecommunications. Fewer employees. Greater productivity. Corporations have more cash. And everyone will be tested by the internet supplier's abilities to deliver the least expensive goods anywhere.* "And the funny thing is that people don't get it."

Angie asked, "Why Jeff?" Jeff took a deep breath. "They can't see past their own self perceptions. They don't realize that millions of other people will jump on this. And people don't read. They phoo poo new things they can't understand. They don't understand the computer processor speed doubling through new chip invention every 18 months. They don't know what a processor is or what it looks like. So you have new products racing in that are faster better and cheaper. It isn't planned obsolescence. Faster processing was needed so people did not have to stand around and wait for information to appear on a monitor one line at a time every two minutes.

Jeff continued to read. "Rowe says," *Sharp reversals in confidence (of bets made and placed) happen abruptly with no advanced notice.*

"Now all of these guru's are saying that if the market drops below 10,600 there will be a huge selloff. And the reason is because of the 175 trillion hedge fund/derivatives debt problem. Officials are afraid because no one has come up with a solution."

Clinton cannot find anyone who wants to take the job of regional Federal Bank President or Federal Bank Governors because of the situation. Greenspan bullies the 18 other members of the Fed's Open Market Committee.

"Greenspan had a monster of a problem. The hedge fund crisis. Highly leveraged trades means that a small amount of dollars *is actually used to secure the contract along with a lame promise to pay the rest.*" Jeff shook his head. "And they call this an investment. This is nothing more than rolling the dice for potentially enormous profits."

Angie clarified, "And on the flip side of the coin there are enormous losses that cannot be paid for. Is that like buying a new car with a small down payment and never paying the balance?"

*They destroyed south East Asia in 1997, just to make a profit. Now they are working on South America. 500 to one leverage. And **guess** where the borrowed money comes from? **The super banks. The world's 20 largest banks.***

"Hey, Angie. Here is **October, 1997**. It was behind 1999. "There is some interesting stuff. Rowe says," *Asian world leaders had to learn to fight inflation in the 60's, 70's and 80's and now they have to learn how to fight deflation. They are putting up trade barriers to protect their currencies from other cheaper currencies, but that reduces USA and Europe countries output and reduces jobs everywhere. All Asian countries have deflating currencies (at this time), deflating economies and they move their money out of country to buy a stronger currency or a bond or T bill that pays more interest.*

"Rowe says," *Out of the G7 countries only UK, USA, Helmut Kohl of Germany and Greenspan are saying the right things about getting Asia on its feet, keeping global markets open and ending all tariffs.*

Russia cannot collect enough taxes to run its own government. Russia's output, the pride of communism, is insignificant in the world economy.

Angie spoke up. "Richard would say, 'So much for communism. And so much for the liberal progressive communist party in the USA and the democrats who want big business to give everything to them and the poor people, the under achieving juvenile delinquents'."

Despite president Clinton's File Gate, Travel Gate, China Gate, Whitewater Gate, Foster Gate and the Lewinsky Date, he is still around because he is 'popular' even though his ratings have dropped. The stock market dropped **40%** *during Nixon's resignation.*

"Here are a couple of little tidbits."

Record liquidity *has been a more powerful force on the stock market* **than the economic growth** *in the USA.*

"Isn't that a little bit stupid? Why Bet on the moon when things are just dragging along?"

Three powerful forces push US interest rates down. Global slump in demand for commodities which has driven down inflation world wide. The biggest is obviously oil. The Economists commodity price is down 23% in the last 12 months.

And Second is the Asia recession spreading to Europe. They are pushing their lower price goods into Europe. And that is hurting USA business sales in Europe as prices are being squeezed everywhere. Third, currency markets are putting pressure on the USA to lower its interest rates.

"He doesn't have a buy signal yet. He says," *The big companies like Cisco, Dell, Lucent and Microsof*t (remember this is 1998 tele communications and internet stocks) *are the mutual fund favorites because there is easy liquidity (ability to trade easily, plentiful number of shares), in and out without harming the indexes or the share prices.*

"He says the other possibility," *is a fast run in the small and mid cap stocks.* "Angie, I have watched the mid caps. The big boys get positions before they ever breath a word to the public that mid caps are underpriced and worth accumulating. The big boys are always ready to sell midcaps to you. Whenever new money comes in, the big boys are able to sell out at a profit."

"He's recommending a British company. Vodafone. That one was a biggie." *Sales increasing at 36% Earnings growing at 20%. 200,000 new users each quarter. Annual sales over 4 billion for a cell phone company in 1998. Pay as you talk. No monthly contract.* "Wow, I was still in high school. I sure wish I could have bought 10 shares."

US exports to Asia have been cut back, **but they still exceed exports to Europe**. "He is predicting a global recession including the USA in 2000."

Jeff shuffled the last newsletters. "Just a couple more sweetheart and we are done. Here is November 1999."

AOL PE 332 YAHOO PE 471

Greenspan promised to open his checkbook and bail out Japan and other G 7 countries with liquidity problems by buying the USA Bonds that those countries hold in their treasuries. This was during the 1997 China currency collapse in Asia. Japan was in a depression at that time."

The USA money supply is exploding at a rate never seen before. "We read that before."

"Okay here we go for December 1998. Rowe is saying that," *November December and January are the three best months of the market.*

"I think he means that there is usually a drop that originates in September and October. Then it is an up and down thing from November to the Christmas rally and then on through the new year into January. After August, September and October, anything looks good."

There is a lot of whipsaw action because (supposedly) people rearrange their portfolios. "This is pure bunk. It is profit taking. Make no mistake They are going to cash or buying bonds."

"It's only 3:30. I guess we studied enough for today."

Angie stood up and stretched. She spun the triangles. She walked over to the wall chart. "I love this chart." "Jeff, you are right. The tax liens are the end result of the big calamity, the big crash."

"Calamity. I like that word. We are thinking the same thing." They both realized that the tax liens are the completion of the economic cycle. "Economy up, economy down. Job losses, foreclosures and then tax liens. And thus came the saying, *Every cloud has a silver lining.*"

"Jeff, you have a good idea about touring the rural areas this weekend. Let's do it. We can make sandwiches and carry them in the cooler."

"Want to go now and grab a motel out in the boonies later?"

"You are on, Mr!"

"I will gather things up and gas up the car now."

"I will get the non perishable food for two days."

"Don't forget to pack your midnight blue negligee."

LIGHTS OUT TRICK

It was the evening before Thanksgiving. Angelique and Veronica were comparing notes over the phone on the Wall Street Digest newsletter.

"Why don't you drag your husband over here, Angie? Rich is napping in front of the TV. We aren't doing anything. Come on over and we can watch those two silver haired gorillas talk about the stock market."

"Ha Ha! You always make things fun Ronnie!"

"It's the secret to keeping a marriage together. You have to know how to poke the gorilla."

"Ha ha! Do you want us to bring anything? Are you serving beverages?

"We are having iced tea and PBJ. There is probably some wine around. Sometimes I hide it from the gorilla. Come on over and we can talk trash about Mr. Rowe."

"Veronica hung up the phone. "Quick, Richard! The Thompson's are on their way over. Hide and don't answer the door." Richard hit the TV button and the living room light switch. Ronnie ran through the house and turned off all the lights. They ran to the bedroom and changed into pajamas. The Thompson's hoofed it across their yard to the Whiting's front door. The dark windows presented an eerie feeling. Angie rang the doorbell. There was no response. She rang it again.

Jeff questioned the dark windows. "Are you sure Ronnie called from the house?" Angie poked the front door bell repeatedly to vent a little irritation. "You don't know Ronnie as well as I do." Jeff turned mildly apprehensive and turned to go. Angie continued to pound on the door and ring the doorbell. She was really getting into it. She yelled at the top of her lungs. "Open the door you jokers!"

After thirty rings the Whiting's answered the door together. They were yawning in their bedtime pajamas and robes. Big smiles and chuckles covered their faces. "What is up with you people? Do you like to break door bells?" Angie said acidly. "Hi. Ronnie. Looks like you put on some weight. I hope we woke you up." Angie barreled through the doorway to the living room. "Hi, Richard. How is your ankle?"

"Oh, my. A little abrasive this evening are we? Can't take a little joke?" Jeff handed Livermore's biography and the Wall Street Digest newsletters to Richard. "Come on in. Sit down and make yourselves comfortable." Richard placed the Livermore book and the newsletters on his desk. "Thanks, Jeff. I hope you enjoyed the newsletters. Ronnie and I have been through the Dead Cat Bounce and the Erdman books. Good entertainment." Richard set the books on the corner of the table for the Thompson's to take home. "This Dead Cat Bounce is a pretty good start up book. Only three things jumped out at me. First was the timing of the earnings reports. It stated that the earnings reports are 45 days after the end of the quarter. That was true way back when, but I think they appear a little sooner nowadays." Jeff agreed. "And the chart on the NASD Composite has the volume missing across the bottom of the chart. There must have been some foul up at printing time or something. I did find a chart. It shows that the monthly volume from 2000 on was just about three times the size of the volume in 1998 and the years prior." Richard paused as if thinking deeply. "The four year business cycle. That is kind of old hat. It was a topic in Econ 102 when I was in college and back then it might have represented earlier times. But that was a couple of decades ago."

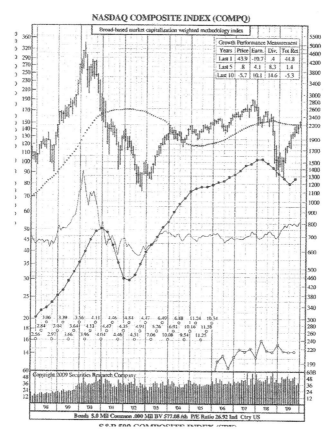

NASDAQ 100

Chart provided by Securities Research Company
(SRC). Please visit www.srcstockcharts.com

"Anything else, Richard?"

"Well, maybe. Now don't take offense, Jeff. I believe that the theory of the 4 year business cycle has forced you to believe that the market has seen its last days after that 500 point sell off. Ronnie and I know it is a little too early for that. But what I really want to tell you, is that the investing world is so huge now, that I believe that *it takes a longer time for this worldly financial community, I mean the institutions, the big shots, to sell their winners.*"

Ronnie was deliberately stirring the pot as always. "I did get a real kick out of those triangles, Jeff. It finally occurred to me that Richard and I should bring them into the new millennia. So we decided to bring your triangles up to date." Ronnie picked up two pieces of cardboard off the top of the file cabinet. "What do you think of these?" She handed a triangle to Jeff and one to Angie.

"We wanted to represent a seven year stretch of *so called bull stock market*. Richard and I both agreed that Area D should be at least two years long. Also Area B and Area C. Area A, at the bottom of the market is still one year so everything adds up to seven years.

Richard related the thought behind seven years. "Ronnie and I believe that there are so many investors from all countries and from all age groups, so many institutions pursuing investment in the world markets to try to become millionaires that it takes two years for the big boys to sneak out their profits without crashing the market. Rowe mentioned in one newsletter that there was an increase of 1.5 billion new investors due to the ease of access provided by the internet boom."

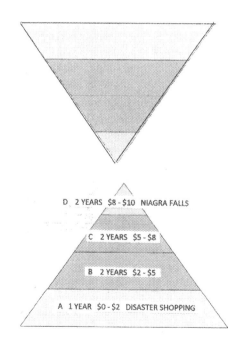

RONNIE'S SEVEN YEAR TRIANGLES

Richard continued. "In 1999 the NYSE and NASDAQ market capitalization was *10 trillion dollars*. ($10,000,000,000,000). We put some quick numbers together using 10 trillion dollars and this is what we came up with. Say you have 100 institutions. Each of them have a **billion** shares at $100 a share equals **100 billion dollars** *times 100 institutions* equals **ten trillion dollars**. Say they do pure selling once a week and in 100 weeks which is two years, they have their money out." Richard paused. "We know this is not the true picture. But we feel this assumption would hold for 100 institutions selling one billion shares of stock every week. If you say, '*Well, it is probably 200 institutions*' then we will say, all right then, *the share price is now $50 a share*. This elementary model has given us some sense of perspective. You can vary the amount of the institutions and share price and still come up with 10 trillion dollars."

Jeff responded, "I will have to think about that one for a while. Not every institutions has 100 billion dollars in the stock market at today's prices. The average is more like 20 million or less."

Ronnie cut in. "We have more slim reasoning. GM was upside down in 2003. Their debt was 7 times higher than the total assets of the company. Unbelievable!" Seven to one in terms of debt to assets But GM didn't tank until three and a half years later in 2006. Who turned on the light? That is just mystifying to me." She paused with her thoughts. "The only thing that Richard and I could come up with is that the mutual funds were able to sell off very carefully as much as they could before GM crashed. We are certain that millions of mutual fund investors had no idea if GM was in their mutual fund. They never know the difference. It is as Erdman said in *The Crash of 1989, Where are you going to find more stupid, greedy people with money to throw away besides the USA?*"

Angie smiled. "Oh. Shame on those mutual fund managers for not alerting their investors."

Ronnie invited everyone to the kitchen. "Come into the kitchen and make a sandwich." The Whiting's had thrown together chicken salad, appetizers, wine and iced tea. Jeff and Angie expressed their thanks verbally and with big smiles. Veronica had placed all of the makings for sandwiches on the kitchen table. In the center was a bowl of tuna salad and a bowl of chicken salad. Two pitchers of iced tea and two wine bottles were on the counter with the knives, forks, spoons and the paper plates.

"You guys look funny in your PJ's. We should get a picture. Jeff, get a picture of these two yay hoos."

Jeff snapped with his cellphone while the Whiting's posed with comical faces. Jeff inquired, "Where's the china? An important person like me can't be eating on a paper plate. Are you cutting the expense account to match the sparse winter income?"

"China is across the ocean in the Eastern hemisphere. You are welcome to swim over there. If you don't like the paper plates, then you will have to use a napkin and your pinkies. Angie has told me about your disgusting eating habits. Angie, have you been on anymore tax lien hunts?"

Angie decided it was a good time to spring her independent decision on her husband. "Ronnie, you would not believe how much is out there. There are two lots we are thinking about making a move on."

A questioning look of surprise appeared on Jeff's face. "Are you sure?"

"I am, honey. I guess I forgot to ask you if we could use the money that you moved into the savings account. I think the lake lots would be a good move. The two that are close to the county line." She looked at Veronica. "We are thinking that if we ever built a cabin that we could sell one of the lots to help with building materials cost."

"Angie. There is no electricity or water out there."

"I figure you could rig up one of those diesel powered electric generators for us. We can figure out where to pick up water and how to store it. Can't we, honey?"

Ronnie interrupted, "Wow! Good for you two. Now, everybody go on into the living room and make yourselves comfortable. Gab a folding tray and my butler will bring the iced tea and glasses out to you."

Richard had a sheepish grin on his face. "Have your money ready folks. It is two bucks for a glass of tea and three if you want ice cubes."

Ronnie and Richard sat at their strategy tables. Everyone relaxed and enjoyed tuna fish and ham salad sandwiches chased with wine spritzers before the first round of questions were unleashed.

Jeff took the opportunity to interrupt Richard as he was just about to take another bite of food. "Hey, Richard! Did you see any articles on Japan recently?"

"You know I did, Jeff. I know everything that goes on in the Eastern Hemisphere."

"Isn't it just amazing? The market dropped the first week of October and everyone from the President to the paper press and the TV news media told the public that there is absolutely nothing to fear. They swore that the economy is healthy and that the global economy is healthy. That gave me a really snug, secure feeling and I slept better. I didn't need my teddy bear. I think I even released some pent up gas. How about you?"

Ronnie laughed. "It is called denial and keeping the lid on. Throw some more bull manure on the mushrooms." Richard devoured a bite before he answered. "Yes, yes. See, the market is defiant. It is like an expanding colony of amoebas in a petri dish. It rallied back to a new high. It is the highest it has ever been in 200 years!"

Jeff Gave Richard a strange look and answered, "All I know is when the DJIA Index hits a new high, all of the other stocks are still in their same old rut."

Angie spoke. "Isn't it funny? Just two days ago we were blindsided with an AP article in the local paper that says Japan is now 'entering a recession'."

Richard nodded. "That is just like the media. Everything will continue *to be just great until they are forced to print the **really bad news**.*"

This raised Angie's ire. "How can the associated press print and out and out lies in the newspapers? How can the president utter the words, 'The global economy is growing'?"

Jeff responded. "It is easy! Politicians lie! They love to lie. Especially to people who are better citizens than they are. And let me tell you the reason why. It is because your politicians don't know anything but dollars and lobbyists. They even lie to themselves and say they deserve their salary because they have worked hard all their lives and that they are smarter than everyone else." Richard commented, "It is a vicious circle at the bottom of the food chain." Laughter broke out.

Jeff looked at Ronnie and Richard. "So, what about the Fed Reserve and interest rates. Are they cooling the stock market or stopping other nations from loading up on Treasuries?"

"Both. The two items are inextricably linked. If the rates go up, there are fewer loans and less money to spend. People cut back on travel. Groceries. They don't remodel the kitchen. Mom and Pop shops and the service industries see a decrease in cash flow. Corporate sales decrease. Their revenues may hold up for another six months if the extra shifts are shut down and worker hours are cut back. Time and a half goes out the window and then the company announces the ultimatum, 'Accept this temporary situation or you can quit'." Ronnie laughed. "We have no advanced degrees in money theory so we are just guessing."

Richard sipped his wine. "Short of reading up on banking theory I will say a couple of things. Any creation of money out of thin air is an infusion of dollar bills into the USA economy regardless of whether it goes overseas or stays in the USA. Those creations by the Fed are paid back with USA citizen taxes and corporate taxes or proceeds from the Fed's sale of USA Treasuries. I will even stick my neck out and say the more bills you have in circulation, the easier it is to move prices higher. These bailouts of banks around the world raise inflation as much as social programs, war, food stamps and unemployment compensation from the government."

Angie reminded everyone. "If you all recall, Rowe said every time interest rates go up, the market takes a dive."

"Right, Angie. Richard and I are going to help you with that concept after the snacks. Richard thinks it is because there are too many deals between the financial institutions, businesses and the Super 20 banks. He thinks that the deals are so interest rate sensitive that they begin to fall apart during rate increases. I happen to believe that these banks will always start a new deal anytime they can rub two pennies together. They are greedy. Too greedy. They are always maxed out. And if anyone of them misses a current payment or the balance due, then they begin to fail like dominos."

Angie changed the subject. "You know something that is really ironic. Martin Weiss's father made his first bundle when he went short in 1929 on the overzealous market."

"Yes." Richard recalled. "I forgot about that. Isn't that funny? Martin still goes short in his personal account as the market corrections begin. He even makes put option suggestions in his newsletter."

Angie waited until everyone had a bite of food and piped up. "Jeff and I found out a slick way to short the market. It doesn't leave you naked." Ronnie's jaw dropped. Richard's eyes opened. Jeff spit some cookie crumbs and began to choke. "You are covered and there is no unlimited liability."

"Tell us about it. Don't keep us in suspense."

"We made some calls two weeks ago and finally we found someone at B. C. Christopher who explained to us how to short stock. It is easy. And you know something? It helped me to understand the pullbacks and the rallies." Angie munched her tuna fish sandwich and spoke in between gulps and bites. "And all the financial pros tell their clients that the best thing to do is just *to hang on* or *average down* when prices drop. It is like Ronnie said. Life goes on."

Jeff commented. "I shorted Citigroup based on the class action lawsuits. There are three or four class action lawsuits out there. Right after the lawsuit Citigroup stock price ticked up *like it was lawsuit proof.*"

Angie swallowed a bite of her chicken salad sandwich. "I shorted 3d Systems. It was one of the first charts I saw in the Blue Book. The PE is 70. Livermore said to avoid high PE's so it seemed like a good choice. Everyone nodded their head in approval. "Now Jeff and I have a few questions for you two guru's."

Ronnie opened up her laptop. "Okay, Angie. Fire away! Don't hold back! Give us the big questions first and if we can't answer them, I will do the internet search and get back to you."

"Okay here we go. Jeff and I couldn't figure this one out. We are totally stumped. Rowe said *'There was an infusion of cash into the economy'* to the tune of 4 trillion dollars to pump liquidity into the market, as he likes to say. We can't figure out what he meant. He also mentioned that Brazil was bailed out from their economic crash. Then he mentions a multiplier effect of 50,000. All of this was in one sentence or in about the same breath."

Ronnie looked up. "That may have been the amount that the USA Treasury paid for T Bills and Treasury Bonds bought from the Asian countries to help them avoid a depression back in 1997 and 98. They also helped out in South America. 4 trillion dollars is a pretty hefty cash infusion."

Ronnie searched for more info. "Now, back in 1998, The Federal Reserve Bank had just taken on the mission to print USA money to buy USA Bonds and T Bills from the Chinese and the Japanese because those countries were ready to fall into **depression** and they needed cash urgently. Here you go, Jeff. 12 billion to Mexico in 1995. Mexico put up all of its oil reserves as collateral. No one really seemed to know how much oil is in the ground. Mexico's oil revenues were deposited through the Federal Reserve Bank in New York as collateral for the loan. There is more. November, 1998. 5 billion in USA taxpayer money. During the time of the Dot Com Crash, the Fed was becoming one of the world's bail out champions. It says here there were 11 countries that pitched in, the British, the World Bank the IMF. I think the 4 trillion that Rowe was talking about was mostly used to bail out China and Japan and the 1997 fiasco in Asia. That is, if that much of the money ever made it over to Asia. You know there are many official people who stick their hands into a big bundle of money like that. At that time, 4 trillion was half of what the market capitalization was for both USA stock markets."

Jeff shook his head. "I don't think that is right. That is a whale of a lot of money, but then again Asia is a whale of a lot of nations and there was a whale of a lot of money during the Dot Com Boom. You know, come to think of it, Rowe said that M3 expanded by 18 billion dollars. What happened to the other 3.9 trillion?"

Ronnie answered. "I will search for that later. Okay, for now let's talk Brazil for a while. You know south America was having problems too. You have to understand that most of South America's neighbors depend on Brazil. If Brazil tanks so does South America." She took a new bite of sandwich and continued. "Back in the 50's, 60's and 70's Americans would vacation in Acapulco, Cancun and Mazatlán."

"Is that where matzah balls came from?"

"Oh, Angie! You are so intuitive! Now it is Rio, baby! Sleazy movies like *Ten* with Dudley Moore and Bo Derek and that song, *The girl from Ipanema* brought millions of vacationers to Brazil. Okay! I found Brazil today. *China powered most of the Brazil expansion during the early*

2000's. Currently, in 2013, economic growth is near zero. Today, Brazil is close to another sharp recession. Who knows for some reason USA, Great Britain and others not mentioned here went on a crusade to bail out distressed countries. Maybe the result of a G7 or G20 decision. Usually the philosophy was to help the afflicted nation so they don't storm your border and start a war. Or get them flush with cash so they can buy your products."

"Listen up. Brazil is currently in the longest recession in decades. Politically, they would rather do business with China than UK or USA. Eleven percent of the nation's 473 companies trade at less than half of book value."

Angie inquired. "Would that be a reason why everyone is fleeing South America and crossing border with their inherent rights as humans to homestead in California or Texas?"

"Here is more. In 2003, 21% of Brazil's citizens were in poverty. In 2009, only 11%. Venezuela currently has close to 100% inflation. Duke energy put 4400 megawatts of their Brazil system up for sale to the Chinese. Population in China is currently 300 billion. It is expected to go to 500 billion in the next decade."

Jeff had his own suspicions about the meaning of the population growth. "Could that be a reason for the Chinese waterway expansion to the south China Seas? Suburban flight to the Philippines and South America?"

"Here you go, Angie. Brazil. Rio de Janeiro gets a big 42 billion dollar cash bail out. Brazil claims to have 40 billion in oil and gas reserves in the ground."

Richard answered. "I might throw in at this point that Bernie Sanders, (democratic presidential candidate) firmly believes that no agency of the USA government should be allowed to bail out a foreign country or corporation without approval of congress. And I personally believe that corporations should offer employees a program to match funds on employee balance paydown of home mortgages instead of dumping free stock in employee IRA or Keogh accounts."

"There is more. China is now the top owner of Brazil assets. I imagine the USA and UK were back in 1999. That would be the reason the UK and USA ran to the bailout rescue."

Richard interrupted. "Okay. Let me provide a little bit of factual background into what was taking place at that time." Three pair of eyes rolled to the ceiling. "Clinton searched for people to take the Federal Bank Regional Chairmanships. Those who volunteered didn't have the qualifications. No one would answer Clinton's calls to replace Greenspan. No qualified people wanted Greenspan's job. To cut to the quick, Greenspan came up with a simple solution. Make no mistake about it. Greenspan was the man of the hour! *The problem was hedge fund* **currency** *speculations.* The hedge funds borrowed money from the 20 Super Banks to increase their hedging."

"Each of the big 20 banks was assigned a team of expert auditors. Auditors studied the lists of collateral used by the Super Banks to justify their swollen loans to secret offshore accounts around the world, not just the Caribbean (see Appendix Panama Papers). The Banks were required to *explain any discrepancies and resolve the problems.* **And the banks were forced by the auditors to call the money back**. Well, anyway, the blow out in the market arrived just after the banks start collapsing. You will find this association to be timeless. The two are intertwined, obviously."

"Okay. What is the next question?

"Ronnie, what are they talking about when they say record debt?"

"That one is easy. Record debt is actually public debt here in the USA. Do not confuse this with government debt. It is the amount of money USA citizens have borrowed for *everything.* The total debt from borrowing to pay for houses cars credit card debt, you name it."

"And Rowe was talking about the banks printing up 4 billion credit cards."

"What people don't comprehend is that this happens in at least 160 nations around the world. Can you even imagine a million credit cards issued in each country? That would be 160,000,000 million credit cards. Throw $10 on everyone's card and that would be 1.6 billion dollars. $100 would be 16 billion."

"That includes auto debt, credit card debt, bank loan debt, college debt, debt for the sailboat and debt for Sears or Target or Macy's and gasoline cards. You name it."

Ronnie went on line. "Hey, just imagine this. There are 424.3 million accounts in the USA. Credit card debt in last 3 months was only 182 million accounts used. Visa account uses numbered 89.8 million. The use of master card in the last 3 months was 48.5 million times. Citi and Capital One about 30 million. This shows that credit cards were seldom used and that is because consumer spending is at an all time low right now. Charging on the credit card has really backed off."

"Put $500 on 4 billion cards and that total is 2 trillion dollars. How is that for public debt? Throw $1,000 dollars on each card and that would be 4 trillion dollars. Just imagine. Cars, mortgages, student loans. Jeff, maybe 4 trillion is not so absurd after all. Maybe some of it went to the banks."

Angie asked, "So how about that lawsuit on Rowe? There were four or five investors who were asking for 6 million in damages. Something like that."

"Richard and I know little of the actual incriminations or details of the scandal. But we do agree on one thing. A young guru with a decent track record influenced Rowe. Rowe mentioned a couple of the suggestions in his newsletter. A few subscribers picked up the recommendations and invested a couple of million and the recommendations went south. That is what we think. We don't know the scope or the details. Richard always thought that in the years leading up to the crash it was easy to make great recommendations. But all investors face the same problem in the C and D area. Share price upturns are smaller and shorter in duration. Plus, Richard still thinks it was the entire market that went south not just the new guy's recommendations. We just don't know for certain what happened."

"It is unfortunate that this whole thing happened of course. Rowe is one of the many accomplished guru's in the pack. Most of them are educated and heavily experienced. They do pass some knowledge on to subscribers. I imagine Rowe will remain a consultant to his most moneyed followers at their request. I really think Rowe should write a book or just publish a summary of the Wall Street Digest newsletters. It is an intriguing time in the market and world economy.

"Well." Richard jumped in.

Next question. Now keep in mind that there was 10 trillion in the NYSE and the NASD. The GDP was 7.7 trillion, liquid assets were 4 trillion. The derivatives problem was 175 trillion.

"Okay next question."

Angie read from her notes. "Rowe said it was illegal for derivatives accounts or funds to be in any Federal Insured Bank because FDIC would not pay for any derivative losses. There were few laws on the books to regulate derivatives. The derivatives were in off shore banks whose laws prohibited tracking where the money came from, who owned it, and where it disappeared to. The funds and the money were kept in banks around the world (unregulated banks). Still the fund managers borrowed money from the big 20 Banks. This is all about greed and lawlessness for unjust enrichment.

Rowe said the sums of money were so large that *those in power and in the position in the world to do something were just too scared to do anything or to solve the problem.* No one had any worldly idea what to do. Rowe said that this was enough money to destroy every bank in the world and many countries. Rowe mentioned that the derivatives plays in currency wars in South East Asia in 1997 took the Asian currencies down. Then supposedly derivatives traders experimented with South America.

Angie looked up at Ronnie. "Ronnie, Jeff has explained options to me so I have an entry level understanding of options. But I have no idea what derivatives are. So, Ronnie, what are derivatives? What form do they take and what about this 175 trillion dollar hedge fund crisis? Why are derivatives still in use today and what in the world are credit swaps?"

"Okay. Now, get two chairs from the kitchen and let's sit around the strategy tables together. Angie, sit over here with my laptop and Jeff you take Richard's." Jeff and Angie answered, "Yes, Miss Ronnie."

Richard stood up and walked to the file cabinet. He returned with copies of two newsletters. He handed two newsletters to Jeff and two to Angie. Richard explained, "Rowe wanted to predict the exact month that the market would collapse during the Dot Com Boom. Who really cares? Now, Weiss. Crafty Martin D. Weiss sent out a warning six months in advance of the 2000 collapse."

Ronnie interrupted. "Angie, we are going to answer your question on derivatives in a couple of minutes. But first, Richard and I want to talk about Area D and investment advisors. After that, we will approach the financial world and stock market environment from a different perspective. We simply can't sit here all night and try to explain things. Rich and I went through all of this circle reasoning and arguing together years ago. Thinking and talking in circles and guessing and wondering is just wasteful. So. What we are going to do here is to take you to the environment that exists at the crash and explain it to you."

Richard took his turn. "Newsletter gurus make money by recruiting subscribers. They gain subscribers by the success of their recommendations. Obviously, the day after disaster day it is easy to make a bucket load of promising recommendations that will produce a significant rise in share value in two or three years. That is the easy part. Now making recommendations as the market peaks is risky unless you tell investors to sell. All of the gurus share this problem. The closer you are to Area D, the harder it is to pick a winner. Investors want doubles. They want 100% returns. And there is no way to convert them to become day traders. There is another problem. The pivotal points of the downturns are sharp and fast with little warning." Richard sipped some iced tea. "The only saving grace is the ability to tell the investor to get out and sell everything. Some advisors have a service where flash message warnings of impending disasters are emailed to the subscriber."

"Okay folks. Heads up here. Martin Weiss knows the ins and outs of the stock market going back before the early 80's. Donald Rowe was around in the 90's on the Dot Com run up. Rowe's May 2001 newsletter is almost in denial of a pending disaster. He is charging forward with a battle cry that the market cannot be defeated. He reasons that there is 3 trillion dollars of liquidity on the sidelines. He reasons that the Fed has called the large money centers (regional Federal Banks) and encouraged them to lend more money and have it available ***even though consumer debt is at an all time high!*** He reasons that there is so much cash on the sidelines that investors will not believe how fast the indexes will recover after any correction. Rowe is literally delusional with this premise. That premise is still around today but it is an incorrect assumption. Investors choose to wait until the smoke clears." Richard sipped his wine. "Now.

Angelique. Read the headline on the second newsletter, please. And remember the Dow is 11,000. It has been between 10,000 and 11,000 **for two solid years**. The date is late December, 1999."

Angie read. "*Martin D. Weiss accurately forecast the failures of Executive Life, Mutual Benefit Life, and the Bank of New England.* Next he explains, and this title is in bold type, **Why a banking collapse 12,000 miles away from Wall Street is about to knock 3000 points off the DOW!**"

Richard cautioned. "Okay. Remember how Rowe told you about the Asian recession, the deflation and the devaluation of the Chinese dollar? He also mentioned that Asia has 1/3 of world output? Think about that when you read the rest."

Angie continued. *Four huge Japanese banks, far* **larger** *than Citicorp, Wells Fargo and the Bank of America* **combined** *have been smashed by the financial crisis in Asia. They have been downgraded to the same status as junk bonds, by Moody's. They hold an estimated 300 billion of American stocks and bonds.* "Let me paraphrase here. He goes on," *If the banks sell those assets to keep from going under, then IBM, General Motors and five other huge stocks are going to lose 70% of their value.* **The DOW will plunge by 3000 points.**

"Okay. Just like teenagers who think that hostile threats from overseas countries will not cause an invasion to the USA or a war that they might have to personally go fight, so it is the same for new gullible investors to reject a belief that a bank crash on the other side of the world will cause the USA stock market to crash. And their reasoning is as follows. *Well, our banking system is protected. It is not linked to any overseas banks. And our politicians and our congress are not supposed to let harm come to the American people.* Now this is the usual thinking and gibberish of the younger idealistic minds and the older adults who have very little education. It is all rational and logical. But their conclusions are all wrong. They are wrong because their arguments are based on the emotions of the way they think things should be. They are not using the true facts of the environment."

Angie read the paragraph at the bottom of the page. "*Sakura Bank, Approximately 50% larger than Citicorp (then the largest bank in the US), is now closing 23 international offices, firing hundreds of employees, and closing or selling subsidiaries."*

"Okay now, Jeff. Tell me what your thoughts are."

"With Rowe, I see a person with the view and the belief that the USA has reached the point where it has conquered any possibility of failure. We are now so advanced that we control and handle our financial future without harm to the USA. A quick look at page five. There is one of those dream charts that shows the NASDAQ is on target of projected growth to reach 25,000 by the year 2009. On page four, he is calling the bottom here in April of 2001, based on the Arms Index. It flashed one of its super signals Friday, March 16 2001. The 10 day moving average moved to positive territory and Rowe calls it the sign of the bull. He explains **that in every case in the last 40 years a significant low occurred within the next 20 days**. And in the last 19 years, the low occurred in the next 4 days. There has been only one time when the signal occurred on the day of the drop."

Jeff continued. "Rowe says he thinks that *April 3 will finally be the date of the final DJIA bottom low point*. Rowe says *Wall Street pros know that the DOW will not collapse. Pros know that the stock market will not crash when the Fed is creating new money on top of the 3 trillion on the sidelines.* He further states that he is *disappointed in market analysts who tell their clients that it will take 2 to 3 years for before the technology sector recovers*. Rowe is talking about the high flyers of the internet bouncing back fast or at least climbing back quickly. The MRM Asset Allocation Group is forecasting NASDAQ 8000 on the next leg up.

Jeff sipped his wine. "On page seven he speaks up about the Bernard Connally case. Seems there is some unrest and disbelief in the new European Union about anyone from any of the EU countries being able to bad mouth the European Union. No one has the right to disrespect the European Union. Don't talk trash about the European union!"

Ronnie remarked, "This was the early stage of globalization in Europe. Bernard Conolly is a British economist who criticized the EU posture. He was dragged into court and handed a gag order. He was fired from his job for having the nerve to *criticize eroded rights of the people of the European Union from the **very first day** that the Union* *was formed*. The EU Court of Justice ruled that, *It is okay for the EU to suppress political criticism.*"

Angie spoke up. "Maybe this big up market prediction was what got Rowe into trouble. Maybe he was paid off by the Street to give a buy signal!" Laughter filled the living room. "I bet that is the real reason behind the law suits. Any stock you bought in April, 2000 was at the bottom of the ocean seven months later. Can any of you tell me why the associated press never mentioned that a Japanese bank was going broke and that it would cause the market to take a powder?"

Ronnie interrupted. "Okay. Angie. That is fine, but stay with us here. What did you glean from these two newsletters?"

Angie cut in. "Weiss is telling everyone that the crash is a certainty and to go short! He even wrote a book! **The Third Great Crash**. And on the back of this newsletter there is a post script. His father, Irving Weiss, went short in 1929 and Martin watched his father go short in 1987 and together they made a bundle. He claims his father, Irvin, was the only person who made a fortune in both crashes."

Ronnie stared into the air as if she was a navigator charting star formations. "Okay. This is what we are going to search for on the laptop right now. We are going to find a new perspective in the financial environment that exists six months before the very day of the stock market crash. This perspective is not discussed very much. So, in the search box, type in the words, you are going to love this, Angelique, type in **large banks in default position**."

"Okay. Who found any banks in banks in default positions in our world today? You both did. Okay good. Angie, on the website www. thismatter.com, select the title, *Bank Risks* and read it to us."

"There is something here about a bank in China that loaned money on oil well servicing companies from 2012 to 2014. It is going broke!

"What do you see, Jeff?"

Jeff announced, "I am looking at several topics. One is, **Framework for Measuring and Controlling Large Exposures,** published by Bank for International Settlements (BIS) in Basel, Switzerland. There is another one by the Federal Reserve on website www.federalreserve. gov. called **The Modern Trading Business of Large Banks**. Here is an interesting one. **Banks Liquidity Positions for Biggest Banks in America**. They have huge leveraged credit default swaps. Another is **Too Big to Fail.**"

Ronnie took over again. Okay, good. Now both of you click on **Greg Hunter's USA Watchdog**. Perfect. Jeff, why don't you paraphrase this one essay titled **Four Biggest Banks in the US Have Huge Leverage.**"

Jeff skimmed the article and whistled. "Oh, my gosh. This is a big one. You know the **16 trillion bailout we had in 2008**? Well 16 trillion **was still not enough money for the total derivatives bailout**. The current figure in the world today, *of over the counter derivative exposure*, is pegged by **BIS (Bank of International settlements, Basel Switzerland) at 600 trillion dollars**. *It is an **unregulated dark pool of money with no public market**. These are bets of debt on such things as credit risks, currencies, interest rates and commodities.*" Jeff shook his head in disbelief. "**Four banks in USA, have 235 trillion** and the whole USA nation is tagged at 250 trillion. **JP Morgan, Citibank, Bank of America and Goldman Sachs.** The total assets of these 4 banks are only 5 trillion dollars." Jeff looked at the group. "Does anyone sense something is wrong here? There is this explanation given. *Banks hold many assets on the books at a subjective value (their interpretation), but the banks swear that they have hedged their bets and they use a term called bi-lateral netting.*" Jeff read on. "AIG was hours away from making 3 trillion dollars (under contracts) worthless. *As far as the Euro currency goes* **it cannot be saved**. If EU goes under the banks in US will too. Listen to this. **The current related post oil derivatives exposure is twice as big as the sub prime crisis was in 2008**. Wow!"

Angie blurted out. "I have indigestion. My stomach has turned sour and I feel like I am going to throw up. I am totally disgusted! I am just horribly sickened by all of this dreadful information on the banks going berserk and trying to make another dime every time they have two extra pennies to rub together. Then what happens? The banking system collapses. The stock markets take a dive. The workforce is cut by 10% so companies can survive. This total greed should be punished. Does anyone go to jail when 10 million Americans and all the other people in all the other countries in the world lose their jobs and homes? No! And only one or two white collar criminals get jail time! This is insane! **You people have fed me a poison pill**! You suckered and scammed me into this whole stock market thing. *I hate you all for doing this to me!*"

Ronnie criticized, "Angie! Remember who causes these terrible catastrophes. You have to know the reasons so that you can protect yourself and the future that you and Jeff have together. It is totally unfair. Yes. But that does not mean you can get mad and throw in the towel like a spoiled athlete or juvenile delinquent. **Hang in there and outsmart the circumstances**. That had always been the deciding factor between winners and losers. Between people who survive and those that go right down the drain and those who are able to just keep their chins above water all of their lives." Ronnie glared at Angelique. "Do you want happiness or do you want despair in your life? Angie, Get a grip! Get your big girl panties on!"

Angie stiffened a bit. "*Why doesn't somebody do something*? **This is sickening**!"

Richard tried the light hearted approach and educated the group. "Milton Friedman addressed this concern back in the 60's and 70's. You can find his thoughts on YOUTUBE. I kid you not! *He declared the Federal Reserve Board to be staffed with just regular citizens who were and still are ill equipped to do anything to combat this predicament or eradicate the dirty rats who continue to screw the citizens of many countries.* Isn't it pitiful? This is the reason they nixed any help from Martin Weiss. Anyone who upstages the Federal Reserve Board is resented for being **the bright person who has a solution**. The dull person does not know if it will work or not and is scared to take a chance. The members have no creative instincts or problem solving ability and moreover they are afraid to go off the end of the high diving board and take any chances. Instead they just do nothing and shrug their shoulders."

Ronnie interrupted. "Okay everyone. Let's go back to the article **Bank Risks**. This is an article by www.thismatters.com. Wipe your tears, Angie. You go with this one." Angie skimmed the article and muttered 'wow' several times. "Bank failure was one of the major causes of the 2007-2009 credit crisis. Hold on to your hats. Royal Bank of Scotland (Barclay's) the largest bank in the world, with assets of 2.4 trillion was suffered a loss of 8 billion pounds (3% of its assets) because it was leveraged to the hilt. The risks are liquidity risks." Angie paused. "And then there are the derivatives risks. There are two types and both are swaps. Swap risks are mainly interest rate swaps and credit default swaps. This is a funny agreement. If party number two is unable to pay the debt due to party number one, then a third party will guarantee the payoff of party number two's debt. We are talking the monthly principle payment of a bond to the bondholder. Well, I guess it could be the quarterly or the yearly payment. The amount and the time period are not discussed."

Angie continued her rant. "Cripes, Ronnie. This makes my head ache. It goes even further talking about the Federal Reserve Bank and its relation with the national banks. Banks have commitments called *off balance sheet risks such as loan commitments, letters of credit* that may or may not have been honored. This is supposedly, so called insurance that a person or entity will pay off any loss incurred by another and save the loan status. *It is buying protection and guaranteed payment of overdrafts and losses.* Like a cosigner? **Can you believe that?** It talks about repurchase agreements. Repos. It talks about credit default risks and way down here at the bottom interest rate risks. So it spells out the situations and the problems that exist. Arms! Adjustable rate mortgages." Angie sipped her wine. "There is more. *A bank's trading ratio is limited by law but it can earn greater profits by trading securities.* **Banks cannot by law own stocks**, but they get around that. They can buy debt instruments, securities and derivatives. **Obviously, this is part of the big problem**. So, believe it or not, banks hire traders and believe it or not rogue traders can cause stupendous losses. Barings Bank, established in 1762 was stable and the safest. Enter **Nick Leeson** who lost more than *860 million*, **close to 1 trillion pounds** in 1995. He was trading of all things, Japanese equities in Singapore of all places. Barings Bank could not cover the loss and went under. The most popular derivatives traded are mortgage backed securities, interest rate swaps and credit default swaps, more commonly known as credit derivatives. In 2004 derivatives were 2 trillion. In 2008 they were 8 trillion."

Jeff commented. "I think I know where the 4 trillion Rowe was talking about disappeared to."

Richard finished up the rest of the article. "Next it goes into foreign exchange risks, then sovereign risk including foreign loans out to unstable governments. They call these operational risks."

Ronnie called it a night. "Okay boys and girls. That is all for tonight. We have done enough exploring. We will have to continue this another evening. Richard and I make a yearly trek to the library to read the Barron's January Issues. Why don't the four of us go together and read the January Round Table discussions? You would love the mutual fund round up and all of the wizard's projections of 6 to twelve months down the road. And, of course, the touts of stocks poised to advance for one reason or another. Let's plan on that the last weekend in January."

The Whiting's and the Thompson's gathered for the holidays to wish each other well and celebrate. They promised to get together the last week in January for a trip to the library together. They would be able to get the skinny on fourth quarter earnings. Barron's always conducted The Round Table in January which was a comprehensive review of the stock market. The Round Table included some of the top people in the financial world. There were plenty of articles with differing views of everything going on in the business world.

THE LIBRARY

I t was a normal Saturday, January 24, 2015. The holidays were past and all New Year's resolutions had been broken. The market had made it safely through October and the holidays. In the USA, the Republican Party was now the majority in the Senate. The stock market had remained calm and undisturbed. The DOW did not take off into the stratosphere.

Things were back to normal. The state of the union address was over. So was President Obama. Israel Prime Minister Netanyahu was on his way to congress in March, 2015 against the USA President's wishes. Was the world on its way to World War Three as predicted by a fringe grass roots group of leftist progressive global extremists?

The Whiting's were finally on their way to the new library building in the back seat of the Thompson's clunker. The tires crunched through the frozen snow. Ronnie and Angie were immersed in conversation. "Well, Angie, let me tell you how much I really miss the tropical temperatures in Phoenix. Right now, Richard and I would be in the back yard or on the front porch relaxing."

Angie questioned Ronnie. "Does that mean that Richard would be stumbling around the front yards bothering the neighbors?" Richard laughed. "You probably are not used to being in such luxury, are you, Ronnie? I know you are jealous and holding it in. I bet we see an old beat up clunker in your driveway next week."

Jeff congratulated Richard. "Well, Richard, you were right. All of your predictions about the holiday market and the new year were right on. What about the disaster case at El Chapultepec? Should we buy that?"

"Somebody seriously messed up. They had food poisonings at so many different locations. Let's look that chart up when we get inside." Richard congratulated Jeff. "I've been watching your Citi, Jeff. Nice job, buddy! You are going to have to start giving me some of your tips."

"Sure thing, Richard. I covered the short sale last week at 46 7/8."

"You did? Good for you!"

"I had to. The volume picked up and the price was holding. It was pretty obvious that Citi was base building. I had to get out. I just wanted to get my first short sale into play so I could learn the mechanics on this first go round. I was hoping for a 20 point drop, but it became obvious that would not happen. I thought it was really going to drop more, but it is just too popular a stock. Lots of trading around the world on Citigroup." Jeff thought for a moment. "You know, if I was playing short term trades, I would buy it now at $48 and play the upside back to $56, maybe even $60."

Ronnie gave Richard the cut your heart out look. "Let's do it, Richard. *Let's buy that piece of junk and ride it **back to $60**. Jeff, you don't realize how right you are. It should hit resistance at $57 to $60, but it will break out above that. With a whole year of trading as one of the 100 'big boy stocks' as you like to call them, it will see $70 easily because it is one of the heavily traded stocks and it is a major financial institution worldwide. Richard, you know that Wall Street will still be setting record highs every day for a year and a half to suck some more loser cash into the market. Let's do it!"

Richard shot Jeff a glance. "I can see it in her eyes, Jeff. She means it. It is a sure thing." Richard agreed with Ronnie. "You are right. It will be one of the few stocks out of 2600 that might make 20% this year."

Ronnie looked at Richard. "What little damage there was to the stock price is done. Go for $20,000 Richard or I will divorce you." Laughter erupted. "Fifteen percent on our money is acceptable risk on a small investment. Tonight we will get the skinny on the lake lots and we will steal them from the Thompson's." The car filled with laughter.

In order to annoy Richard and Veronica, Jeff acted as if the new library building belonged to him. "Now I want to tell you folks that this library is a new modern design. It is a combination of 50% steel sheeting and 50% large square flat concrete skin on the outside. On the second floor, there is one section that has a huge vertical wall of windows from the floor to the ceiling. When you stand in front of the window, it feels like you are standing in the air thirty feet off the ground."

As they pulled into the parking area, Ronnie spoke up. "Richard says it reminds him of an aircraft carrier."

Angie questioned Richard's sanity. "Richard, have you ever taken any of those ink blot tests? Ronnie, I think you should get Richard to take an ink blot test. It might give you a clue as to any peculiar personality traits."

"You need not worry, Angie. Richard has plenty of those. He did not get short changed in that area."

Jeff calmed the group. "Folks, let's stay neutral here. It is too early for jousting." Jeff parked the car. Everyone removed themselves and they donned their back packs. Snow crunched under their boots as they walked through the cold air to the library. Jeff continued. "Our favorite spot is on the second floor. There is a nice area with comfortable chairs and a few large tables. Be sure to wipe your feet inside." The Whiting's laughed. "How much are you going to charge for your tour, Jeff?"

Angie spoke up. "Our second favorite spot is on the third floor. It is the genealogy section and it is pretty quiet except the staff gets loud once in a while. We traced Jeff's lineage back to the red ass baboon family tree." Angie's line snared some chuckles. Ronnie asked, "Isn't that the same tree that the president heralds from?"

They made it to the second floor. Ronnie picked a table big enough for four in the news media area. "This will do fine." They took off their back packs and arranged their laptops and spiral notebooks on the table.

Jeff and Ronnie strolled off to the newspaper shelves and brought back the Barron's issues. "It's all right here folks!" piped Ronnie. "Just look at the front page of these babies. 'Barron's hosts the **Mutual Fund Roundup**.' They do this every year. It is a forecast of what is to be in the next twelve months by leading analysts." Ronnie laid four issues of Barron's on the table. Everyone grabbed an issue and the foursome began a spontaneous round robin discussion.

Ronnie broke out laughing. "Look at this Barron's cover! **Blame strong weather**. They are blaming the sub-zero temperatures and the deep snows for the poor holiday shopping turn out. They do that every year. Americans must be turning into faggots and weaklings! Richard used to walk to the grocery in the sub-zero to bring back the fambly groceries in his widdle wed wagon. And that was uphill both ways!" Chuckles surrounded the table.

Each one read to the others the interesting articles in the issue they held. Richard kicked off first to lead by example. "So this is a **year over year decline** with the 4th quarter. A nice way of saying that 4th quarter earnings are lower than last. This is the first year over year decline since the 3rd quarter of 2012, just two years ago. *Always, always, always compare results to previous quarters and the same quarter a year ago or even two years ago!* Keep track of the quarterly earnings. You have to know the trend of the share prices." Richard yawned. "Judging from what this issue says, it looks like things are slowing down. **Here is the big picture**. *The mutual funds think there are some stocks that were oversold or have gone unnoticed.* They are pointed out right here so you gamblers can sling your money into them. Hey! Let me warn you. These might be stocks that the mutual funds still hold and they want to get rid of them. They tout them as being oversold to get the young and foolish to invest so the mutual funds can sell into the new buyer money."

Ronnie reminded everyone, "Also, you have to be wise and stay vigilant. These are not Barron's recommendations. A few readers **will get confused on this point**. These are articles with forecasts and different points of view from different leaders with different concerns and issues. Barron's is a collection of forecasts and views. You could be reading ordinary lies, so don't be tricked into something that doesn't seem right. Buyer beware. Don't bend over for the soap, Angie!" Laughter erupted at the table. "Now don't get me wrong. Barron's staff and editors make good recommendations, but you always have to consider what phase of the market you are in."

The librarian shot a dirty look at the outburst. "Please be considerate of others and keep your voices down."

Angie entered the round robin discussion. "*Interest might go up to half a percent. A quarter of a percent is likely by the end of the year.* There will be a whole lot of Yellin' on whether or not the interest rate gets an uptick." Angie thought for a moment. "This subject has been a topic every month in the local paper. They played this fiddle all year long. It makes for good filler. No one gives a spit about half a point when the interest rate has been zero for the last five years. So, why Ronnie, has the rate been zero for the last five years?"

"Hhhmmmmmm. Actually, the sole purpose *might be* so foreign countries will not buy USA Treasuries. But I know you are messing with me, Angie. Listen up. This is the last time I will tell you. If you have debt, then now is the time to refinance as much as you possibly can. Use the new money to pay off all your old loans that have high interest. Banks want to lend. They are discarding bad credit reports. They are issuing credit cards that will pay money as a reward to the buyer of goods. The whole world is refinancing. The whole world is on back order. Besides. It makes good filler." Laughter rose at the table.

Richard clarified. "Look. There is talk of the interest rate being raised. That will not happen before the presidential election. Just a gut feeling. The DJIA Index usually drops about six months after the election. The reasons given will be that the economy is overheating or that inflation is gaining. The federal Reserve has kept the overnight lending (weekend three day lending) at 0 for six years in a row. Back in the day, the weekend or the overnight lending rate was used by many companies to earn a little bit of interest off of the money set aside for the upcoming employee payroll. We are talking million dollar payrolls and the interest payment was quite a boost to the sundry (discretionary) cash account. Big business lost that little perk.

Jeff relayed information to the group. "Barron's is touting the stocks that dropped 10% in January. The drop is due to the unexpected low earnings that Barron's warned everyone about back in August, 2014 and again in October. The stocks should recover by April or May." *From that point on into the end of July the favored big stocks might gain another 10%. That gain will dwindle down to 6% by October.* "So it seems like the market is going to be stagnant for awhile. You know, not one AP article ever addressed this eventuality. Everything is about keeping people cheerful for the holidays."

Richard looked at the table. "It is going to be slim pickings for the whole year folks. The short term investors will be playing the big stocks like buzzards picking scraps off of road kill skeletons."

Angie spoke up. "Damn, Jeffy! 10% for the whole year? We need to make a down payment on those lake lots and get the title in our names. Let's call the realtor tonight before someone else beats us to them. Like our rude neighbors."

Richard agreed. "That would be the best move you could make."

"You know, Angie. You make good sense. Why do investors even care about a 6% swell in only 200 or 300 stocks? Let's go get the lake lots. Let's call that realtor tonight. It will be a low monthly payment. We will save our hard earned money and truly diversify."

Ronnie pulled out the Market Week section. "Listen to this everyone! *'FOLLOW THE MONEY OUTFLOW '* Pay attention to this little tidbit. This should have you short term investors salivating. The title is **Mutual fund** outflows *for the month.* *'Money coming into mutual fund programs totals 7.6 million a month for the last five months.'* This is roughly **40 million dollars** total. If you think that is a lot of money, then be sure to listen to the second part. '**The *net outflows*** for the last five months *are **one billion dollars'**.* Off the top of my head the outflows average about **200 million a month.** *1 billion more outflow for the last five months than the inflow of 40 million.* So here you have all the reasons for the October selloff on a silver platter!"

Angie whined. "Ronnie, these Barron's articles are totally opposite of what has been said in all of the Associated Press articles in the business section of the local newspapers since the 500 point drop."

Ronnie mimicked the average media and brokerage house rebuttal. "Oh, Angie. The brokerage house said this is normal. It is a little profit taking and portfolios are diversifying into medium sized companies. You are going to see some portfolio balancing." They all laughed and the librarian peeked around the corner and cast a dirty glance.

Angie was disgusted. "I believe what you said, Ronnie. It sounds like the mutual funds are telling us what stocks they still have to liquidate so they can catch any fresh money that gullible investors throw at their suggestions. I mean, what is to keep an interview in Barron's truthful? Why not lie and name a couple of stocks poised for 10% return. Especially if the fund needs to cash out of the stock? The funds take their long term profits and throw a few pennies back to play the market rally and help keep the DJIA Index high so they can pull out another 40% over the next two or three months."

"Do you like big money, anyone?" Jeff read his issue of Barron's. *'Outflows of equities were tallied as 8 billion in money markets, and 8.5 billion in taxable bonds.* **16 billion total**. That would have started back in August."

Ronnie looked at Angie. "What does that tell you, Angie? Did the mutual funds do any profit taking? Has that been announced in any local newspapers? We all know that the Associated Press has not run one article of mutual fund profit taking. Instead they have called it portfolio adjusting. What are you gonna do, Angie? Half the people in the USA do not know what a portfolio is."

Angie guessed, "It sounds like some conservative bond funds dropped all of their low risk portfolios. Maybe some thought that Yellin' would raise interest rates. On second thought. Maybe they are going to cash so they can do some heavy short term trading for this year. Anyway, they will have cash ready for the disaster day shopping spree!"

Richard advised, "I think the bond investors have to make their move early. Their window of opportunity is short."

On Jeff's lap top they pulled up the DJIA Index chart his online brokerage account. The chart has a cursor ability that allows the viewer to see the index figure and the date when the cursor is placed anywhere along the index curve. Jeff and Angie read the ups and downs between 16000 and 17500 in the DJIA Index from the October sell off to the end of the year. "What do you think about these drops, Angie?" Angie had a quick answer. "It is pretty obvious there are two drops of 500 points. But, if you consider the all of the rallies and the drops, it was 2000 points up and 2000 points down in this what, 60 day trading period over three months and all of the holidays. This isn't portfolio arranging. This is profit taking. Especially since we know the earnings and share prices have slipped going into this first month of the year."

Angie turned to Ronnie. "This is crazy, Ronnie. I can't believe the analysts are still haggling over the fourth quarter results.." Ronnie responded. "Remember, Angie. In the fourth quarter, there were **steady downward revisions** *of earnings estimates* while the media hyped the Santa Claus rally. They are refining and combing the truth out of all of the fluff and innuendos kicked up by the media all last year. They are disputing the intentional misdirections handed to investors."

"And the lies?"

"No, no, Angie. Not lies! *Misrepresentation*s. Just like any other business. Such and such car gets so many miles to the gallon. Whether the mutual funds put money back into the market under the auspices of 'portfolio adjusting' remains to be seen. What you do is keep track of the cash on hand in their financial statements to see if they are accumulating more cash. If that is the case, then they are selling and waiting for a better opportunity."

One of the items Jeff was going to investigate was the old adage, '*As goes January, so goes the rest of the year*'. The New Year was celebrated with blaring horns and drums on Wall Street. He did notice that after the New Year's weekend passed that the drums were beating big time and the first couple of days were obviously up slightly each day. The real answer was right in front of him in Barron's. "Out of the last 39 years in the stock market, only six Januarys had made it through the month with any kind of increase in the S+P 500. So about 85% of the time, January finished the month with a slight decline of the indexes."

Jeff leaned over to Angie and whispered, "Here you go, Angie. The trumpets of the marching band have just heralded in the new year. There was a little uptick in the DJIA Index again at the end of the first week of January. It is supposed to give everyone the good feeling that the market is moving up especially for the new year. It perpetuates the century old lie 'as *January goes so goes the market*'. Besides they would never print a warning of a Dow drop on the front page of the business section."

Angie interrupted, "Marty Weiss would. I just can't believe how good these reporters are at putting the American people back to sleep. They say 'Nothing to be worried about. Just a hiccup.' All the while the institutions are actually dumping stocks like a wildfire headed towards Los Angeles."

Ronnie looked at Jeff. "It is the whole month of January that is considered, Jeff. Not just the first week. The Street always goes crazy on the first week of the new year! Most of the brokers are still drunk from the holidays." Chuckles rose around the table. "Yet the share prices immediately began to slide 5% in the second week."

Jeff gave Richard a hard look. "What do you think about the Chinese waterway?"

Richard replied instantaneously. There was no question he did not know the answer to. "Paving the shipping route to Australia via the Philippines? Maybe it would be safer for the Chinese tourists to take the slow boat cruise to Malaysia rather than a plane ride for vacationing. There would be less chance of being blown out of the sky like flight M370." Richard reconsidered. "Make no mistake! The Chinese are widening and lengthening their ocean going global rights. So are the Russkies and Iranians. The Chinese want to live in Australia and South America. *In 20 more years they plan on* **knocking the shit** *out of our millennials who believe in global peace.* We need to train the millennials how to win the next war just using their cellphones."

"Gosh, Ronnie! Sometimes your husband is a pessimistic, crusty old fart!" Laughter broke out.

The librarian appeared. "If I have to ask you to be quiet one more time. I'm going to call security."

Richard paid no attention. "Commie subversive elements and rioters are already in the USA waiting for the flag to drop. All the Russkies and the Chinese have to do is get their troops massed on the Canadian and Mexican borders and get their subs on the east and west coasts"

Ronnie spoke up. "Heck, Jeff. We have no control over that stuff. Let's forget it. The same with Crimea, Ukraine, the middle east and ISIS. We ain't going there. Our leader, Osama Bin Obama is a weenie. As a youth, I bet he was never in a fist fight in his life. Even if this is part of a troop buildup, another war is at least three years away. We can plan a couple of raids on the market before any world war kicks in. Let it go."

"Thank you, Madam Secretary of Defense. I'll put that tidbit in my file folder, 'Wartime Contingencies'. Buy defense stocks and beer." Angie pitched in, "Don't forget stocks in women's cosmetics companies."

Angie read. "Growth is running at 1% of productivity based on an analysis of a moving average that is based on 8 quarters. That would be two years." Jeff looked surprised. "I never heard of a quarterly moving average. That is a new one on me. Be careful because it won't include the bad news of the last quarter. If a large down trend were to develop, then the statistic or the moving average is no longer relative. It is wrong."

Richard threw in, "Maybe they had to use two years to get that one percent productivity figure." Ronnie advised, "Richard is right. GDP growth has been negative contrary to all of the economic recovery reports."

Angie looked at her husband. "Jeff. Do you remember Rowe's idea of 80 60 40?" Angie revealed her theory. "I have a theory on the churning. In the first sell off it is 30% of the holdings. Then the DJIA rallies back. 4 months later 40% of the remaining positions are sold. The rest is shorted from a long position and recovered four months later." Ronnie approved. "That is an interesting approach although I think the managers have begun to take profits and I suspect they will do so just a little bit at a time for the rest of the year."

Jeff read to the group. "Here is a blurb about consumer spending in the Barron's *Up and Down the Street* Column. *'Personal spending has seen the largest **decline** since **September, 2009***'. This is just amazing! The column goes on to explain that the economy is currently, as of January 2015, on the edge of recession as far as durable goods are concerned. It touches on the statistics that consumer buying is way down and it reminds us that just four years ago, a boat load of homeowners lost their houses and their life savings. This made it easy for rent prices to inch upward. Rents continued to climb due to the fact that there were not enough rentals to go around. Also, *some landlords lost their rental property in the meltdown*."

Angie whispered. "Jeff! Look at this. This is funny. Barron's editorial says that **Obama's state of the union address is a fantasy**. *It is very out of touch and predicted that more tax and spend is on the way.* Boy! Talk about smoke and mirrors in the market. This POTUS is just singing lullaby's right in front of the dumb people in this country to get their vote. And they believe him! He claims that the economy is robust and has recovered! His State of the Union Address says *'It is going to be a break through year.'* How many non investors will be encouraged by this blurb and jump into the market?"

Jeff spoke up. "Do you expect Obama or Wells Fargo to tell the truth? This is not misrepresentation or misdirection. It is an out and out lie. They have **author and speaker privilege**. They can say whatever they want to."

Ronnie changed the subject. "Mutual funds are predicting 14% profits in 2015. Barron's predicts 6% for the stock market initially, but goes on to warn that the DJIA may well end up flat for the year." Angie asked, "What in the world does flat mean?" Ronnie answered, "Flat is a word that is neutral in emotional control. Flat is better than saying zero or no gain. It is all about describing a cow chip to look like a cookie."

Richard read. "*Sluggish economic growth around the world. Europe down 1 to 2 percent for the year headed toward recession. Asia up 1 to 2 %.* This contradicts all of the newspaper articles that we read last November and December."

Angie commented. "But just back at the holidays the local papers were saying that the market would **rebound due to overseas growth. A burgeoning European economy.** Global growth was the rallying cry! Someone must have used an old article to write a new blurb and was hoping for the best. Or maybe the journalists were looking for a good plausible excuse to put investors back to sleep while we slip into recession." Angie looked at her husband. "I see what you mean. Newspaper articles are bull manure. Keep the lid on. Don't panic. Just feed the usual feel good statements to the starving public. Don't disturb the peasants. They might grow angry and storm the castle."

Richard intoned, "We are all peaceful globalists now."

Jeff took his turn for a little sarcasm. "DJIA was up 7.5% in 2014! Boy is this a kick ass record high or what? Remember, Angie, I am not trying to flaunt my luck to you, but two of the buys I made saw 100% increase in 14 months. Now compare that to 7%. On the next cycle I will be trading these short term inundations that happen at the market top with about 10% of my money."

"No you won't! I will put you in Weiss recommendations."

"I like you more and more each day, Angie. Can you Whiting's figure out this next blurb on Exchange Traded Funds? 'ETF's and dollar strength spell out the following scenario. Previous months were **10 billion dollar inflows per month**. For how long it doesn't say. This January inflow is only *1.1 billion*.' Those ETF funds have more money in them than the stocks do."

Ronnie spoke up. "Those are SPDR funds. ETF's have grown more popular since 2000."

They don't trade on the NYSE. Hey! Just a minute! I want Angie to assess this Wells Fargo article. Here Angie. Read this and tell us what you think. We will critique your assessment!"

The Thompson's began to skim the Barron's Wells Fargo article. Angie remarked, "Do you believe it? Wells Fargo admits that the USA economy is on the very edge of recession heading into 2015." Angie Paused. "The bank claims to be in fine shape and openly denies being vulnerable to a slow or unprofitable year." Angie gave her opinion. "What else is a bank going to say? Their final statement of positive spin for the bank is *that they are so diversified that nothing will scathe them in 2015.* So, as far as things appear in the current financial environment, their armor will be impenetrable." Angie continued. "The bank can meet or beat our goals for 2015. *2016 will be the presidential nominations* and **baring any unforeseen circumstances or influences from outside events beyond our control** *we will arrive to 2017 in fine shape.*"

Richard lectured. "That was a pretty big qualifier they used. You have to remember. The government and the newspapers are trying to win the election already and it is still a year and a half away. You will not hear much bad news. They are college educated liberals. 60% of the women will get degrees in social science to be liberal social workers." Ronnie and Angie gave Richard cold stares.

"Very good, Angie." Ronnie added, "Now the thing to remember here is to assess this blurb the correct way. Here is how you receive this kind of news. *Wells Fargo has been gracious to issue a note of caution.* They give a brief prediction of good health in the market for the next six months to a year. Dialogue wise, **this is a very standard time frame approach in looking down the road.** *Six months to a year.* They warn of the slowing economic situation, *which is a good tip.* At the end, they declare that *the USA economy is on track* for 2015 (FEB 9 Barron's). This statement *'on track'* is one you will hear and read quite often this year. *It does not say the economy is on fire and will break records.* Nor does it say that the country will experience negative growth. All in all, this is pretty standard comment that means the entity will make it through the year as is, **if we are lucky.**"

"Gotcha, Ronnie Greenspan. It seems that everyone is reluctant to admit the possibility that things are not so great. We are in the D Area and pickings are slim. Share prices will drop somewhat, even in the big stocks. No more long term buying, only very calculated short term trading."

Jeff held Angie's hand and they stood up together. He crushed his lips to Angie's. Then he stepped back and said, "Excellent, Angie. I will kill for you!" Just at that moment a security guard walked through their area.

Angie called Jeff's attention to the Standard and Poors 1. 6 **billion** dollar lawsuit. "Gosh, Jeff. Marty Weiss talked about that in his *Ultimate Safe Money* book. The lawsuit fourteen years ago in 2001 was for 77 **million**. It looks like they have another one. This must be their second and it is for **1.6 billion**."

Richard sarcastically commented. "Oh, dear! Have companies been buying the influence of Standard and Poor's Corporate Wealth reference work again? Mercy! Heaven forbid! Oh, goodness me! There is no hope for us honest people anywhere in the world anymore. The entire world has gone corrupt."

Angie announced to the table. "Quantitative easing," supposedly Obama's brainchild was '*The largest unconventional money policy ever and was quickly retracted within a year.*' This is mentioned disrespectfully in several articles in this issue." Angie asked, "So how much money do the institutions use to play these short swings? How much do they throw back in to play the new rally? It says 7.5 million a month went back in to mutual funds in January. Is this to help play the rally back and help the DJIA Index rally?"

Richard commented, "That sounds plausible. I think they sacrifice 7.5 million for the short term rally. It would move the DJIA Index back up. Then they can take another stab at selling 30% of their long term profit again."

Angie says, "So *technically*, **they are not lying** when they say it is just a little portfolio adjusting. **It just isn't the truth**."

"Aha! But think about it! The real risk is getting the next 40% slice of their position out of the market. They need to foment a rally. You know they will. They need to feed the glutinous creature some nourishment to keep new investors throwing their money into stocks while the band screams 'This is the best global market **in the history of the world**! Ante up everybody!'

"This is fanaticism!" Angie said to Richard. "I am convinced that they all jump back in to play a rally."

"Yes but remember it is just the Dow stocks and the big stocks. Only what? 250 or 300 out of 2600 at the most are played for 5% to 10%. And any recommendation they give you will probably be a stock that is still in the fund. They will sell that stock into fresh buyers. So why not start a rumor?"

Richard knew that the independent market news letters were still pumping stocks of the new start up situations. One or two recommendations would take off like rockets this year. He knew that all of the broker houses were looking at 2015 as an up year *with higher record setting moves every day for the DJIA Index* and S+P 500 stocks. There would be no *victory for the 2400 others* with the exception of the mergers, rockets and special situations. He paused and continued. "Here is something else that you have to understand. In this new millennia, companies are pros at cutting back and downsizing. They are more adept than ever at closing down the night shift, cutting extra shifts, cutting employee hours in half. If they are so adept now at maintaining breakeven on earnings. If the earnings figure does not drop, then the stock price might hold its present price. Anything more than that, say 20% would cause a drop in earnings and sales. So, you see, some companies may only be at 80% of their usual output. They will still break even or show a couple of dollars profit but they are operating at 80% capacity. Sales revenues is what you have to watch. That might give you a clue of how much downsizing has taken place."

Jeff got a word in edgewise. "Hey, Ronnie. Here's a blurb on consumer confidence. Consumer confidence is at the highest level since September 2009." Jeff looked at Ronnie straight in the eyes. "You have been around for a while. What do you think about this confidence index?" Richard and Angie chuckled, but Ronnie cut them with a cold stare.

"Richard and I think the USA is suffering inflation. Look at home prices. They hopped right back up. So did the new car prices. Rent inflation is just unbelievable, but this is market action. It is true market supply and demand action. The government and everybody's brother wants low housing and rent prices, but that is not the reality that exists in our world of the big metroplexes unless you tough it out in low rent neighborhoods."

Richard picked up to express some thoughts. "Jeff, a contradiction has always existed between the state of the economy and the world wide polling of citizens. Especially between consumer spending and consumer confidence statistics. The stats will make you scratch your head. How could consumer confidence be at an all time high when consumer spending is at an all time low? These two statements flip flop and criss cross at every market peak. Right along with them is the fine line that the Fed is going to raise interest rates because inflation has reared its ugly head. Most of the time it is the bank shenanigans that bring us down. It is like Erdman said, *Once the Americans find out what the banks have done to them it will be too late.*"

Ronnie took over. "So you see these little indicators are disjointed in logic. They make for bytes of seemingly logical information but the little bytes do not fit together in a pattern of continuity. They really are not even linked logically. The real link is an abundance of media manure. It has been used for a century. The peasants' minds are dulled. It enables the facts to be hidden but what it really does is to eliminate any desire for the peasants to actively seek a truth that goes against an established river of lies and deceit. It is more like witchcraft and sorcery!"

Angie responded. "You should know Ronnie!"

Ronnie jumped back because she wanted to pound this topic into the earth. "Let me tell you all about the polling and the opinions. The polls are conducted monthly or quarterly in a few countries around the world. France has one. Great Britain has one. There is one in Spain and India. The Neilson global poll surveys 60 countries. And the questions they ask are all all subjective. There are no stats that quantifies the questions about hard goods, production, jobs and things like that. There is no question asked that requires extrapolation from factual data. Each month a minimum of 500 phone calls are made by Wisconsin students for the Gallop Poll in the USA. The responses are all emotional and subjective. How absolutely ridiculous! The pollsters mathematically divide up the yes and no by locality and they say that the division of localities makes the polls a hard statistic! That is a joke. A business statistics teacher would fall over dead."

Richard cut in. "The irony of these polls is that the people regurgitate the news that the media has fed to them for the last two years. This is the reason why the peasants think that the market is at an all time high and that the economy is recovered. Sure, economic production is up, but it is not operating at 100% capacity. Production has increased and we are out of the hole, but compared to what? We are far from a burgeoning economy. There are no reliable facts or statistical data as the basis of these polls. These statements are baseless. The polls simply help to put the peasants back to sleep. A sedative if you will. It all reminds me of that TV show *The Family Feud. Survey says!*"

"We are getting a real value deal with price of gas at the pump. That is one big reason consumers think the economy is good. But oil, gold and rent prices are not in the Consumer Price index. And right now oil and gold are deflating commodities. The financial world uses them to point out something good is happening. True we benefit greatly on the low gasoline prices. It provides a cut in the monthly family expense accounts. But inflation is still rising and there are absolutely two reasons for this. And they are the printing of money for social programs, i.e. food stamps, unemployment disability, social security and welfare just to name a few social programs. And then there is the printing of money to bail out ailing economies around the world to stop widespread depressions and bailing out wall street firms and banks when their credit swaps fail. And, of course, the money printed for wars which I happen to think are a good cause especially if they are not on USA soil. But look at the wars we are fighting in our country now. Radical insurgents from foreign countries and the illegals crossing the border. The government payrolls are expanding at home. And truth be known, our meager peasant income tax offerings to the IRS just don't scratch the surface."

Angie goaded Richard. "Richard, why has the Dow changed from AT&T to Apple?" Richard revolted. "I am sick and tired of you people messing with me. The global financial world is all about **stock market heritage and pride!**" Write that down you buffoons. I really believe that all of you are trying to drive me crazy by asking me this same frivolous question time and time again." There were several light snickers in the group. Angie said, "If it is not representative of 2600, it is cheating."

"Wrong! It is to keep the Dow Index in strong stocks. We don't want any weenies. Now listen. These stocks are popular and they trade. So let it go. So what if this group is only 4 or 500 big companies? So what if the share prices of 2100 other companies are dropping? This has been the MO since the 1920's. Let it go, Angie! **It is only a set up**. And by the way. If you take the time to search the net on 'the historical components of the Dow Jones, you will find that since the 1890's there have been 51 changes in the makeup of the 30 industrials."

As the big articles passed played out, the foursome read the one liners. They continued to interrupt one another and share the small article headlines.

The number of mutual funds worldwide reached 79,669. *Vacation flights were down.* The average drop in share prices during a steep market decline is 43%. *The average life span of the hedge funds is 40 months. About three years.* The market is going to tank. The naysayers predict DJIA 8000. The astute in the know predict 13,000 to 15000. *Twitter down 13% from last year IPO.* Workman's Compensation is at highest level in seven years (2015 January). *Intercontinental Exchange bought out Standard and Poor's. They have exchanges and clearing houses worldwide that connect companies around the globe with loans.*

Ronnie was ready to shut down the library visit. "You know we have a good handle on 2015. We know the environment. And we have an average guess on 2016. The presidential candidate races will keep the trading activity on a positive note for the DJIA Index. Let's call it a day. But before we go, Angie, would you explain what we have covered today?"

"Well, I am going to rely on the drift of what we have read and discussed this morning. The weather forecast is that the waters are choppy. We are in area D. The greedy mutual funds turned their triangle upside down and dumped a whale of a load of stock in the market to cash out. Oops! I mean they confirmed their return on their investments. The lifeboats will be full of brand new crisp bills from the Fed to save the failing institutions and citizens. The defibrillator paddles are applied as many times as necessary to resuscitate the monster. We are at the market top and the money is leaving the smart hands who are taking profits and the inexperienced hands are buying the shares. The drums are still beating. The market is on fire. Don't be left out!"

Laughter erupted at the table. The librarian appeared on the spot. "All right. You people have to leave. You are no longer welcome. I have asked for security to see you out."

The group picked up their pens and spirals and stuffed them in their backpacks and left the library.

"WHEN YOU CAN NOT FIGURE OUT THE MARKET DIRECTION AND THE MARKET IS GOING SIDEWAYS BE OUT OF STOCK." JESSE LIVERMORE

"BY THE TIME THE AMERICANS FIGURE OUT WHAT THE BANKS HAVE DONE TO THEM, IT WILL BE TOO LATE." PAUL ERDMAN

EPILOGUE

The last week in March, 2015, the Dow shed 414 points for the week March 23 through March 27, supposedly on the Jobs Report which is only a convenient blurb to fog up the bathroom. The first issue of Barron's in April, 2015, printed that there were two reasons for the decline. Earnings had been glossed over and losses had gone unreported by companies and brokerage houses. Second was the announcement of further closings of large department stores across the USA, i.e. Macy's, JC Penny, Sears, Kmart and Safeway, just to name a few.

AUTHORS NOTE

You must make your investment decisions early in life and for the right reasons.

What is the value of a car after 10 years and 200,000? Is it less than 65% of the original value? A car will eventually end up in a salvage yard.

A plot of land will hold value. It will be more valuable if a subdivision or shopping center is built nearby.

If the cost of living and inflation are 2% a year then that will be a 20% increase in ten years. In 20 years the increase could be as much as 40%. Is this increase the same as the **appreciation in value of a hard asset?** Sure. Inflation and the cost of living are part of the increase of the value of a hard asset.

If you wait until after the age of 30 to buy a hard asset You will be paying 15 to 20 % more than the item cost 10 years before.

If you never purchase a hard asset, you will never have any asset to trade that is free and clear. You will lose ground to the rising cost of inflation and the cost of living. You will become one of the 30% of Americans **in your generation** who do not have a pot to piss in when they reach the age of 65.

APPENDIX

The short essays below will reveal the answers to the question, 'Why does the stock market crash?'.

Lucent Technologies   Search the internet for **What Really Happened to Lucent Technologies** by Doug Pitt. This essay is on <u>www.scribed.com.</u> (An app invitation appears on screen with the article. Click on 'Continue on Browser' and avoid the app. You will find the article above all the advertisements) **This article is a must read!**

Long Term Capital Management   Search internet for **Long-Term Capital: It's a Short Term Memory** by Roger Lowenstein September 6, 2008 **This article is a must read!**

Cendant   Search internet for **Chairman of Cendant is convicted of fraud – Business International Herald Tribune** by Stacey Stowe.

Inside Job   Search internet for **Inside Job: The looting of America's Savings and Loans** by Steven Pizzo

BARCLAYS   Search internet for Wed May 20, 2015 Reuters, **Global banks admit guilt in forex probe, fined nearly $6 billion** and CNBC. com **Barclay's used blockchain tech to trade derivatives.**

ROYAL BANK OF SCOTLAND   Search internet for **Bank crimes pay: Under the Thumb of the Global Financial Mafiocracy** by Andrew Gavin Marshall

<u>www.corp-research.org</u>   **The scandal In Home Mortgage Financing: A Look at Freddie Mac**. Corporate Research E Letter No 43 Jan 2004

www.investopedia.com   **Fannie Mae Freddie Mac And the Credit Crisis of 2008** by Barry Nielsen

www.youtube.com   **Inflation** by Milton Friedman. **Federal Reserve Bank** by Milton Friedman.

www.panamapapers.icij.org   **Giant Leak of Offshore Financial Records** Reveals secret hideaway tax havens and money laundering activities by celebrities, heads of state and international drug cartels.

www.treasurytoday.com   **Regulating Derivatives in Asia**

GLOSSARY

Use www.nasd.com Locate the Glossary on the NASD home page. There are explanations for 6000 words and terms.

Printed in the United States
By Bookmasters